Web Campaigning

Acting with Technology
Bonnie Nardi, Victor Kaptelinin, and Kirsten Foot, editors

Web Campaigning

Kirsten A. Foot and Steven M. Schneider

The MIT Press
Cambridge, Massachusetts
London, England

For information on quantity discounts, please email special_sales@mitpress.mit.edu.

This book was set in Stone Serif and Stone Sans on 3B2 by Asco Typesetters, Hong Kong and was printed and bound in the USA.

Library of Congress Cataloging-in-Publication data

Foot, Kirsten A.
Web campaigning / Kirsten A. Foot and Steven M. Schneider.
    p.   cm. — (Acting with technology series)
Includes bibliographical references and index.
ISBN-13: 978-0-262-06258-9 (hc : alk. paper) — 978-0-262-56220-1 (pbk. : alk. paper)
ISBN-10: 0-262-06258-5 (hc : alk. paper) — 0-262-56220-0 (pbk. : alk. paper)
1. Political campaigns—United States—Computer network resources. 2. Internet in political campaigns—United States. I. Schneider, Steven M. II. Title. III. Series: Acting with technology.

JK2281.F66 2006
324.70285'4678—dc22   2006044927

10 9 8 7 6 5 4 3 2 1

To W. Russell Neuman, for opening doors and letting many flowers bloom, and to Sean Treglia, for trusting us.

Contents

Digital Resource

A digital resource presenting a collection of annotated artifacts drawn from campaign Web sites produced during the study period of this book is available at http://mitpress.mit.edu/webcampaigning. We have inserted a symbol, , in the margin to indicate the availability of these objects. In addition, all Web pages referenced in endnotes in the text are digitally linked to archived objects in our digital resource. Interested readers may enter the corresponding endnote number to view these archived pages. In addition to illuminating our findings, we hope the practice of digital schol-arship is advanced through the presentation of these digital materials. We think that studies of the Web are enhanced by reference to Web objects, and we appreciate that MIT Press is willing to engage in this experimental form of authorship and publishing with us.

Acknowledgments

We each came to the study of the Web in elections in a rather roundabout way. Although we had done prior research in technology and politics (Steve) and the politics of technology (Kirsten), neither of us had studied Web technologies or electoral politics previously. Asked by W. Russell Neuman of the University of Pennsylvania in the autumn of 1999 to help coordinate a research team studying the impact of the Web on elections, we quickly decided we would need to begin archiving election-related Web sites in order to conduct a developmental analysis. Neither Russ nor we could have guessed at the time that we would continue to pursue questions about the Web over the course of three elections—sometimes an object set in motion remains in motion a very long time. We soon found ourselves in the middle of a maze of complex theoretical, methodological, technical, and legal questions about the Web and politics, archiving Web materials, analyzing Web archives, and creating digital representations of knowledge.

Six years into the maze, we now have a deep sense of fulfillment at the opportunity this book has provided to integrate the various kinds of knowledge we have garnered along the way. To conduct the digital scholarship presented in this book and at http://mitpress.mit.edu/webcampaigning, we developed a set of software tools called the WebArchivist Toolkit (see http://webarchivist.org). With these tools, we are able to create archives of Web objects in which links are preserved. Then we can sort, annotate, and interlink the objects preserved in our archives—as well as in other Web archives—in a variety of ways. This book reflects the integration of our analyses of campaigns' Web strategies with the fruits of our learning adventures in software development and Web archive creation.

We are grateful for the support and assistance that many have provided us through the research, software, and archive development that led to this book. Our spouses, Ralph Puchalski and Laura Horvath, and Steve's daughters, Addy, Marlise, and Avery, have encouraged us unceasingly and put up with too many late night work sessions over the years. Their enthusiasm buoyed us in the moments we considered escaping out of the maze by finding a research topic that was not quite so political nor technical.

A grant from the Pew Charitable Trusts to the Information and Society Program at the Annenberg Public Policy Center (APPC), University of Pennsylvania, supported the study of the 2000 election under Russ Neuman's direction. Hugh Donahue and Lara Scott provided vital administrative support for the APPC project. We were fortunate to work with terrific graduate students at the APPC. Kirkland Ahern, Laura Duchessi, Josephine Ferrigno, Rachel Gans, Masaki Hidaka, Chris Hunter, Kim Kirn, Elena Larsen, Corina Matiesanu, Frances Mesa, Leslie Sillaman, Jennifer Stromer-Galley, and Tresa Undem each played a key role in the project. We also benefited from a very talented group of undergraduate research assistants, including Margaret Allen, Anthony Gill, Jonathan Karush, Ilyse Stempler, and Eileen Weinstein. Gretchen Haas, a graduate student at the University of Minnesota, kindly conducted some interviews and a focus group for us. Additional coding assistance was provided by Barbara Bosma, Ivan Bosma, Marissa Condosta, Pam Plymell, Patricia Seybolt, and Susan Schultes.

Our study of the 2002 election was based at the Center for Communication and Civic Engagement at the University of Washington and the SUNY Institute of Technology, and supported by a grant from the Pew Charitable Trusts. Lance Bennett, David Levy, and Barbara Warnick each provided insightful advice at critical junctures. Project managers Blake Hayes and Wendy Marker kept us on track and on time. Graduate students Meghan Dougherty and Mike Xenos outdid themselves in data collection, analysis, and dissemination as we produced weekly reports on Web campaigning for three months leading up to the election. Elena Larsen again contributed her survey design and XML expertise, and seemingly infinite patience. Bindu Sundaresen masterfully trained and managed a team of 29 coding assistants: Jennifer Armstrong, Mario Augustin, Claire Blatz, Barbara Bosma, Ivan Bosma, Kathy Casey, Peter Dalbhanjan, Kustav Das, Joanne Freeman, Debra Horvath, Stepen Keblish, Irfan Khan, Vishal Khattri, Sharon Kosinski, Christine Lloyd-Newberry, Gowsalya Mathusamy, Christopher McGrath, Rishi Mehta, Kelly Moore, Barbara Murray, Aaron Neslin, Beatrice Opee, Shawn Petronella, Pam Plymell, Upasana Raina, Deepak

Seshadri, Loren Sutton, Saket Wakharka, and Donovan White. Karen Sosted Foot, Kirsten's mother, graciously housed and fed our research team of six in Minnesota for three days of post-election data analysis, providing east coast and west coast team members the opportunity to meet face-to-face for the first time after months of intensive collaboration online.

Having refined our research questions, our study of the 2004 U.S. election was conducted on a smaller scale domestically, but in the context of a cross-national comparative project we helped coordinate with colleagues from 20 countries across Asia and Europe. Support for our research on the U.S. case came from the University of Washington's Royalty Research Fund. Amazingly, Meghan Dougherty and Mike Xenos agreed to work with us again in 2004. The continuity they provided, and their collective intelligence, made the 2004 study relatively easy and quite enjoyable. Graduate student Jim Carroll, and undergraduates Meghan McLaughlin and Andrew Waits, contributed by coding and annotating sites and by bringing fresh insights to the project.

The APPC technology staff, Rich Cardoza, Kyle Cassidy, and Jon Stromer-Galley, provided a stable infrastructure and technical expertise for various aspects of our research on the 2000 election. Jeff Stanger and Ben Harnett contributed significant artistic, programming, and analytical skills during the 2000 election, and Ben continued to assist us through 2003. Chunyang Chen, Russell Clarvoe, Paul Ford, Tanya Hallberg, Michael Hand, Bill Harnett, Brian Lloyd-Newberry, Hlaing Than, and Myo Thein supplied their technical expertise during the 2002 and 2004 election studies. Ron Kline at the University of Washington and Nick Merante at SUNY Institute of Technology were invaluable as system administrators during the 2002 and 2004 elections.

As this book took shape, many colleagues provided invaluable comments on various ideas and draft texts. Nick Jankowski and Randy Kluver helped us articulate our concepts of online structures and electoral Web spheres more robustly as we designed and implemented the cross-national study with them in 2004, examining the Web in elections across Europe and Asia based on these concepts. We appreciate the time and effort that Lance Bennett, Meghan Dougherty, Tarleton Gillespie, Philip Howard, Victor Kaptelinin, Bonnie Nardi, Gina Neff, Jennifer Stromer-Galley, Barbara Warnick, and several anonymous reviewers invested to help us improve the manuscript. Nancy Bixler saved us weeks of work with her editorial expertise, and kept us entertained with her witty marginalia during the final push to birth this book. Cheryl Aupperle provided timely assistance with indexing and locating materials for the digital resource.

We appreciate the wonderful intellectual and institutional support we have received from the Department of Communication and the College of Arts and Sciences at the University of Washington, and the School of Arts and Sciences at the SUNY Institute of Technology. The digital scholarship that we present in this book also required inter-institutional collaboration and legal support to develop. Chuck Williams and Dana Bostrom of the Digital Ventures Office at the University of Washington, Guven Yalcintas and Mary Klopfer of the Research Foundation of SUNY, and Deborah Tyksinski of the Office of Sponsored Research at SUNYIT, facilitated this book by encouraging and enabling us to create an inter-institutional technology administration agreement to jointly manage the WebArchivist software system developed as a platform for social research of Web phenomena. Dana also helped us structure our collaboration with the Library of Congress and the Internet Archive to create the Election 2002 Web Archive.

Finally, this book would not have been possible without the foresightful, diligent efforts of the MINERVA group at the Library of Congress and the Internet Archive to preserve and display Web materials produced in relation to the 2000, 2002, and 2004 elections. In this regard, we are especially grateful to Brewster Kahle and Michele Kimpton at the Internet Archive, Cassy Ammen, Abbie Grotke, Allene Hayes, Diane Kresh, Rebecca Guenther, Gina Jones, and Deborah Thomas at MINERVA, and Margaret Williams and Dan Rader, at the Office of General Counsel, the Library of Congress.

Some of the data we present in this book was generated in partnership with other scholars. The series of focus groups and the user survey from 2000 on which we report was conducted with Jennifer Stromer-Galley. Interviews she conducted with Lynn Reed and Max Fose that year were very helpful to us. We collaborated again with Jennifer and Philip Howard on a survey of Web producers in 2004. We appreciate Jennifer and Phil's willingness to let us use these data in this study.

All of the survey data employed in this book were collected via the Web from respondents whose identities were unknown to us. When presenting excerpts from focus group and interview transcripts, we have masked the personal identities and campaign affiliations of our focus group participants and interviewees, with the exception of a few site producers who gave us permission to quote them directly. Since there is not yet an agreed-upon standard for the spelling, capitalization and spacing of many Internet-related terms, we have not altered the renderings employed by others when we quote from published texts or written survey responses.

Portions of the evidence and analysis presented in this book have appeared in prior publications. We introduced the concept of a Web sphere in Foot, Kirsten A., and Steven M. Schneider, 2002, Online Action in Campaign 2000: An Exploratory Analysis of the U.S. Political Web Sphere, *Journal of Broadcasting & Electronic Media* 46 (2):222–244. We elaborated the Web sphere concept further in Schneider, Steven M., and Kirsten A. Foot, 2005, Web Sphere Analysis: An Approach to Studying Online Action, in *Virtual Methods: Issues in Social Research on the Internet*, edited by C. Hine, Oxford, Berg, pp. 157–170. The concept of online structure was first introduced in Schneider, Steven M., and Kirsten A. Foot, 2002, Online Structure for Political Action: Exploring Presidential Web Sites from the 2000 American Election, *Javnost (The Public)* 9 (2):43–60. Some focus group data was presented in Stromer-Galley, Jennifer, and Kirsten A. Foot, 2002, Citizen Perceptions of Online Interactivity and Implications for Political Campaign Communication, *Journal of Computer-Mediated Communication* 8 (1), http://jcmc.indiana.edu/vol8/issue1/stromerandfoot.html. Some data on campaign linking strategies was presented in Foot, Kirsten A., Steven M. Schneider, Meghan Dougherty, Michael Xenos, and Elena Larsen, 2003, Analyzing Linking Practices: Candidate Sites in the 2002 U.S. Electoral Web Sphere, *Journal of Computer-Mediated Communication* 8 (4), http://jcmc.indiana.edu/vol8/issue4/foot.html.

Foreword

Michael Cornfield

With each passing moment, the extent of public life affected by behavior conducted on the Internet is expanding, and the ways of making and reacting to political decisions without recourse to the Internet are contracting. The online population continues to climb, as does the amount of time people spend online in an average day (see http://www.pewinternet.org and www.digitalcenter.org). The number of things people do while online increases with a high-speed high-volume connection, and the number of people who have this so-called "broadband" service is rising as well. The pace of technological adoption—that is, of individuals deciding both to go online and to obtain a broadband connection—seems to be slowing as we enter the second decade of the Web's availability. But digital communication is so thoroughly inhabited by the young that the expansion trend is inexorable no matter the pace. The Internet is here. And we are there.

Politicking accounts for only a slender wedge of the online activity pie. But a few people use the Internet regularly and proficiently for political communication, and they wield disproportionate influence over the civic opinions, agendas, and movements of the many. A voter does not have to know what a blog is, much less read one, to be affected by the ninja-style debates occurring in the blogosphere. That's because the "influencers" whom voters pay attention to—campaigners and their donors, journalists and their owners, government officials and their staff, policy experts and their sources—are increasingly involved with blogging (writing on the Web in diary form). These opinion leaders are emailing and Web searching, too, of course. The point is, if you accept the two-step model of influence at the core of political communication scholarship, the heavy migration of opinion leaders to the Internet is another indication of its importance.

It behooves us to learn what these influencers (along with everyone else) find from campaigners when they go online. This book provides an unparalleled look at the development of campaign Web content in the years 2000 to 2004.

It is often useful to speak of the net and the Web as media: conduits for the delivery of information comparable to the postal service, telegraph, and the mass media of newspapers, magazines, radio, and television. But the net has also emerged as a place for work, commerce, and political action. The authors have coined the term "Web sphere" to refer to the totality of Web sites, links, and other digital resources with respect to a particular topic during a particular timeframe. A Web sphere is a social space—looser than a community or organization, but tighter than a population or a one-time gathering around a topic or event.

This concept will continue to be handy in coming years thanks to the revolution in search symbolized by Google. In just the second half of the timespan of this book, it has become much easier and more common for users to find information on the Web using key words. What's more, it has become much easier and more common for marketers (a category which includes campaigners in many respects) to locate individuals through the searches they undertake. That means the routes and traffic between Web sites is as important as the messages on them. So beyond the substantive findings of this book on the topic of Web campaigning, the scholarly apparatus the authors employ, which enables us to study both sites and links, is an important advance.

What happened in the U.S. campaign politics Web sphere between 2000 and 2004? Much the same as what happened offline: the informing, involving, connecting, and mobilizing of supporters, to use the authors' terms. But the authors demonstrate that things change when these campaign functions are performed online.

First, online informing is continuous, even more so than live radio, television, or wire services, which are restricted by procedures and gates. Nothing gets on the AP wire unless it runs through the proper channels. On the net, on the Web, and even on a single site configured with certain software applications, the channel is a stream: more organic in its flows and boundaries. (It is also becoming more festooned with audio and video as opposed to just text and pictures.) On the net, information is not produced so much as managed, absorbed instead of consumed.

Another major lesson is that, with isolated and occasionally dramatic exceptions, Web campaigning has scarcely moved beyond informing and basic-level involving (for example, campaign email signup and donation interfaces). In 2002 only one in fifty campaign Web sites had a robust set of connecting and mobilizing features. The authors help us understand why by noting the additional resources, arrangements, and software required to support these activities, and by describing the intensified dilemmas of campaign control they entail. Yet campaigners know that in order to win they must expose enough supporters to the right messages at stage one to help them at stage four to turn out the right voters on election day. The enormous impact of the Dean campaign's elaborate and successful online network on the Kerry and Bush campaigns was clear by autumn 2004; we should see similar impacts in other elections with the full 2004 data and sets from forthcoming election cycles.

The need for campaign core staff to trust in what this book terms "coproduction" will increase with the popularity of what has been termed Web 2.0: a new wave of dispersed action tools like Blogger (for public diaries), Friendster (for socializing), Flickr (sharing photographs), and wikis (collaborating on texts). By March 2005, more than half of U.S. broadband users (57 percent) and nearly half of all net users (44 percent) had created content and posted it online (http://www.pewinternet.org). This is an ordinary social behavior which campaigns need to adjust to or risk appearing backward—or, worse, uninterested in what potential and actual supporters have to say to them, their fellow supporters, and everyone else paying attention to the election.

While *Web Campaigning* displays some fascinating snapshots of politics in this time of technology-associated transition, its approach, method, and companion resources are also significant contributions to Web studies in general. A camera is a tool and a snapshot is an artifact. Foot and Schneider have built a camera, a digital installation hosted on The MIT Press site consisting of artifacts, snapshots of Web sites, for analysts of online politics so that they—we—may explore for ourselves. Foot and Schneider invite us to approach the subject of online politics as virtual archaeologists who examine Web artifacts in order to infer what campaigners did with the tools of computer hardware and software. The authors want to move us beyond the simplistic explanations of technological determinism (which effectively presumes that a tool has an innate or essential function that everyone adopts as soon as they pick it up) and celebrity history (everyone imitates the big winners). The archaeological approach gives intrinsic properties and great achievers their due, but allows for variations in usage. That makes good sense, especially with such complex and multipurpose instruments as the Internet houses. Microsoft has come close to monopolizing basic operating software for personal computers, but the corporate giant has had to release different versions of Windows in response to technological innovations, marketplace challenges, and emergent usages (those uses consumers come up with which producers did not anticipate). And there are many, many different things one can do with a single version of Windows. The same goes for Web campaigning. The first decade has been more than what Jesse Ventura, John McCain, MoveOn.org, Howard Dean, and the Bush-Cheney campaigns have done online.

The primary artifacts examined by Foot and Schneider are thousands of campaign and campaign-related Web sites. Like other scholars, the authors read out campaign strategies and tactics from the forms and contents of the Web pages preserved in the collection. But these authors go further, and give us the wherewithal to join them, so that linkage routes between and within Web sites may be studied as well. This is crucial. Politics is about relationships, which links both symbolize and actualize. To fully understand Web campaigning, it is necessary to examine these relationships closely and systematically.

The political Web sphere will eventually be contiguous with the public sphere. It is already a preferred region of the public sphere as far as movers and shakers are concerned. This book advances our understanding of the implications of these trends. Further understanding will be made possible as others archive and study the Web as virtual archaeologists, as these authors have done.

Michael Cornfield is the author of *Politics Moves Online: Campaigning and the Internet* (Century Foundation Press 2004). He is an adjunct professor of political management at The George Washington University and a senior research consultant to the Pew Internet & American Life Project.

Web Campaigning

1 Web Campaigning: Introduction and Overview

Caught in the Web

On October 5, 2004, during the only televised vice-presidential debate of the 2004 U.S. campaign season, Dick Cheney attempted to send debate viewers to the Web site of a non-partisan research group associated with the Annenberg Public Policy Center (APPC) at the University of Pennsylvania, called factcheck.org. Cheney sought to defend himself against claims his opponent, John Edwards, made about Halliburton—an oil-services company that also provides construction and military support services—and Cheney's involvement with it. According to a transcript of the debate posted on the Web site of the Public Broadcasting Service,[1] Edwards said,

While [Cheney] was CEO of Halliburton, they paid millions of dollars in fines for providing false information on their company, just like Enron and Ken Lay. They did business with Libya and Iran, two sworn enemies of the United States. They're now under investigation for having bribed foreign officials during that period of time. Not only that, they've gotten a seven-and-a-half billion dollar no-bid contract in Iraq. And instead of part of their money being withheld, which is the way it's normally done because they're under investigation, they've—they've continued to get their money.

Cheney's Web troubles began with a slip of the tongue when he replied,

Well, the reason they keep mentioning Halliburton is because they're trying to throw up a smoke screen. They know the charges are false. They know that if you go, for example, to *factcheck.com*, an independent Web site sponsored by the University of Pennsylvania, you can get the specific details with respect to Halliburton. It's an effort that they've made repeatedly to try to confuse the voters and to raise questions, but there's no substance to the charges.

As most Web users know from experience, making an error in the last part or top level of a domain name can lead to an unintended and sometimes undesired Web location. The Web site referenced by Cheney, factcheck.com, turned out to be produced by an advertising company, Name Administration, run by a business in the Cayman Islands. The producers of factcheck.com were not expecting hundreds of thousands of visitors to their Web site that night. Within minutes of Cheney's reference in the televised debate, the producers noticed a significant spike in traffic. Having learned of Cheney's inadvertent reference to their site, and in the hope of avoiding a penalty fee from their Internet Service Provider, the producers of Name Administration created a re-direct from their site to georgesoros.com—a site produced by a supporter of the Kerry-Edwards effort.

Cheney's attempted use of factcheck.org—an independent, authoritative source—points to an expansion of Web campaigning. By attempting to create a cognitive bridge between the Bush-Cheney campaign and factcheck.org, Cheney sought to add veracity to his claims. In fact, Cheney's reference to factcheck was not the first interaction between the campaign and the independent Web site. The campaign had previously appropriated content from factcheck.org on its Web site, georgewbush.com, by copying headlines and providing links to selected postings on the independent Web site. The use of the Web to provide these connections, and the fact that one such connection was established via an offline medium (in this case, broadcast television), illuminate both the practice of connecting different political actors to each other on the Web and the convergence of modes associated with campaigning.

Reactions to Cheney's misstatement further illustrate how the complex network of relationships among political actors is extended by Web campaigning. Cheney's words implicated three specific actors, two directly—the producers of factcheck.org and the producers of factcheck.com—and one indirectly drawn into the fray—the producers of georgesoros.com. Additionally, they evoked reactions from various others, including press organizations, civic and advocacy groups, individual citizens, and government agencies.

The response by the producers of factcheck.org was threefold.[2] First, they noted, unhappily, "Cheney got our domain name wrong—calling us 'FactCheck.com.'" Second, the producers indicated that Cheney had "wrongly implied that we [factcheck.org] had rebutted allegations Edwards was making about what Cheney had done as chief executive officer of Halliburton." Third, the producers of factcheck.org had a technical crisis on their hands: Their servers were not equipped to handle the deluge of page requests resulting from the Cheney reference.

Prior to the televised debate, factcheck.org averaged 30,000 hits per day. During the twenty-four hours after the debate, the site received 8.5 million hits. For the following two days, the site was effectively inaccessible to the Web public. The flood of site activity by individuals seeking information about the domain also significantly negatively affected other networks at the University of Pennsylvania and the APPC. The APPC's project budget for factcheck.org could not cover the formidable cost of handling this surge in traffic. Eventually, the APPC changed hosts to a provider who could handle the traffic requests at a cost in line with the project budget.

The producers of factcheck.com, similarly experiencing a spike in traffic—and thus in their hosting costs, as well—reacted by redirecting traffic from their site to another site. In a twist that further illustrates the complexities of Web campaigning, the producers of factcheck.com redirected Web traffic coming to their site *not* to factcheck.org, but to georgesoros.com—a site maintained by the well-known financier, George Soros, who had independently contributed over $20 million to organizations actively supporting the Kerry-Edwards campaign.[3]

Within minutes of Cheney's reference in the televised debate, Web users who followed Cheney's suggestion and went to factcheck.com were greeted by a Web page headlined, "Why We Must Not Re-Elect President Bush." Clearly, this was not the intention of Vice President Cheney. This incident illustrates the risks associated with providing connections to independent actors on the Web. A citizen site producer, commenting on the incident, suggested, "this will be the last time that one of the political candidates, Republican or Democrat, refers people to a Web site they don't control."[4]

The choice made by the producers of factcheck.com caused a political controversy, and in fact became a story itself. Several days after the debate, when Web traffic to factcheck.com had returned to manageable levels, Name Administration posted a notice on its site explaining its decision to redirect to georgesoros.com:

Name Administration administrators redirected those visitors to a website relevant to U.S. politics. Name Administration chose the website of investor, philanthropist and political activist Mr. George Soros, because his website is well-funded, does not seek to raise funds from visitors, and had greater capacity to absorb the load of visitors, reaching over 100 visitors per second during peak times after the debate. An administrator for the Annenberg Public Policy Center has since informed us that their web server system would have been severely crippled by the load, had we directed the traffic to them. Contrary to some imaginative rumors spun by some, our actions were undertaken on a voluntary and emergency basis, with no prior communication or consultation with the Soros organization. As confirmed by our legal counsel in response to media inquiries, Name Administration Inc. has not been offered, and has not sought, any inducement, compensation, or other consideration from any individual or organization, for re-directed [sic] the resulting web traffic. Traffic to factcheck.com has begun to return to normal levels, and Name Administration Inc. wishes the citizens of the United States well in the selection of their leaders, whose actions can sometimes have unintended consequences beyond the borders of the United States.

Name Administration Inc. later told the system administrator of the factcheck.org site that they were unaware of its existence prior to the incident, and had no idea where Cheney had meant to send the debate viewers.

Press organizations, civic and advocacy groups, and government agencies made interesting choices about how to handle the misstatement in their transcripts of the debate. As noted, the Public Broadcasting Service posted a transcript of the debate as studio and television audiences had witnessed it. Other political actors felt the need to assist Cheney in setting the record straight. The Commission on Presidential Debates, for example, transcribed Cheney's rendering of the factcheck site accurately, but inserted [sic] after the *.com*.[5] The White House took what we believe to be an unprecedented step of not only inserting a textual correction in parentheses after the original statement, "(** factcheck.org is the correct Web address)" but also inserted a tag in the HTML associated with *factcheck.com* that linked the textual URL to factcheck .org instead, in effect correcting the error in the underlying code but leaving it visible in the presented text.[6]

Defining Web Campaigning

The 2004 election in the United States was, if nothing else, notable for the significant expansion of Web campaigning. We define Web campaigning as those activities with political objectives that are manifested in, inscribed on, and enabled through the World Wide Web. Various actors engage in Web campaigning in a range of sociopolitical contexts. In this book we focus on the Web campaigning activities of candidates and their campaign organizations as they seek to accomplish electoral objectives. The factcheck incident, while a footnote to both the 2004 election in general and even as viewed from the Web, nevertheless encapsulates the evolving phenomenon of electoral Web campaigning. It illustrates the range of political actors that coproduce what we introduce later as an electoral Web sphere, and the political and technical dilemmas that lead to differences in their production choices.

This book centers on issues regarding how U.S. electoral campaigns employ Web technologies to enact and extend campaign activities. Our aim is to advance understanding of the complex and evolving nature of Web campaigning, in order to trace the trajectory emerging from the first ten years of practice. The overarching question we seek to address is how the use of the Web reflects, resolves, or aggravates challenges and tensions in the campaigning process. Our study is further shaped by two additional questions: What factors help explain why Web campaigning in the United States has emerged in particular and specific ways and not in others? And what might Web campaigning look like in the future and under different organizational, political, and technological circumstances? To address our central questions, we engage in practice-based theorizing, a form of theory development in which we investigate campaigns' Web production practices in order to understand the evolving relationship between the Web and electoral politics.

We base our analysis primarily on extensive and systematic observations of hundreds of campaign sites produced by candidates during the 2000, 2002, and 2004 elections in the United States. We view campaign Web sites as both surfaces on which campaigns' production practices are inscribed over time and evolving structures that simultaneously manifest and enable political action. In approaching Web campaigning this way, we seek a more in-depth and nuanced understanding of it as neither solely "politics as usual," (Margolis and Resnick 2000) nor wholly revolutionary. We aim to identify practices that can be used as analytical lenses, to further practice-based theorizing on the relationship between technology and electoral politics, as well as to make methodological contributions to the study of the Web. We also seek to advance the practice of digital scholarship through the presentation of a collection of annotated artifacts drawn from campaign Web sites produced during the study period that is integrated with the present text.

In an analysis of the use of the Web and offline media by campaigns associated with four races in 2000, Bimber and Davis (2003) found that campaigns integrated Internet applications into traditional campaign activities, primarily reinforcing messages conveyed via traditional, that is, offline, media. However, they also noted that Internet technologies offered important and highly effective tools for "mobilizing activists" (p. 166).

Iozzi and Bennett (2004) argue that in embracing such tools, which they term "interactive social networking technologies," campaign organizations cede to others some of the control they have traditionally sought to maintain. We concur in part with Iozzi and Bennett, but we also demonstrate that some campaigns employ innovative Web production techniques in ways that retain or even increase their own control, such as by extending their ability to manage transactional relationships with site visitors. Web production decisions made by a campaign reflect the inherent tensions between a desire to maintain control over messages and resources and the generally decentralizing dynamic of Web-based communication. On one hand, campaigns want to inform as many prospective voters as possible; on the other hand, they want to control the information that is disseminated about the candidate. While campaigns want to involve a large number of supporters, they also want to establish the terms of that involvement. They desire to multiply their resources by mobilizing supporters to promote the candidate in the supporters' spheres of influence, but they also want to manage and track these promotional activities.

Different strategies for mitigating these tensions are evidenced within and across various campaigns' Web presences. The production of any individual Web site, much less a Web presence across multiple sites, involves a myriad of choices on multiple levels, including strategic, rhetorical, structural, and aesthetic. In the process of producing a campaign Web site, many production decisions may entail trade-offs regarding exploiting the affordances of the Web versus managing the candidate's image and maintaining the campaign's strategic communication focus.

The remainder of this chapter serves to place the phenomenon of Web campaigning in a historical context and to introduce the theoretical approach we take in examining this phenomenon. We briefly trace the contours of Web campaigning and its relationship to campaigning in general. We demonstrate that campaigns have been developing as sociotechnical networks, involving both human and technological elements, for many decades. We describe the four practices of Web campaigning that are the foci of this study. To conclude, we present a general overview of the book.

Web Campaigning, 1994–2004

Web campaigning has grown dramatically in each campaign cycle since the first campaign Web sites appeared in 1994. As indicated by Howard (2006), the percentage of candidates with campaign-produced Web sites dedicated to promoting their candidacy has increased dramatically since 1996. Most recently, 71 percent of Senate candidates, 68 percent of House candidates, and 68 percent of gubernatorial candidates produced Web sites. Election-oriented Web materials have been developed since 1994 by a wide range of actors—such as political parties, the Federal Election Commission and other government bodies, news organizations, civic and advocacy groups, educational institutions, and individual citizens.

Of course the adoption and strategic use of information and communication technologies by political campaign organizations precedes the digital era. In some respects, the history of campaigning could be understood as the diffusion of technology into the political sphere. Within the U.S., there has been tight interlinking between advances in communication technologies and the practices of political communication (Abramson, Arterton, and Orren 1988). In colonial America in the 1770s, agitators advocating independence from England used pamphleteering techniques to mobilize and inform supporters (Foner 2004). Federalists campaigning for ratification of the U.S. Constitution disseminated their perspectives through the publication of position papers that came to be known as The Federalist Papers (West 2001). Postal laws, including the franking privilege, were shaped by the desire of government officials to communicate with their supporters at little to no cost (Fuller 1972; Starr 2004). By the 1840s, U.S. political parties had created close relationships with newspaper publishers and established the parameters of the party press (Pasley 2001). Control over campaign management began to shift from parties to candidates, coincident with the arrival of telephones and then especially radio and television, and campaigns began to emerge as sociotechnical networks (discussed in more detail later). Telephones were integrated into campaign organizations by the 1890s (Jones 1964). The strategic uses of Roosevelt's "great radio voice" (Lazarsfeld, Berelson, and Gaudet 1944) and Kennedy's television persona (Selnow 1998) further illustrate this trend in the pre-digital era.

As communication and information technology evolved, campaigns continued to engage in comparable practices, albeit using significantly different techniques. Thus, the practice of informing other actors of the candidate's basic issue positions and biographical characteristics was maintained: The techniques simply shifted from printing pamphlets and posters to producing films to developing Web presentations powered by sophisticated databases accounting for individual visitors' preferences and characteristics. As the techniques associated with practices changed, the organizational structure of campaigns changed correspondingly. The rise of candidate-centered campaign structures paralleled the emergence of new communication media that allowed candidates to establish direct contact with prospective supporters (Schier 2000).

With the emergence of the World Wide Web in the early 1990s, electoral campaigns built upon the already established experiences of other political actors' use of the Internet. As outlined in numerous sources (Castells 1996; Abbate 1999), the history of the Internet begins with the advent of the ARPANET in the United States in the mid-1960s. The first overtly political uses of the Internet are usually traced back to Usenet, which was first introduced in 1979. By 1986, communities with explicit political agendas had adopted email and bulletin board systems and were using these Internet applications intensively. Even then, many users and contemporaneous scholars believed that computer networking technology had the potential to dramatically alter the nature and shape of political discourse—and of democracy itself—by engaging and energizing new participants in the political process (Abramson, Arterton, and Orren 1988; Downing 1989; Meadow 1986). In 1992 the Clinton presidential campaign used the Internet to create discussion groups among elite supporters and email, to a limited extent, as a campaign communication medium (Casey 1996). Following the January 1994 introduction of Mosaic 2.0—the first Web browser that presented integrated graphics—a few campaigns launched Web sites, including Democratic Senators Diane Feinstein (California) and Edward M. Kennedy (Massachusetts). Among the first House candidates with campaign sites were two candidates in a 1995 special election in California: Tom Campbell (Republican) and Jerry Estruth (Democrat) (Politics Online 2000; D'Alessio 1997; Casey 1996).

By 1996, the campaign Web site was considerably more common: Both major party and several minor party presidential candidates had Web sites, as well as nearly half of the Senate and about 15 percent of the House candidates (D'Alessio 2000; Kamarck 1999). Analysts examining sites from this era describe them as mostly "brochureware" or "virtual billboards," simply replicating in electronic form materials already distributed in print (Sadow and James 1999; Kamarck 1999). Web campaigning was largely seen as a gimmick or, at best, an ancillary to "real" campaigning. Attempting to draw additional attention to his campaign, one candidate for the Republican presidential nomination in 1996, Lamar Alexander, announced his candidacy on America Online (LaPointe 1999), even though 88 percent of American households did not have access to the network and 70 percent of the households did not even have a computer in their home (Pew Research Center for People and the Press 1995). Bob Dole, the 1996 Republican presidential nominee, attempted to plug his campaign site at the end of his closing remarks during the first presidential debate. Unfortunately for Dole, he missed the final "dot" in his attempt to say www.dolekemp96.org, perhaps creating frustration for the mostly inexperienced Web-using public at the time (Besag 2001; Kamarck 1999; LaPointe 1999). One candidate for State Assembly in California launched a one-page Web site simply stating that "Jim is a wonderful guy" (Mitchell 1998, cited by LaPointe 1999). For most candidates in 1996, merely being on the Web, or demonstrating knowledge of the Web, was Web campaigning. Only marginal change was noted in the types of Web campaigning in 1998: Although the percentage of candidates with Web sites increased significantly (Kamarck 1999), scholarly analyses concluded that most served as virtual billboards, with little overall, noticeable development in sophistication or features (Sadow and James 1999; LaPointe 1999; Kamarck 1999; D'Alessio 2000).

As the 2000 election season dawned, the dot-com boom was in full swing. Many critics proclaimed 2000 to be the "first Internet election," and the comparison to the role of television in 1960 was often made. Though much of this commentary proved to be hyperbole, the 2000 election did mark a significant shift in the attention paid to the Web by political candidates. All major party candidates for the presidential nomination established a Web presence early in the campaign cycle. Several—notably Bill Bradley, Pat Buchanan, George W. Bush, Steve Forbes, Al Gore, John McCain, and Ralph Nader—invested significant resources in and, based on our analysis of the features provided on their campaign sites, placed considerable strategic value on Web campaigns. Many candidates for House and Senate in 2000 (55 percent and 75 percent, respectively), launched Web sites, and expanded their campaigns' practices of Web campaigning beyond those that had been established in 1996 and 1998.

Since the 2000 election, campaigns have continued to experiment online to figure out how best to accomplish their aims on the Web. As a congressional campaign site producer in 2000 explained, experimentation is risky:

At this point, as important as it is to use the Internet and the Web site to get people to vote for [our candidate], in the back of my mind, I'm also thinking it's every bit as important for us to not do something really stupid on the Internet. Like violating copyright laws, like doing something that people who are very Internet savvy would look at and say, "these guys don't have a clue as to how this should work." And then we lose a voter because, our theme about the new economy, they think, well these guys are talking about the new economy, but they don't understand how [the Internet] works totally. It's not a big fear, but we don't want to stub our toe on it either.

This campaign producer was not sure his candidate could win on the basis of the campaign's Web strategy, though he was sure he could lose if the campaign failed in its online experimentation.

By 2002, we found that uses of Web technologies pioneered in the 2000 presidential campaign had become more commonplace among gubernatorial, Senate, and House campaigns. In 2004, some campaigns took yet another leap forward in the complexity and strategic value of their uses of the Web. Candidates for the Democratic presidential nomination developed extensive and multifaceted Web presences leading up to the primary elections. Howard Dean, former governor of Vermont, became established as a serious contender for the nomination—indeed as the frontrunner for a time in late 2003—demonstrating legitimacy as a candidate largely on the basis of his campaign's Web strategy. The Dean campaign dramatically altered the landscape of the political Internet. During its peak, the extent and strength of the campaign was demonstrated not only by the Web sites produced by the campaign, but also by Web sites and other materials produced by independent supporters across the Web. The Dean campaign demonstrated, on a national level, how a political organization could use the Web as the platform for a large-scale national movement (Trippi 2004). In just ten years, some campaign organizations had moved beyond thinking of the Web as an electronic brochure to viewing it as an electronic headquarters.

Concurrently with an expansion in the number of candidates establishing Web presences, usage of the Web by American adults dramatically increased. In 1995, fewer than 15 percent of American adults had access to the Internet; by 2001, that number was up to 60 percent. In 2004 the proportion of American adults online had increased to 65 percent, with more than one-third of adult Americans having high-speed Internet access from home or work (Pew Internet and American Life Project 2005).

Given the increasing rates of broadband access in the U.S. in recent years, a majority of Americans experience the Internet—and specifically, the Web—as a multimedia environment in which they can engage in almost every kind of social, cultural, economic, and political activity (Wellman and Haythornthwaite 2002; Howard and Jones 2003). With the integration of the Internet into every aspect of society, the Web has become a realm in which it is necessary for all kinds of political actors to have a presence—at least in order to be credible among the growing population of Internet users in the U.S. In the words of a young citizen participating in a focus group on presidential campaign sites in 2000, "I expect the next leader of the free world to be able to pick an expert Web designer." Campaigns have increasingly responded to that logic. As a congressional campaign site producer confided in 2000, "It would be silly for us to be running a new economy campaign and then we don't have a Web site. We sort of have to do it."

The Internet was clearly a significant source of political information and a location of political action in the 2004 election. According to the Pew Internet and American Life Project reports, more than one-third of American adults used the Internet for political purposes during the 2004 election, particularly for getting news or information about the elections and using email to discuss politics. In a national telephone survey during November 2004, over 40 percent of Internet users reported that the Internet was an important source of political information for them, and 27 percent of those who accessed political information online said it made a difference in how they voted (Rainie, Cornfield, and Horrigan 2005).

In addition to campaigns, all types of political actors are increasingly likely to have a Web presence: civic and advocacy groups, political parties, citizens, government bodies, and news producers—including those that were originally established in print and broadcast media, as well as those that were "born digital." Understanding how campaigns use the Web, and why they use it in particular ways, is thus a foundational step toward understanding the relationship between the Web and electoral politics.

Theorizing Web Campaigning

In our investigation of the research questions described previously we employ paradigms developed in science and technology studies (STS) and scholarship on situated practices to suggest that by viewing campaigns as sociotechnical networks both historically and in contemporary configurations, we can understand Web campaigning more fully. As we explain later, we view campaign Web sites as strategically crafted artifacts that reflect the cultural-historical context and as campaign resources that function as tools for communication. In this section we offer an overview of our approach and introduce key concepts regarding practice and structure on the Web.

We employ a practice-based approach to the study of Web campaigning that is consistent with the "practice turn in contemporary theory" across the social sciences and humanities (Schatzki, Knorr Cetina, and von Savigny 2001). In recent years, a number of scholars from different disciplines, such as communication, sociology, anthropology, philosophy, and science studies, have developed explanations of social and cultural phenomena based on the notion of practices (see, as examples, Nicolini et al. (2003) and the February 2001 theme issue of *Communication Theory* on practical theory). Several contemporary strands of practice-based theorizing emphasize the heterogeneous nature of practices. Cultural-historical activity theory suggests that tools—both material and symbolic—are created and transformed within practices, as are the techniques associated with particular tools or technologies. These tools and techniques carry with them not only technological affordances, but also particular vestiges of sociocultural and political values and resources—what Nicolini and Holti (2001) describe as "historical remains from their development" (p. 6). As an emerging practice becomes widespread—that is, institutionalized or normative—its tools constitute a means of accumulation and transmission of social knowledge, participating as formative elements in the practice itself (Miettinen 1998; Kuutti 1996).

Both the focus of this study on campaigns as Web producers and our practice-based theoretical approach distinguish this book from current literature on the Internet and politics. In the field of political communication, the relationship between politics and "new" media has been a focus of research since the 1940s. Political communication scholarship has typically centered on questions of media effects on users' political knowledge, attitudes, or behavior, and has primarily employed methods of quantitative content analysis, surveys, and experiments (Graber and Smith 2005). As this tradition of scholarship has been applied to the Internet in recent years, Web technologies and production techniques have often been "black-boxed" (Pinch and Bijker 1987) by researchers in order to regularize content for statistical analyses, or to standardize stimuli by which to assess effects. As a result, the practices and techniques by which the Web is produced, and the structures and sociotechnical dynamics of Web production, have been largely overlooked. Scholarship in STS, although strong on the social shaping of technology, and on the politics of infrastructure, tool development, and configuration, has not typically focused on technology in distinctly political contexts, much less in elections.

We attempt to contribute to both STS and political communication scholarship by studying the Web in elections (an under-researched topic in STS), through practice-based theorizing (an underused approach in political communication). Political communication scholars may be surprised to find that we do not attempt to assess the impact of the Web on users' political behavior or election outcomes. STS scholars may be surprised to find that we use regression analysis to assess correlations between Web campaigning practices and several sets of factors. Our purpose is to take an in-depth look at campaigns' Web productions in order to unpack their techniques, thereby understanding and explaining Web campaigning practices.

We aim to illuminate the ways in which campaigns are evolving in and through Web technologies. To the extent that campaign organizations structure the electoral experience for other political actors (including citizens, press organizations, and civic and advocacy groups), developments in the Web practices of campaign organizations constitute the impact of the Web on politics. Alternative foci—on, for example, voter knowledge, citizen efficacy, or participatory actions—correlated with individual level measures of Web exposure or usage, while important, fail to capture the broader, but perhaps more subtle, system-level changes that we believe a focus on Web practices affords. Further, we are particularly interested in campaigns' experimentation and innovation, which means paying attention to what some scholars would consider "outlier cases." The prevalence of many of the Web features we examine is low; however, we view the margins as growth edges of practices.

The sum of campaign organizations' decisions to engage in Web campaigning, across a series of election cycles, manifests technology adoption and deployment patterns that can be understood more deeply by viewing campaigns as sociotechnical networks. Campaign innovation and appropriation of specific techniques of Web production provide evidence of an emergent and evolving set of norms across campaign organizations. We suggest that the Web practices adopted by campaign organizations reflect particular political strategies as well as the increasing integration, or convergence, of the offline and online realms.

In our effort to understand the evolving relationship between the Web and electoral politics, we employ practice-based theorizing. Nicolini et al. (2003) suggest that "Practice is both our production of the world and the results of this process. It is always the product of specific historical conditions resulting from previous practice and transformed into present practice. The material process of production involves both the production of goods and the reproduction of society" (p. 8). In this book, we present a "general and abstract account of [particular] practices;" in other words, what Schatzki (2001) calls a "practice theory." As Schatzki explains, this definition of theory departs from notions that tie theory to explanation and prediction, as well as from the conflation of theory-building with hypothesis-testing. Although we take up questions of why some campaigns employ certain Web practices in particular ways, and offer some explanations, we do so through an empirically grounded account of the techniques employed in Web campaigning practices in a way that is consistent with Schatzki's characterization of practice theory. The conceptualizations of these practices—and the techniques that constitute them—provide lenses that may be useful in examining other dimensions of the relationship between electoral politics and the Web, as well as other, nonpolitical, Web practices.

Electoral campaigns vary considerably in their size, funding, status, and internal structure, but as a type of organization they share several characteristics. All have an outward orientation, in that their success depends on informing, persuading, and involving others in the promotion of a candidate. All employ some type of information and communication technology (ICT) in those actions, whether handwritten flyers, radio advertisements, or Internet applications such as the Web. For this reason, we view each campaign as a sociotechnical network, as that term has been conceptualized in the field of social informatics to describe "an interrelated and interdependent milieu of people, their social and work practices, the norms of use, hardware and software, the support systems that aid users, and the maintenance systems that keep their ICTs operating" (Lamb, Sawyer, and Kling 2000). This notion of sociotechnical networks builds on earlier conceptualizations from the perspectives of social shaping of technology (Williams and Edge 1996; MacKenzie and Wajcman 1985) and sociotechnical systems (Moldashcl and Weber 1998), and emphasizes interconnection in contrast to what are sometimes arbitrary distinctions between the social and technical aspects of how people build things and organizations, communicate ideas, and accomplish goals together.

To fully consider campaigns, not just as organizations that use technologies, but also as inherently sociotechnical networks, we have to think about how technologies are both functional implements of human practice and mediating artifacts that intervene in and reshape practices. Cultural-historical activity theory (CHAT) offers conceptual resources to keep both of these dynamics in play. Electoral campaigning, construed as a practice, can be viewed through the lens of CHAT as constituted through particular collective, tool-mediated activities, each of which are oriented toward a shared "object" (Engeström 2005; Leont'ev 1978). In some forms of the CHAT framework, the concept of an object is understood as a collectively constructed entity, in material and/or ideal form, through which the meeting of a particular collective need is pursued. Any individual electoral campaign could be analyzed as an activity system situated within in a heterogeneous network of activity systems involving different, and sometimes overlapping, sets of political actors. Various actors within a campaign may have differing motives in relation to the campaign site as the object of activity. Although there may be many kinds of actors beyond the campaign—such as journalists, citizens, or opponents—for whom a particular campaign site has salience or who coproduce parts of the campaign site with the campaign, in this analysis we position campaigns as the primary subjects in campaign activity systems involving Web production.

Tools are also conceptualized in both material and ideal form and in various levels of concreteness or abstraction in CHAT scholarship (Kuutti 1996; Engeström 1990). The term *tool* is often used synonymously with *artifact*, connoting that all tools are produced through human activity and mediate human activity. Taylor and van Every (2000) explain that "Human interaction mobilizes constellations of [artifacts] which endure after and extend beyond the time and place of the interaction, and as they do, serve to frame future interactions" (p. 163). In this study, both the artifact of a hard-copy campaign brochure and the sociotechnical system for creating and disseminating it constitute tools. Similarly, a candidate biography feature on a campaign site, the mechanism that enables a site visitor to send that biography to a friend via email, the campaign site itself, and a campaign's capacity to produce a Web site all constitute various kinds of tools.

As Engeström (1990) observes, a particular artifact is at times a tool and at other times an object in an activity system. The identification of an artifact as tool or object within an activity system is thus a question of when or under which circumstances, rather than a question of the artifact's properties or affordances. In the activity systems of many campaigns, the creation and maintenance of one or more Web sites—and the overall Web presence of a campaign—is the primary object of at least some part of the campaign organization, if not of the campaign as a whole. Once a campaign's Web presence is established, it becomes a tool employed toward the overarching object of the whole campaign. While the foremost aim of most campaigns is to maximize votes in order to win elections (Downs 1957), the object of some campaigns' activity may instead be influencing the party platform, gaining visibility, or advancing an issue agenda, depending on the particular campaign and the point in time during an election season. For example, a minor party candidate in 2002 described the object of his campaign as shaping political debate: "My opponent ... didn't see me as a viable opponent, because of money. But I used my little computer to provide input to the political debate, my way."

The role of a campaign Web site evolves over the course of a campaign. As a presidential campaign Web producer in 2000 explained,

[A campaign Web site] has a communications role and that communications role changes throughout the life of the campaign. In the early life of the campaign, when the general public really isn't paying attention, it's about communicating with activists and communicating with the press.... In the latter part of the campaign, when it's actually the time when people are voting, hopefully, if you have done your work right, it is a place for undecided voters to go, who are trying to learn more information about the candidates and make up their minds (Reed 2000).

Recognizing that diverse objects animate campaigns during different phases in the election season, and that the appropriation of Web technologies varies within campaigns, we focus on the development of Web practices across campaigns and election cycles, rather than on the evolving activity system of a particular campaign. Although political parties sometimes seek to promote affiliated candidates on the Web, this study foregrounds the Web campaigning practices of candidate-centered campaigns in distinction from those of parties.

We begin with the assumption that Web practices encompass the acts of making (Pickering 1995), by which Web site producers create, appropriate, manipulate, link to, and display digital objects that can be accessed by Web browsers. We view Web objects—whether pages, features, texts, or links—produced by actors in electoral contexts as artifacts manifesting political strategies and actions. Many, but certainly not all, aspects of Web-producing activity can be inferred through careful observation of Web objects. In our observational analyses, we engage in a kind of "Web archae-ology" whereby we infer practices from artifacts, that is, Web objects. Campaign sites are surfaces on which campaigns' Web production practices are inscribed dynamically during (and beyond) an electoral cycle. They carry online structures that simultaneously evidence the communicative and po-litical actions of the campaigns that produce them and enable the organiza-tion of sociopolitical actions on the part of site visitors—some of which may also become inscribed on the campaign site.

Giddens's (1984) structuration theory illuminated the recursive relation-ship between practices and structures, whether social, institutional, or po-litical. Giddens's notion of structure is a macro, system-level concept that connotes hierarchies of people, assumed divisions of labor, and patterned distributions of resources. Structuration theory provides a way of under-standing the emergence and evolution of macro structures such as the elec-toral arena through iterative practices, as well as the shaping of practices through structures. Orlikowski (1992) developed what can be considered a more meso-level "structurational model of technology" in organizations, in which she posited a dialectical relationship between technology devel-opment and use on one hand, and organizational structure and practices on the other. We extend Orlikowski's model of structure, practice, and technology by focusing on campaign organizations and the relationship between the structure of the electoral arena (in Giddens's sense) and meso-level structures created online through sociotechnical practices embedded in code. Orlikowski (1992) and Yates (1989) demonstrated that corporate

organizational structure is manifested in and enacted through material
objects. We suggest that a similar dynamic exists between campaign organizations and their Web productions. We contend that campaigns' acts of
making on the Web reflect the electoral arena, existing organizational
structures, and prior practices, and result in particular organizational and
online structures. These acts of making in turn enable and constrain
actions in ways that may shape future iterations of practices—and thereby
the evolution of structures—both offline and online, and at both the macro
level on which Giddens focuses and the meso level addressed by both
Orlikowski and Yates. More specifically, the Web practices of campaigns
(and other political actors) are shaped by existing structures and cultural
resources in that they reflect strategies and campaign practices developed
over decades of electoral activity. They also manifest technology adoption
patterns within sociotechnical organizations or networks that may have
deep historical and cultural roots. Concurrently, campaigns' Web practices
instantiate an emergent and evolving set of norms and create online structures for political action, some of which may be quite innovative.

To summarize the relationships we posit between tool, technique, activity, practice, and organization as discussed previously, we take the CHAT
perspective that artifacts and technologies are tools for which and with
which techniques are developed that mediate human activity. A practice
is a set of related activities, and an organization is a system of practices
(Nicolini, Gherardi, and Yanow 2003). Building on Orlikowski's (1992)
model, we argue that Web campaigning practices both manifest campaigns'
organizational practices and (re)structure those organizational practices.
The evolution of Web campaigning practices alters campaigns themselves
as sociotechnical networks. With this framework in mind, we now turn
our attention to the concepts of online structures and Web spheres, and
the relationships between them.

Online Structures and Web Spheres

We conceptualize an online structure as a set of features, links, and texts
that provides users opportunities to associate and to act. An individual
Web site can constitute an online structure, as can a set of features, links,
and texts within a site, as well as a coproduced set that spans multiple sites.
Like Web features and sites, online structures are also tools with artifact and

capability aspects. On the Web, relations between Web producers, as well as between producers and users, are enacted and mediated through online structures. Furthermore, each online structure enables and constrains the potential for various kinds of political action, both online and offline.

This notion of online structure is derived from the literature on social movements and the literature examining the potential of the Internet to foster political change. In particular, it builds on the work within the social movements literature distinguishing between "structure" and "action" (Klandermans, Kriesi, and Tarrow 1998). Much theoretical work in the social movements literature focuses on the relationship among political mobilization, formal organizations, external political processes, and internal organizational features (McAdam, McCarthy, and Zald 1996; Mueller 1992; Johnston and Klandermans 1995). Toward this end, McAdam, McCarthy, and Zald (1996) provide a comparative analysis of different theoretical approaches to using the structure of mobilization processes as an analytic tool. This literature suggests the utility of distinguishing between the structure for action and the action itself, and draws attention to the characteristics of the "micromobilization contexts" (McAdam 1988), "free spaces" (Evans and Boyte 1986) and other associational forms (Oldenburg 1989, 2001; Cohen and Rogers 1995) that facilitate political action.

Political campaigns have, of course, always provided offline structures for political action. Campaign offices serve as physical spaces within which activist citizens can engage in political action. For example, activists staff phone banks, produce and distribute literature, and interact with campaign professionals in these spaces. Some of these political actions that are enabled by structures created in campaign offices are engaged within the office itself; others are engaged outside of the campaign office. And, of course, campaigns use structures other than their offices to invite and provide opportunities for citizen action, such as television commercials, direct mail, and billboards. Similarly, campaigns' Web practices result in various types of online structure that enable or constrain a range of political actions both online and offline, such as information gathering, engaging in political talk, and advocacy. Some of the political action made possible or explicitly encouraged by campaign sites is intended to be carried out while online, either through further use of the same site or through other Internet services such as the Web, email, chat, newsgroups, or instant messaging. Other action engendered by the sites requires offline engagement, whether through face-to-face or telephonic conversation, the display and distribution of hard-copy materials, or bodily presence at rallies and other campaign events. Thus, campaigns' Web practices result in online structure for both online action and offline action.

The context within which we analyze online structures is a Web sphere. The concept of a Web sphere emerged from our explorations of the Web during the 2000 election, and we have also employed it as a framework or unit of analysis for studies of other kinds of Web phenomena (Foot and Schneider 2004; Siegl and Foot 2004). We conceptualize a Web sphere as not simply a collection of Web sites, but as a set of dynamically defined digital resources spanning multiple Web sites deemed relevant or related to a central event, concept, or theme. Although some of these resources may be hyperlinked to each other—and the presence (or absence) of links within a sphere may indicate some of its characteristics—links do not define the sphere. Rather, the boundaries of a Web sphere are generally delimited by a shared topical orientation across Web resources and a temporal framework. An electoral Web sphere has a topical orientation toward the election and includes sites produced by actors with a role in the electoral arena, such as candidates, civic and advocacy groups, press organizations, citizens, and government bodies. The electoral arena also includes the sociotechnical systems and instruments produced or appropriated by the many actors associated with the electoral process; in other words, everything from the buses that carry candidates and their entourage in caravans through the countryside, to Congressional legislation governing campaign spending, to the voting guides produced by civic and advocacy organizations such as the League of Women Voters and the Christian Coalition. As Internet technologies such as the Web have developed, the electoral arena has expanded to include online dimensions. We envision the electoral Web sphere as one realm of the electoral arena. By keeping the context of the electoral Web sphere in mind while examining campaigns' Web practices, we are able to analyze the ways that Web campaigning mediates relations between political actors, both within and beyond campaign organizations.

In table 1.1, we summarize the distinctions we make between Web features, online structures, and electoral Web spheres, and compare each with their offline corollaries through the example of facilitating letters to newspaper editors (LTEs). Campaigns have traditionally sought to encourage supporters to send candidate-promoting LTEs and many campaigns have

Table 1.1
Comparing Campaigns' Offline and Online Facilitation of Letters to Editors

Offline	Online
Instrument	*Feature*
Campaign brochure encouraging recipients to send letters to newspaper editors	Web object encouraging visitors to send letters to newspaper editors
Offline Structure	*Online Structure*
Sociotechnical network required to facilitate the creation and distribution of campaign brochure encouraging letters to be sent to editors of newspapers, and monitoring publication of letters	Code, text, and links required to implement a feature on a campaign Web site enabling visitors to send letters directly to editors of newspapers via email, and tracking usage of feature by visitors
Electoral Arena	*Electoral Web Sphere*
Electoral systems, mechanisms and artifacts produced by actors associated with the election (e.g., candidates, press, parties, government agencies, civic and advocacy groups, citizens)	Online structures and other digital resources produced by actors associated with the election (e.g., candidates, press, parties, government agencies, civic and advocacy groups, and citizens)

begun doing this online as well. Working offline to catalyze LTEs, a campaign may create the instrument of a paper brochure with text urging supporters to write to newspaper editors, and including guidelines for letters and contact information for local editors. On the campaign's Web site, an LTE feature may be created for the same purpose through text, HTML code, and links. Neither the paper brochure nor the Web feature facilitating LTEs drop out of the sky fully formed, nor disseminate themselves automatically to supporters. Both are produced and made available for distribution through the campaign organization, which is a sociotechnical network that interfaces with other sociotechnical systems. Thus the paper brochure is situated in organizational structures along with other media produced by the campaign, and the Web feature is situated both in those offline structures and in online structures comprised of other texts, links, and code. The offline structures within which the paper brochure on LTEs is produced are constituent elements of the electoral arena—that is, the electoral systems, mechanisms, and artifacts produced by all actors associated with the election. The online structures with which the LTE Web feature is associated are part of an electoral Web sphere as well as part of the general electoral arena. The online structures and other digital resources produced by all actors associated with an election constitute an electoral Web sphere.

To understand Web campaigning practices within an electoral Web sphere and to explore the wide range of causal factors that we think are necessary to explain differences in Web practices among campaigns, we engage in a close analysis of specific types of practices. The essence of campaigning is persuading. Within the general framework of persuasion, we define and examine four practices in Web campaigning—informing, involving, connecting, and mobilizing—suggesting that each practice involves a distinct type of relationship between campaign organizations and other political actors. Campaign organizations engage in the practice of informing by creating online structures consisting of features that present information. The elementary form of this practice invokes the classic transmission models of communication, in which a communicator or producer transmits a message to a receiver or recipient (Shannon and Weaver 1949; Lasswell 1948). Providing information, such as candidate biography, issue statements, and news or press releases, exemplifies the basic Web practice of informing, but, as we will demonstrate, this practice is evolving in ways that move far beyond transmission models of communication.

The practice of involving is manifested in online structures that facilitate affiliation between the site producer and site visitors. Involving as a campaign practice concerns the opportunity to establish interaction between campaign organizations and campaign site visitors; campaigns employ this practice to cultivate supporters. Involving practices on the Web include allowing users to sign up to receive email or to contribute funds to the campaign. The relationship between the producing organization and the actor using the site is sometimes reminiscent of the swapping between roles of source/encoder and receiver/decoder envisioned by Osgood and Schramm (1954) in their model of communication (McQuail and Windahl 1981). However, some online structures associated with the practice of involving enable site visitors to become coproducers of the campaign site with the campaign, turning role-swapping into spirals of exchange.

The Web practice of connecting involves a campaign in the creation of an online structure that serves as a bridge between the user of the site and a third actor. In other words, the campaign organization uses its Web presence to connect a site user with some other actor, such as a press organization, political party, government agency, or even an electoral opponent. In social network theory, these bridges are the ties between nodes of the network (Rogers 1986; Barnes 1954). In our analysis, any other actor, whether offline or online, constitutes a node to which a campaign Web site may be connected, and the online structure facilitating the connection acts as the tie between nodes. The practice of connecting on the Web is most familiarly invoked using the technique of linking, as described later. However our conception is considerably broader, in that we suggest campaigns create both cognitive and transversal bridges between users and third actors. Transversal connections provide the online structure to facilitate movement through cyberspace, from one place (Web page) to another (Saco 2002), while cognitive connections provide only the mental or psychological bridge, relying on users to complete the connection. For example, a campaign can provide a transversal connection with a link embedding an email address, or a cognitive connection by providing a street address and telephone number.

Futhermore, some campaigns engage in the practice of mobilizing, providing online structure facilitating a user's efforts to involve another actor in the goals and objectives of the campaign. In this type of practice, the campaign has moved beyond involving itself with the user and even beyond making it possible for the user to become connected with a third party actor. Mobilizing practices include structures allowing individuals to send Web pages to friends, print campaign brochures for offline distribution, and obtain names and telephone numbers of potential supporters to be telephoned or emailed.

In tracing a campaign's Web practices, we examined the Web presence produced by a campaign within the electoral Web sphere, not just the main campaign Web site. In the 2000 presidential primary, Max Fose, the Web producer for John McCain's campaign, created two campaign sites (mccain2000.com and mccaininteractive.com). In subsequent elections, the number of campaigns distributing their Web presence across multiple sites increased. Although most campaigns to date have focused their Web presence on producing and maintaining a single campaign Web site, the Web presence of even single-site campaigns is manifested in and mediated by other sites via coproduced content, features, links, or sites produced by other actors. Thus, a more comprehensive understanding of the Web practices of campaigns is possible when campaign Web sites are situated analytically within a Web sphere.

Differences among campaign organizations in their instantiation of these practices distinguish relationships among three types of political actors: (1)

the campaign organizations as producers of online structures for political action; (2) the political actors who choose to take action within the online structures produced by campaigns; and, in some cases, (3) additional third party actors who may become involved through production decisions of the campaign organization. These differences are evident not only through the practices in which campaigns engage, but also through the Web production techniques deployed by the campaigns. To explore these differences, we examine each Web campaigning practice by analyzing the techniques involved in it, as evidenced on campaign sites and discussed by site producers. These four practices share some common techniques—coproduction, linking, convergence—and each involves unique techniques as well.

Campaign organizations use the technique of coproduction when including content produced by other organizations on their own Web pages. This could be accomplished, for example, by appropriating significant amounts of content from a news organization, or by displaying a graphical image that is produced by a national party organization. Linking as a technique involves providing a mechanism through which a user could move within the Web from a page produced by the campaign to a page produced by another actor. A third technique, convergence, involves not only media integration but also bringing together the online and the offline realms of production. Candidates who reference their Web site on campaign yard signs, as well as candidates who draw attention to televised debates on their Web sites, are using the technique of convergence.

Structure of the Book

This study is an examination of campaign Web practices. We trace the emergence and evolution of campaigns' online presences and practices, and the tensions to which they point, through their inscriptions on the Web. Through the production of Web objects, campaigns' strategies of informing prospective voters, involving supporters, connecting Internet users with other political actors, and mobilizing advocates are manifested on the Web in differing ways and to varying degrees. Each of these Web practices is analyzed in view of techniques of linking, coproduction, and convergence, as well as other, practice-specific techniques.

In chapter 2, we elaborate on the techniques of Web production as ways of tracing practices within the conceptual framework of Web sphere analysis. In chapters 3–6, we analyze each Web campaigning practice in-depth, examining the particular ways that the production techniques of linking, coproducing, and convergence mediate the practices of informing, involving, connecting, and mobilizing. Each of these chapters analyzes strategies campaign organizations employ to negotiate the tensions manifested as these practices are engaged on the Web. In chapter 7, we explore the impact of four broad types of factors on the variance in Web campaigning: characteristics of Web producers, aspects of political campaigns, the dynamics of the Web environment, and the structuring effects of practice on practice.

We conclude in chapter 8 by returning to our original questions regarding the relationship between the Web and electoral politics. We use our close analysis of the Web practices and techniques employed by campaign organizations as they instantiated these practices over the course of three elections to draw conclusions about the changes in Web campaigning itself and in campaign organizations as a result of Web campaigning. We consider various potential futures for Web campaigning, taking into consideration the trajectory emerging from the first ten years of practice and the possible developments in organizational, political, and technological circumstances. Finally, we suggest ways in which our conclusions contribute to a political theory of technology and a technologically grounded theory of electoral politics.

2   Tracing Practices within a Web Sphere

In this chapter, we explain further the notion of a Web sphere introduced in chapter 1. We discuss several dimensions of Web spheres, as well as methods for demarcating them and identifying the constituent elements within them. After introducing the set of techniques through which we analyze Web campaigning practices, we then lay out the specific approach we employ to analyze campaign Web practices as they occur within electoral Web spheres. We describe our methods of collecting and observing Web objects, and the interviews, focus groups, and surveys we conducted with campaign site producers and Web users. We conclude the chapter with an overview of the data corpus we compiled in our research on Web campaigning in the 2000, 2002, and 2004 electoral Web spheres in the United States.

Web Sphere Analysis

As explained in chapter 1, we conceptualize a Web sphere as not simply a collection of Web sites, but as a set of dynamically defined, digital resources spanning multiple Web sites deemed relevant or related to a central event, concept, or theme. In this book, we employ the electoral Web sphere as a framework within which we focus on the Web practices of electoral campaigns. Web sphere analysis is a conceptual lens for this and other studies of Web phenomena, enabling analysis of communicative actions and relations between Web producers and users developmentally over time. Web sphere analysis provides an approach for investigating relations between producers and users of Web materials as potentiated and mediated by the structural and feature elements of Web sites, hypertexts, and the links between them.

In the first stage of the multimethod approach of Web sphere analysis, researchers identify Web objects (usually either sites or pages) related to the topical focus of the sphere. These objects are archived at regular intervals during the period of the study in a manner that maintains their hyperlinked context, allowing the researchers to reproduce at some point in the future the experience users might have had (Arms et al. 2001). This enables both contemporaneous and retrospective analyses of developments in the Web sphere over time. Then metadata are created through the annotation of archived objects (again, usually sites or pages) with human or computer-generated notes and/or codes of various kinds. These metadata correspond to the units and levels of analysis anticipated by the researchers. Finally, interviews, focus groups, experiments, or surveys are conducted with site producers and Web users and triangulated with Web annotations and objects to interpret the sphere.

December's (1996) typology of units of analysis for Internet-related research is useful for understanding the nature of a Web sphere as a unit of analysis. The five types of units of analysis December identifies are:

(1) a media space, consisting of the set of all servers of a particular type that may provide information in one or more protocols, the corresponding clients that are capable of accessing these servers, and the associated content available for access on these servers;

(2) a media class—a particular set of content, servers, and clients;

(3) a media object—a specific unit in a media class with which the user can observe and interact;

(4) a media instance—a media object at a particular time; and

(5) a media experience—a particular user's perception of a set of media instances.

In correspondence with December's definitions, a Web sphere could be considered a subset of an Internet media space, constituted by a set of Web sites (a single media class), each of which are composed of elements or objects such as links, features, and texts. Boundaries based on a thematic or event orientation and a temporal framework differentiate our concept of a Web sphere from December's definition of a Web space.

The Web sphere can function as a macro, aggregate unit of analysis, by which historical and intersphere comparisons can be made. For example, the Web sphere of the 2000 elections in the United States can be comparatively analyzed with the electoral Web sphere of 2004 and those that will develop in later years. Similarly, comparative analyses can be conducted on electoral Web spheres internationally. A significant element in our conceptualization of a Web sphere is the dynamic nature of the sites that constitute the sphere. This dynamism comes from three sources. First, researchers involved in identifying the boundaries of the sphere are likely to continually find additional sites to be included within it. Second, new sites related to the topic of the sphere may be produced as it develops. Third, the process of defining a Web sphere is recursive, in that pages that are referenced by included sites, as well as pages that reference included sites, may be considered part of the sphere under evaluation. Thus, as a Web sphere is analyzed over time, its boundaries may be dynamically shaped by researchers' identification strategies, the production of new sites, and changes in the sites themselves.

The more micro and/or molar units—such as texts, features, links, sites, or even the multisite Web presence of an actor—can be employed in analyses simultaneously within a Web sphere. Defining any of these units operationally can be challenging, particularly when the temporal and malleable aspects of Web objects are considered. For example, any Web text or feature can appear stable but actually be modified by its producer or rendered differently by technologies such as Web browsers employed by users at a particular moment. Therefore, the point in time and the way in which a Web object is observed must be part of the unit's definition for research purposes. Units such as an actor's Web presence must also reflect the potential for change over time by being situated in a particular temporal period. For instance, the Web presence of a political party might be appropriately specified by the particular week or month within an election cycle. The hyperlinked and multilevel nature of the Web makes the identification and demarcation of units of analysis a critical but difficult task, even within a Web sphere. Seemingly straightforward questions, such as what constitutes a Web site and from what or whose perspective (robot, browser, or human) that question will be framed, require careful consideration. In addition, the coproduced nature of the Web—evidenced in the joint production by multiple actors of many features and much content—makes the attribution of agency to producers of specific bits problematic.

Bounding Web Spheres

In Web sphere analysis, the process of demarcating boundaries, that is, identifying elements such as sites or pages to be included, is part discovery and part creation. Three dimensions of Web spheres have bearing on how researchers go about this process: thematic anticipatability, actor predictability, and the stability of constituent Web objects. These three dimensions can each be viewed as a continuum. The position of a Web sphere of interest on these three continua may help researchers develop strategies for identification of elements to be included in the analysis.

The degree to which it is possible to anticipate the emergence of a Web sphere is the measure of *thematic anticipatability*. Some Web spheres can be easily anticipated in view of prior and current dynamics on the Web, and others cannot. Part of the anticipatability of a Web sphere is dependent on the extent to which it is defined by a specific event. Events such as elections and the Olympics are regular occurrences and thus anticipated, while others, such as accidents, tragedies, and scientific discoveries, are less likely to be anticipated. Triggering events (Gamson and Modigliani 1989) such as major new discoveries, which in general are unanticipated, may also provide the stimulus for a thematic Web sphere. For example, a Web sphere focused on cloning may have emerged in response to the announcement of Dolly, the first cloned mammal. Web spheres that emerge in the aftermath of an event may be triggered by but not focused on that specific event. In the absence of generalized and systematic Web archiving (Kahle 1997; Schneider et al. 2003), anticipatability is often a crucial factor in whether a Web sphere is researched. Web spheres emerging quickly after an unanticipated event may be challenging to study because a rapid investment of resources (time, money, topical expertise) is required and the boundaries are difficult to demarcate.

Actor predictability is concerned with the ability of researchers to predict the types of actors who will produce materials encompassed within a Web sphere in advance of its emergence. Some Web spheres will be produced by a highly predictable set of actor types. Web spheres organized around electoral campaigns, for example, are highly actor-predictable because they may (depending on the localized political context) include sites produced by parties, candidates, press organizations, advocacy groups, citizens, and government agencies. Web spheres emerging around unanticipated natural disasters and accidents are likely to include sites produced by a predictable set of actors: government agencies, relief and charity organizations, press organizations, and citizens, for example. Other Web spheres will be produced by a less predictable set of actor types. Following the terrorist attacks of September 11, we observed significant and unpredicted activity on Web sites produced by corporations and businesses, along with more predictable activity on sites produced by religious organizations, educational institutions, and government agencies (Foot and Schneider 2004). Actor predictability can greatly affect the thoroughness with which relevant sites can be identified. A predictable set of actors enables researchers to identify a universe of sites to examine for evidence of Web activity within a demarcated Web sphere. A less-predictable set of actors makes this task more difficult and requires additional searching and identification activities.

A third dimension of Web spheres is the *level of stability* in the development of sites, links, and other objects within the Web sphere. The level of stability has an impact on how frequently the boundaries of the Web sphere need to be reconsidered and how often the sites within the Web sphere need to be examined. We have identified three determinants of the level of stability within a Web sphere. First, consideration should be given to the frequency of entry and exit of new producers. The extent of new entrants into the Web sphere (represented by specific producers, rather than types of producers) and the extent to which producers stop updating, maintaining, or serving their sites, are measures of the stability of the sphere: Highly stable spheres have less entry and exit than unstable spheres. Second, stability is measured by the degree to which sites being analyzed add or remove links to other sites within the Web sphere. Frequent additions or deletions of links reduce stability. Third, the frequency and breadth of changes to content and features within the Web sites under examination contributes to stability. Highly stable Web spheres consist primarily of sites with infrequent and narrowly focused changes to content and features.

The position of a Web sphere along these dimensions influences the researchers' decision either to fix the boundaries of the sphere at the beginning of a study or to engage in a dynamic bounding process. Bounding refers to the process of identifying constituent sites or pages within the Web sphere and specifying a temporal frame for analysis. Although electoral Web spheres can be anticipated and the general categories of actors involved in coproducing these spheres are anticipatable, electoral Web spheres can be quite unstable. Thus researchers still face significant quandaries regarding the bounding of these spheres in time and virtual space, as we explain later. Identifying constituent elements of a Web sphere to be examined may include both establishing the universe of sites or pages about which generalizations can be offered and specifying a method of sampling sites or pages to be analyzed. Constituent elements can be identified prior to analysis by following long-established practices in survey research (Hyman 1955) and content analysis (Berelson 1952). Alternatively, constituent elements can be identified as part of the analytic process, building on well-established techniques used in participant-observation (Whyte 1943) and on snowball sampling (Berg 1988; Atkinson and Flint 2001). Identifying constituent elements prior to analysis—in effect, fixing the boundaries of the Web sphere under study—offers several advantages to the researcher. A clearly defined universe of sites within a Web sphere makes representative sampling of sites possible for both archiving and structured observations. Fixed boundaries may also increase the possibility of replicating findings by subsequent analysts. Finally, fixing the boundaries of the Web sphere may enhance options for collaboration in archiving or analyzing it, particularly with entities such as libraries (Schneider et al. 2003).

On the other hand, dynamic bounding allows the researcher to be responsive to unanticipated developments and emergent trends in the Web sphere. Even within anticipated, predictable, and generally stable Web spheres, unanticipated events precipitate the production or alteration of intertextual and interlinked Web objects, sometimes in a matter of hours or over the course of a few days. We employ the concept of a *Web storm* as a unit of analysis that reflects unanticipated interactor and intersite activity over a relatively brief period of time. For instance, a political scandal is likely to result in a Web storm wherein news organizations, advocacy groups, and individuals post texts, graphics, and links regarding the scandal intensively for several days or weeks. Some Web storms develop into Web spheres that are durable on the Web over a longer period, often through the migration of individual texts and pages pertaining to an event to sites newly produced and dedicated to the event. For example, a Web storm emerged quickly in the wake of the 1988 release of the Starr report, detailing U.S. President Bill Clinton's affair with Monica Lewinsky and raising questions of perjury. The Web storm of commentaries developed into a Web sphere focused on the Clinton impeachment, as sites were produced by different types of actors advocating or opposing the removal of the president from office. Interestingly, some sites, such as moveon.org, emerged from this Web sphere and became part of other political Web spheres, including the U.S. electoral Web spheres in 2000, 2002, and 2004.

A researcher engaged in dynamic bounding is less likely to miss the opportunity to analyze these Web storms, which may actually be significant bursts of online action. Dynamic bounding as a scholarly practice is also more consistent with how the Web functions from a user perspective. It is critical, though, that dynamic bounding be implemented systematically to ensure representativeness and replicability. Researchers need to decide, preferably before beginning a study, how frequently the Web sphere boundaries will be redefined, specifying the circumstances, frequency, criteria, and techniques to be used to identify the pages, sites, or links comprising the sphere. A further factor to consider is the correspondence between research goals and the bounding strategy. For instance, if the goal is to analyze the development of a Web sphere, a fairly dynamic bounding strategy is needed. Finally, researchers should assume that increased dynamism in Web sphere demarcation will increase resource needs (time, effort, and storage), especially if systematic archiving is involved.

The process of discovering and establishing the Web sphere under study also includes defining the steps or procedures necessary for identifying the specific elements to be examined. Depending on the characteristics of the Web sphere, this process can involve a number of strategies. If the producer types are highly predictable and the Web sphere itself highly anticipated, current and maintained directories of sites may be available. For example, for a researcher interested in the Web sphere related to a single season of a professional sports league, a current directory of sites representing each of the participating teams could likely serve as a starting point for identification of relevant sites. Encompassing the pre-existing directory into the research design (by specifying sites to be examined as those identified by the directory on a specific date) serves as a robust specification of identification strategy and provides a universe from which samples of sites can be reliably drawn for systematic examination.

On the other hand, some Web spheres of interest, especially those that are not anticipated or predictable, may require a more search-oriented strategy to identify constituent elements. Using topical key words systematically in search engines may be fruitful in identifying constituent elements of a Web sphere. However, this strategy, which relies on the presence of seemingly relevant content within potential sites, may have significant drawbacks. The absence of relevant content on some Web sites may reflect action on the part of a site producer that is just as strategic as the presence of relevant Web content would be. For example, we would consider a Web site produced by a political party that provides issue information several weeks before an election—but does not mention any candidate or the election itself—a constitutive element of the electoral Web sphere in view of the party's role in the electoral process. In such a case, the absence of election-related content may reflect a strategic aim of general agenda-setting rather than specific candidate promotion. Furthermore, if explicit election-related material were to appear on a particular site at a later date, establishing its absence at the beginning of the study period would be critical for developmental analysis.

One alternative to content relevance as the primary criteria for inclusion in the Web sphere, as suggested by the previous example, is the inclusion of Web sites produced by actors identified as relevant to the sphere. Relevant actor types can be determined in several ways, including through whatever extant literature informs a particular study, as well as through methods of social network analysis. Once relevant actor types are established, the Web sites of particular actors within each type can be selected through various indices and sampling techniques. Web sites produced by relevant actors may be significant in structuring online action—or the lack thereof—within the Web sphere even if those actors have not (yet) produced Web materials relevant to the theme of the sphere at the beginning of the study.

Another strategy for identifying constituent elements in a Web sphere is to analyze patterns of linking to and from a set of URLs representing core sites in the Web sphere. For instance, the Web sphere of a sports team could be defined by tracing the links to and from the URLs of the home pages of each player and of the team itself. The linked-from and linked-to pages can be analyzed in the context of their base sites to identify their producers and thereby specify the producer type. Further analysis of these producers' Web presence may be helpful to ascertain their position or stance within the Web sphere under study.

In summary, the process of demarcating Web spheres includes establishing a thematic or topical orientation, a temporal range, and a method of identifying constituent elements. The dimensions of a Web sphere, expressed as thematic anticipatability, actor predictability, and the stability of constituent Web materials, all shape the challenge faced by researchers interested in conducting Web sphere analyses. Following an overview of some production techniques employed in the creation of online structures within Web spheres, we assess the particular characteristics of U.S. electoral Web spheres.

Web Production Techniques

We analyze Web practices through the techniques that mediate the production of Web objects or artifacts. One baseline Web technique is simply the production of any kind of content in hypertext markup language. The three techniques on which we focus in each of the following chapters are coproduction, convergence, and linking. These three techniques are particularly significant to electoral campaigning, although they are also associated with many practices and activities. Coproduction is the joint production of Web objects, whether of content, features, links, or sites. Convergence is bringing together the online and the offline realms of production, whether through media, organizations, or activity. Linking as a technique of Web production is the establishment of a mechanism that connects one Web object to another, thus enabling a user to transverse from a page produced by the campaign to a page produced by another actor. Variants of each technique are employed broadly across all four Web campaigning practices—informing, involving, connecting, and mobilizing—although not all variants are evident within each practice. General characteristics of these three techniques are described next. Specific variants of these and other techniques employed uniquely within each practice are analyzed in the following chapters.

The technique of coproducing encompasses creating and maintaining Web objects jointly between actors who are organizationally independent from each other. Collaboration between individuals who are co-located within an organization is not our focus in this technique. Evidence of a coproductive process may be textual, visual, or manifested through links. In 2000, for example, the webwhiteandblue.org site was created to provide comparative information about candidates' issue positions. The multiactor collaboration through which it was produced was described in a text displayed on the site. Its coproduction was also indicated by links to several campaigns and news organizations as well as to the Markle Foundation (the site's primary sponsor). Although some forms of coproduction of Web sites are invisible to site visitors, other forms are manifested clearly, such as when the site producer uses appropriated or syndicated content from external sources. Other observable means of coproduction are through various forms of content contributions, such as postings on message boards, campaign event accounts submitted to the site by people outside the campaign, and blogs that allow reader comments or multiauthored posts. Similarly, coproduction may be evident in features such as a photo gallery with images contributed by supporters, or through reciprocal links between sites produced by different actors.

The second production technique we explore is convergence. Although the term *convergence* is sometimes used to refer to the integration or hybridization of various kinds of media, we conceptualize it more broadly. In our view, convergence involves bringing together aspects of the offline and online realms through organizations, actions, or media. In the context of campaigning, convergence occurs frequently through the incorporation of information objects originally produced offline (such as brochures or television commercials) onto the campaign Web site. Conversely, convergence can also be evidenced through the incorporation of Web media into offline campaign strategies and messages, such as the dissemination of yard signs via the campaign site, the use of a campaign site to organize supporters to canvass a physical neighborhood, or the advertisement of campaign site URLs in print or broadcast media. In other words, the promotion or dissemination in either the online or offline realm of an artifact produced in the other realm instantiates our notion of convergence.

In addition to media integration, convergence is employed in any instance in which a campaign seeks to blend its offline and online presence and activity. For example, posting photos online of an offline campaign event brings an offline experience onto the Web (and invites site visitors to envision themselves at such an offline event). A feature on a campaign site that urges site visitors to telephone local talk radio stations to express support for the candidate is another variant of convergence, using an online structure to catalyze offline action.

Linking is the third Web production technique we assess. Often considered the essence of the Web, linking is one of the most basic of all Web production techniques; it is, arguably, the most studied and the most important to present with a nuanced and detailed approach. An examination of the origin of the hyperlink concept and the literature analyzing the purpose and meaning of hyperlinks illustrates the importance of linking to the study of Web practices.

The term "hypertext" was coined by Ted Nelson in the 1960s, in an Association of Computing Machinery conference presentation where he described his work on developing early text processing software (Keep, McLaughlin, and Parker 1993). In his book *Dream Machines* (Nelson 1978), Nelson described the interconnectedness of ideas in types of links. In his typology, referential links displayed the destination on the originating page. A note link displayed a linked destination in a separate screen (similar to a pop-up window) where non-linked information could be read, comparable to a footnote or endnote in a paper document (Keep, McLaughlin, and Parker 1993). Nelson conceptualized expansion links as supplying the destination information in expandable outline form at the source and command links as running some external function, such as starting another software program.

Nelson's typology of ideas interconnected by links was foundational to Tim Berners-Lee's (2000) vision for the World Wide Web. However, the definition of hyperlink and what comprises its source and destination nodes are still ambiguous in many studies of the Web—perhaps because researchers approach hyperlink analysis from a variety of disciplines. Mitra's (1999) study of intertextuality online characterizes hypertext as inherently dialogical, with site producers engaging in a form of dialogue by linking between texts. Mitra argues that sense-making communities develop around interlinked texts, providing interpretive lenses. The connections between these discourses—that is, the hyperlinks created between texts—may provide meaning for a community.

Rogers and Marres (2000) take a slightly different tack, contending that hyperlinks evidence socioepistemic networks in which actors on the Web acknowledge other actors by linking to their sites, or do not acknowledge others by not linking. Adamic and Adar (2001) also consider links as more than associations between bits of information. Rather, they suggest links convey some kind of social relationship between the producers of the links' nodes, although not necessarily a personal relationship. Through these link structures that are created between producers of sites, some kinds of relationships between site producers can be inferred from hyperlinks in addition to associations between information and activities presented in the linked texts. In a similar vein, Hine (2000) and Beaulieu (2005) examine the methodological issues of an ethnographic approach to Web studies and attend to the context and situatedness of Web sites. They question the aims, strategies, and the resulting identity-construction processes of Web site producers as they are mediated through hyperlinks.

We concur with many of these studies, which emphasize that hyperlinks between sites are not only connectors between texts, but can also be mediators of a wide range of associative relations between producers of Web materials. For the purposes of this book, we draw distinctions between three broad types of linking: internal linking, outlinking, and inlinking. Internal linking creates links between objects or pages within a single site. Links between the front page of a site and any other page that shares the same domain are internal links. Linking between objects or pages within a site structures a visitor's experience in two ways. First, the menu of links that is provided across the top or along the side of many sites is a heuristic, allowing site visitors to efficiently parse the site. As a heuristic, this navigation menu shapes the way a visitor makes sense of a site (Burbules and Callister 2000; Burnett and Marshall 2003). Second, internal linking enables a form of interactivity that Stromer-Galley (2000) labels "media interaction," that is, links between elements of a site—such as images, words, or pages— allow visitors to create their own paths through the site and afford them a sense of motion and navigation (Peng, Tham, and Xiaoming 1999; Saco 2002; Manovich 2001). The experience of navigating hyperlinks can evoke in site visitors a perception of increased informational value and control over the information-seeking process, even though, in actuality, the site producer controls the information that can be found on a particular site (Eveland and Dunwoody 2001; Stromer-Galley and Foot 2002).

Outlinking creates links to pages that are part of a different site, outside of the domain in which the link originates. A campaign site that provides links to sites produced by other entities, such as political parties or government agencies, is outlinking. Outlinking entails a relinquishment of control in two ways: Outlinks make it easy for site visitors to leave the original site, and linked-to sites may be altered in ways the outlinking entity did not anticipate. Inlinking refers to linking into the site being analyzed, so from the perspective of a campaign, any site that links to its site is inlinking. We share Park's (2003) contention that outlinking inscribes communicative and strategic choices on the part of site producers. Proponents of this view suggest that hyperlink networks between sites can serve a communicative social function for the producer and users. Through outlinks, Web producers transform independently produced sites into contiguous elements of a common Web sphere.

We take a user's perspective by including the criterion of functionality in our definition of a link. After all, from a user's perspective, two pages are not connected by a broken link, regardless of the producer's intentions. Although a broken link may be repaired at any future point in time, there is no guarantee that it will; nor is there any way of determining whether the lack of functionality is accidental or intentional on the part of either the outlinking site producer or the linked-to site producer. Thus, the user's experience of the functionality of a link at the moment of observation becomes a decisive criterion. For example, the front page of a campaign site of a congressional candidate in 2004 encapsulated a link to the phrase "Experience we need, leadership we trust," but the link resolved to a "404 page not found" error.[7] To the user, whatever the producer intended to display in conjunction with notions of experience and leadership did not exist. Instead, the broken link may have served as an ironic sign casting doubt on at least the Web production skills of the candidate, if not also the experience and leadership of this candidate. In the context of Web campaigning, we focus on linking as enabling movement between different producers' domains, not merely creating cognitive associations between Web objects.

Techniques such as coproduction, convergence, and linking mediate Web practices. Within our conceptual framework, Web objects—whether sites, pages, or individual features—are viewed as inscriptions of practices produced through techniques. Once implemented on Web sites, the objects that result from a site producer's production techniques both reflect those techniques and function as tools themselves within the producer's overall activity. Web practices can be examined by taking a close look at the techniques that mediate them, which, in turn, can be inferred by observing the particular features associated with them. Having sketched some characteristics of Web spheres and some techniques of Web production within

campaigns, the remainder of this chapter focuses on the specific characteristics of U.S. electoral Web spheres and on the particular methods we used
to collect the data presented in this book.

Methods for Tracing Campaign Practices in U.S. Electoral Web Spheres

Web campaigning, as practiced by organizations advocating for specific
candidates, occurs within the context of an electoral Web sphere. In the
United States, the key nodes, parameters, and growth patterns of electoral
Web spheres are largely anticipatable, fairly predictable, and relatively
stable. Since the first significant use of the Web by political campaigns in
the 1996 U.S. elections, electoral Web spheres have become as anticipatable
as the elections around which they are oriented. The temporal parameters
of each election's Web sphere are fairly easy to establish: Depending on the
level of office being sought, the production of the electoral Web sphere usually begins in conjunction with the declarations of candidates and continues a few days after the election. The general types of actors involved in
producing the electoral Web spheres are, for the most part, predictable. In
addition to campaigns and political parties, electoral Web sphere producers
in the U.S. typically include news organizations, civic and advocacy groups,
government bodies such as the Federal Election Commission and the Secretary of State offices for each state, and individual citizens. However, many
of the specific actors who coproduce each electoral Web sphere are not predictable. Moreover, although there are a few substantial online indices of
the main Web sites produced by campaigns for federal offices, in our experience none of these have been comprehensive at the onset of an election
season, nor have they been kept up-to-date during the months preceding
an election as campaigns take down some sites and produce others. Thus,
the identification of constituent elements of a U.S. electoral Web sphere is
quite challenging and comprehensive identification is impossible.

The recent proliferation of blogs produced by journalists, citizens, and
citizen-journalists has increased the difficulty of comprehensive identification. For most U.S. elections, it is reasonable for a researcher to establish ad-
mittedly arbitrary but generally acceptable start and end dates to demarcate
an electoral Web sphere. For example, a researcher studying an electoral
Web sphere including a presidential primary election might establish a
start date of one year before the New Hampshire primary and an end date

of the last day of the second national convention. It is also possible for a researcher to predict the timing of some of the significant events in the electoral Web sphere based on scheduled events in the election season, such as public debates and campaign finance reporting deadlines.

The growth of the Web sphere may also be somewhat predictable if the activity peaks associated with online campaigning reflect those associated with offline campaigning. The sources of unpredictability found in offline campaigning shape the lack of predictability of actors, events, and growth trajectories of electoral Web spheres. Scandals involving one or more campaigns or parties, changes in electoral regulations during an election season, or deaths of candidates are examples of unpredictable events. These events may create an unanticipated lack of stability within an electoral Web sphere, attract new Web producers to the sphere, or otherwise reshape the sphere's parameters or growth trajectory.

Alternatively, Web campaigning may manifest significantly different patterns of activity than offline campaigning under some circumstances. Although it would appear that, overall, electoral Web spheres involve highly anticipated events with predictable types of producers who create somewhat stable Web artifacts, our experience suggests advantages to a research design that encompasses dynamic bounding and is responsive to potential Web storms. Systematic, ongoing identification of this type of Web sphere at regular intervals during its development enables a researcher to either establish empirically the stability of the sphere or track its changes over time. Some forms of online action within this type of sphere are foreseeable, but the possibility of anticipated forms of online action intensifying or new forms emerging during the development of the sphere requires regular observation. In U.S. electoral Web spheres, when a Web storm erupts, new constituent sites may emerge and linking patterns between political actors may change significantly. For example, the sudden death in October 2002 of the incumbent Senator Paul Wellstone of Minnesota led to the rapid emergence of new producers, including a new candidate, as well as a repurposing of the Wellstone site from candidate promotion to memorial. This Web storm was also evident in new texts on many existing sites and new links between sites within the electoral sphere.

Our analysis of how campaigns engaged in Web practices in the U.S. electoral Web spheres of 2000, 2002, and 2004 was informed by a variety of data sources. To generate observational data from the Web, we first demarcated the electoral Web sphere for each election. Based on this demarcation, we identified as many constituent elements as possible within each sphere, including Web objects with election-related content and Web objects produced by actors with roles in the electoral arena (whether their manifest content seemed election-related or not). We conducted interviews, focus groups, and a survey with site producers. In addition, our analysis was informed by data collected from citizens who were potential users and coproducers of the Web sphere, again through a survey, interviews, and focus groups. The multimethod strategy we employed reflects the approach to Web sphere analysis previously presented. In the remainder of the chapter, we briefly describe our strategies for demarcating Web spheres, analyzing campaign Web sites, and gathering data from Web producers and Web users. (For a more detailed description of our methods and data corpus see Appendix.)

Starting with the 2000 election season, we developed the processes for demarcating a Web sphere through a grounded theory approach. Beginning in the summer of 1999, we started an exploratory process of identifying Web sites related to the presidential, congressional, and gubernatorial elections scheduled for 2000. We used standard Web indexes to locate sites produced by campaigns, parties, advocacy groups, civic organizations, news media outlets, portals, and citizens. We continued this process throughout the election season and for several weeks following election day. In an attempt to preserve the electoral Web sphere that unfolded between July 1999 and December 2000, we archived more than a thousand Web sites for future analysis (Schneider and Foot 2000). Based on this experience, we systematized our identification processes for the 2002 election and, in cooperation with the U.S. Library of Congress, identified more than 2,500 Web sites related to the 2002 election. These sites are preserved for analysis in the publicly available 2002 Election Web Archive (Schneider and Foot 2003). Identification processes were further refined in 2004, in correspondence with shifts in our research design (see Appendix).

Having demarcated electoral Web spheres for the 2000, 2002, and 2004 elections, we conducted systematic observations on samples of Web sites produced by various types of actors during the periods under study. In this book, we report our analyses of campaign Web sites. In each election year, we observed a sample of Web sites produced by candidates running in whichever presidential primary and general election contests were held that year for president, governor, U.S. Senate, and U.S. House of Representatives. In our exploratory study in 2000, we first observed and annotated a set of campaign Web sites to determine both the range of features present and the characteristics of online structures. We then developed measures to estimate the presence or absence of particular features on the selected sample of campaign Web sites, adding new features to our coding schemes as they were discovered by analysts. In 2002, we developed a more comprehensive coding frame of more than sixty features drawn from our analysis of campaign sites in 2000. This coding frame was used to assess the prevalence of features on a large sample of campaign Web sites. Having refined our research questions over two election cycles, in 2004, we focused our analysis on a subset of features from the 2002 coding scheme in order to make structured observations of over a hundred campaign Web sites and unstructured observations of approximately 250 additional sites. Our sampling strategies, coding frames, and operational definitions of each feature we assessed during the three elections are provided in the Appendix.

When referencing particular Web sites as illustrations in this book, we provide the site URL in an endnote, using archival URLs when possible. We include the candidate's name, party affiliation, state, and office sought in the text. Party, state, and office sought are represented in a three-part parenthetical notation, such as R-MN-5 or D-IA-Sen, wherein the first letter(s) designates the candidate's party affiliation (D=Democrat, R=Republican, C=Constitution, Lib=Libertarian, Gr=Green, Ref=Reform, etc.), the middle letters are the U.S. postal code abbreviations for the state, and the third character is either a number representing a congressional district or the abbreviation "Sen" for Senate or "Gov" for governor.

In addition to our analyses of campaign Web sites, we gathered data through focus groups, interviews, and surveys of both producers of campaign Web sites and citizens who were potential users and coproducers of campaign Web sites. Our initial fieldwork with producers and citizens was through several series of focus groups conducted in 2000 with citizens in New Hampshire, New York, Pennsylvania, Minnesota, and California. The primary series on which we draw in this study consisted of eleven focus groups conducted in the homes of New Hampshire voters just prior to the presidential primaries. In this series we employed a snowball sampling strategy to recruit neighbors and friends as participants; we provide a more detailed description of this series in the Appendix.

Other citizen focus groups were conducted in professional facilities by a consultant, using industry-standard recruiting practices. Although we do not report findings from these citizen discussions directly in this study, these discussions are significant in that they were observed by producers of campaign Web sites working in the districts from which participants were recruited. These observing producers were recruited as participants in meta-focus groups held simultaneously with the citizen focus groups; the citizen focus groups served as the stimulus material for the groups of site producers. Producers watched citizens navigate and discuss several kinds of sites in the electoral Web sphere, including campaign sites and sites produced by nonpartisan civic groups, and discussed with us their reactions to citizens' comments about these sites. We draw on the producers' discussions of citizens' responses to political sites in this study.

Along with the focus groups, we conducted thirteen in-depth interviews with campaign site producers from various states during the fall of 2000. Most of the interviewees were Webmasters; some were campaign managers responsible for Web strategy. Those interviewed represented a wide range of experience in producing campaign Web sites, from low-budget, third-party House campaigns to presidential primary contenders.

Finally, we used Web-based surveys to gather data from both citizens and Web producers. During the 2000 election, we conducted a Web-based survey of citizens to assess their interest in using the Web for particular kinds of political and electoral information and activity. Following the 2002 campaign, we conducted a Web-based survey of Web site producers. More detailed methodological descriptions of the focus groups, interviews, and surveys are provided in the Appendix.

Our multimethod approach, involving demarcating electoral Web spheres, closely analyzing campaign Web sites, and gathering data through multiple mechanisms from Web producers and potential users (and coproducers) of the electoral Web sphere, enabled us to capture the emergence and evolution of campaigns' Web practices, and the tensions to which they point. Through techniques such as linking, coproduction, and convergence, campaigns' strategies of informing prospective voters, involving supporters, connecting Web users with other political actors, and mobilizing supporters to become advocates are manifested on the Web in differing ways and to varying degrees. The following four chapters draw on the data sources we have sketched in this chapter to analyze Web campaigning practices through the lens of Web production techniques.

3   Informing

A Practice Observed: Informing

The 2002 Senate campaign site of Colorado Libertarian Rick Stanley was a
model of breadth, depth, and hyperlinked architecture in its information provision. In addition to a biography and overview of the candidate's positions on a
range of issues, the site also featured several other types of information. These
included an explanation of Stanley's reasons for running for the Senate, an
overview of his "new ideas for government," texts of speeches given at campaign events, and endorsements.

Some of the information provided by the Stanley campaign was unusual
enough to differentiate their site from most. A list of "movements, events, and
issues which Rick [was] keeping an eye on" enabled visitors to gain a sense of
the candidate's concerns, values, and affiliations.[8] In one section of the site,
labeled "Most Important Documents," a visitor could read the entire text of
the Declaration of Independence, the U.S. Constitution, and the Bill of Rights.[9]
Another section of the site was devoted to a national "Bill of Rights" campaign
urging Congress to repeal all unconstitutional laws. The text exhorted readers
to volunteer for that effort, noting, "And remember—this is not just for the
Stanley for U.S. Senate campaign—this is for you, your family, your friends,
and your community. It is for our country."[10] The invitation to volunteer with
this issue campaign illustrates how Stanley used his electoral campaign site to
advance an issue agenda.

Stanley's campaign made extensive use of the techniques of linking and coproduction in its implementation of the practice of informing. The primary issue
section on this site featured a grid containing titles for twenty-seven issue
topics, ranging from those commonly addressed on campaign sites (taxes, education, and healthcare) to those that are rarely mentioned (jury nullification,

flag desecration, and drug prohibition). Each issue title on the grid was internally linked to a lengthy page of text describing Stanley's position on that issue. Furthermore, each issue position page had a section at the bottom containing outlinks to other Web sites supporting Stanley's position along with a set of relevant quotes from news articles and famous people.

In contrast, Stanley's Democratic and Republican opponents addressed fewer issues, with less substantiation. The Democratic candidate posted positions on twelve issues on his campaign site, and the incumbent Republican candidate described his Senate committee appointments and the legislation he sponsored but did not provide any distinct issue positions.[11] Both sites lacked the long descriptions, extensive outlinks, and supportive quotes that made Stanley's site so rich in issues.

Coproduction was also employed among the Stanley campaign and other Web producers in the 2002 electoral Web sphere. The campaign appropriated materials from several newspapers—over a dozen news articles and editorials, dated and attributed to the newspapers in question, were re-presented in the "Press Clippings" section of Stanley's site.[12] Two other sections of the site, "Endorsements" and "Letters from the People," also manifested coproduction by displaying texts authored by persons outside the official campaign.[13]

These instances of coproduction were largely unilateral, on the part of Stanley's campaign. However, a form of reciprocal coproduction was evident between the candidate and the producers of the political portal purepolitics.com, self-described as "a non-biased, non-partisan political portal that is not supported by any cause or entity." Both Stanley's site and the portal posted on their Web sites the candidate's responses to a questionnaire that the portal had authored and emailed to candidates across the country.[14]

Though Stanley's site made extensive use of linking and coproduction to provide information, it did not employ convergence beyond the provision of a street address and telephone number. Stanley sought to affiliate himself with like-minded individuals, issue advocacy groups, and Libertarian organizations in many ways, but made no attempt to explicitly compare himself to his opponents.

The Practice of Informing

Web producers engage in the practice of informing when they create online structures to present information to site visitors. In essence, with every element posted on a Web site, site producers create a message and transmit it, upon request, to the site visitor. A campaign's engagement in the basic form of this practice does not require the creation of a structure that facilitates either additional interaction between the producer and the recipient, or any additional action on the part of the recipient beyond the initial request. However, when campaigns engage in the practice of informing through the techniques of coproduction, introduced in chapter 2, and documentation, introduced later, more robust and complex online structures emerge than are suggested by the sender-receiver models of communication (Lasswell 1948; Shannon and Weaver 1949).

We conceptualize informing as foundational to and part of all other Web practices. In other words, all online structures present information. However, because some aspects of Web campaigning are associated with informing alone, it is useful to examine informing as a practice in its own right. To do this, we must consider the overall patterns of informing by campaign organizations over the past few election cycles, as well as the particular techniques employed by campaign organizations as they engage in this practice.

Our examination of informing highlights tensions that the adoption of this practice entails for campaign organizations. In particular, organizations are concerned with pressures to create and maintain a significant quantity of accurate and current information, as well as to provide specific information. Closely related to the pressure for quantity and specificity are campaigns' concerns for providing information to a sufficiently wide audience—including those whose interests may not coincide with the campaign. Addressing these concerns can be especially challenging in a rapidly evolving environment where Web materials are increasingly cached and archived, facilitating analysis by other actors, including current and future opponents, journalists, and regulators. These concerns shape how campaigns seek to inform site visitors, as we will discuss in detail.

Cursory examination of campaign Web sites reveals that most sites engage in the practice of informing. Candidate biographies, issue statements, texts of speeches delivered by the candidate, press releases and other campaign news, and text or video presentations of campaign advertisements released in other media are common examples of this practice. Some are fairly standard in form and structure: Candidate speeches are typically presented as audio files or transcribed texts,[15] campaign advertisements are similar but also may be available as video files,[16] and press releases, typically addressed to journalists, are usually text memos about campaign events or candidate activity.[17] Others show more variety: Candidate biographies range from brief overviews about a candidate's personal life[18] to resume-like listings of professional positions held and political experience,[19] to extensive narratives about the events, beliefs, and values that influenced a candidate's decision to run for office.[20] Issue statements on campaign sites also vary in focus, depth, and breadth.[21]

The very earliest campaign Web sites provide evidence that most of those campaign organizations practiced informing extensively from the inception of Web campaigning. Sites launched to support the efforts of candidates in the 1996 Republican presidential-primary election—the first campaign in which most serious candidates launched Web sites—show a high incidence of informing. Analyses of these sites indicate that most featured candidate biographies, issues sections, speeches, and campaign news (Benoit and Benoit 2000; Margolis, Resnick, and Tu 1997; Selnow 1998; Tedesco, Miller, and Spiker 1998; Klotz 1997). For example, the Web site for Steve Forbes's 1996 primary campaign included sections on issues, press releases, speeches, news articles, a biography, and a Forbes family album.[22]

Nearly universal adoption of informing as a Web campaigning practice continued during the 2000 and 2004 presidential primary campaigns. Informing features were ubiquitous during the 2000 primary season: All of the sites included candidate biographies, issue statements, speeches, and campaign news, and all but two included campaign ads. Presidential campaign Web sites during the 2004 Democratic presidential primary season provide similar evidence that the practice of informing had become widespread and deeply ingrained. Seven of the nine presidential sites evaluated in 2004 included all five features, and all of the sites included at least three of the features.

Similarly, campaign Web sites produced to support gubernatorial candidates and congressional candidates provide further evidence of the early, widespread, and growing adoption of the Web campaigning practice of informing. Our analyses of congressional and gubernatorial campaign Web sites in 2000, 2002, and 2004, when combined with Kamarck's (1999) analysis of 1998 sites, provide a broad overview of more than 2,000 campaign Web sites across four election cycles. Averaged over those cycles, 91 percent of the sites included a candidate biography, and 83 percent included issue statements. The prevalence of the other three indicators of informing (speeches, campaign news, and ads) was less widespread. The percent of sites featuring candidate speeches decline, from 20 percent in 1998 to 10 percent in 2004; overall, speeches were found on 13 percent of sites across the four cycles. Data for campaign news show an increasing trend, from 49 percent of sites in 1998 to 73 percent of sites in 2002.

The stability in the prevalence of biography and issue statements from cycle to cycle at the presidential primary, gubernatorial, and congressional levels shows that these two key indicators of informing were widespread from the earliest emergence of Web campaigning. Further evidence of the importance site producers place on the practice of informing on the Web comes from the Web-based survey we conducted after the 2002 campaign. We asked campaign site producers to rate the importance of eleven potential goals for a campaign site. Three of the four top-rated goals directly reflected the practice of informing: informing Web site visitors, increasing public awareness of issues, and persuading undecided voters. A fourth goal, cost-efficient campaigning, reflects an underlying aspect of informing, that of seeking to expend the minimum resources to reach the maximum desired audience. These findings indicate that the prevalence of informing features on campaign sites reflects the priority most campaigns place on informing.

Our focus in this chapter so far has been on the types of information provided on campaign sites and the prevalence of informing across campaigns. We now turn to an analysis of how the techniques of documentation, position taking, convergence, linking, and coproduction are employed in the practice of informing.

Techniques for Informing

Documentation
In the electoral context, political actors not associated with candidate campaigns make reasoned decisions related to their roles in the election as voters, contributors, organizers, journalists, or even opponents. The processes by which they make these decisions are greatly enhanced by having access to particular types of information. For example, knowing who produced or sponsored the message, the source of the information, points of comparison and contrast between candidates, and details of campaign

financing could usefully contribute to making decisions. We call the cluster of techniques employed in the provision of such information documentation. A primer produced by the Institute for Politics, Democracy, and the Internet (2002) identifies "best practices" for Web campaigning, including those related to informing. Documentation is among these best practices, first, because visitors to campaign Web sites look for such documentation, and second, because when it is provided it enhances the credibility of campaigns.

The affordances of hypertext and the Web make many forms of documentation relatively easy and inexpensive to produce in comparison with print or broadcast media. It is reasonable to suppose, then, that documentation could be various and widespread on campaign Web sites. However, while most campaign sites provide the most basic forms of documentation, other forms are quite rare.

The most common and fundamental forms of documentation are statements expressing the candidate's position on a range of issues. As previously discussed, information about a candidate's position on at least one issue appeared on an average of 83 percent of campaign sites over the 1998, 2000, 2002, and 2004 elections. Our analysis of more than 800 campaign sites produced for House, Senate, and gubernatorial candidates in 2002 indicates that more than three-quarters of those Web sites with any issue statements addressed the candidate's positions on three or more issues. One-third of these sites presented position statements on five to nine issues, and another one-third provided statements on ten or more issues. Furthermore, 86 percent of sites with position statements substantiated the candidate's position by providing some type of rationale on at least one issue.

However, most of the other documentation techniques identified as best practices by the Institute for Politics, Democracy, and the Internet (2002) appeared much less frequently on campaign Web sites. In 2002, very few sites examined referenced an independent publication or Web site in support of claims made in the issue statements. Aligning a candidate's issue position with the views of another political actor, such as a party or advocacy group, was more common than contrasting the candidate's position. On 15 percent of campaign sites, visitors were provided with statements indicating common interests or shared viewpoints between the candidate and another political actor. Only 6 percent of campaign sites contrasted the positions of candidates with their opponents, whereas 11 percent contrasted the candidates' positions with other political actors besides opponents. Because both contrast and alignment entail representing a candidate to site visitors in relation to some other political actor, they are also associated with the practice of connecting, as we discuss in chapter 5.

Another set of features associated with documentation concerns transparency regarding sponsorship and campaign finances. A statement of sponsorship is required by law on all print and broadcast campaign materials and recommended on campaign Web sites as well (Institute for Politics, Democracy, and the Internet 2002); however, just over half (56 percent) of campaign sites produced in 2002 included an explicit message to the visitor acknowledging site sponsorship. And while about 10 percent of the candidate sites posted a position statement on the issue of campaign finance reform, only a handful of sites (less than 1 percent) provided information on their own campaign's contributors, contributions, or expenditures.

A close examination of sites that provided the forms of documentation we have discussed reveals that they were structured in interesting ways. For instance, the sites produced for Cecil Staton's (D-GA-11) primary election campaign and Todd Platt's (R-PA-19) general election campaign each provided a link to an online report by the U.S. Federal Election Commission (FEC) of their respective campaign's receipts. This report provides the names of personal and political action committee (PAC) contributors whose donations were above $200, along with their addresses and employers.[23] Norm Coleman's (R-MN-Sen) campaign site featured a "Financial Disclosure" page with a link labeled "Contributors not otherwise filed as public information with the Federal Election Commission on August 29, 2002 for calendar year 2002," but the site did not link to the FEC report for its campaign.[24] On Eli Bebout's (R-WY-Gov) 2002 campaign Web site, the prime real estate of the upper left corner was devoted to a feature labeled "Campaign Receipts." By October 31, 2002, links to three more financial reports had been posted: An itemized list of receipts through August 2002, created by the campaign with an FEC template that included fields for each personal and PAC contributor's name, city, state, date of contribution, and amount received;[25] and two other itemized lists containing only personal contributions, formatted similarly to the first report but without headings or dates.[26] As a final example, in June 2002, the campaign site of Congressional candidate Tom Tancredo (R-CO-6) featured a link in the main navigation menu labeled "Contributors and Supporters." This link resolved to a page with a long list of personal contributors' names, cities, and contribution amounts, the contents of which remained unchanged throughout the election season.[27] Ironically, none of these candidates who provided financial information addressed the issue of campaign finance on their sites.

Position Taking and Issue Dialogue

The overarching aim of all campaigning strategies is to maximize votes, primarily in order to win elections (Downs 1957). Based on this assumption, researchers have documented the incentives for candidates to remain ambiguous in their issue stances (Page 1978), and to carefully choose when or whether to associate themselves with controversial issues that polarize the electorate (Stokes 1963). The selection of issues on which to take a position and the explication of positions are among the primary means by which candidates construct pluralities of voters that will send or return them to office. As the fundamental currency of campaign issue discourse, the technique of position taking involves articulating statements of advocacy or opinion on political issues of public concern. At campaign events, in press releases, and in advertisements, candidates make issue statements that they believe will win them votes. Although somewhat consistent with offline campaigning, campaign techniques of issue selection and message construction on the Web do not conform entirely to the usual patterns found in print and broadcast media offline (Xenos and Foot 2005).

Simon (2002) refers to instances of opposing candidates referencing each other or each other's issue stances in the course of position taking as campaign issue dialogue. Instances of issue dialogue may be direct, where campaigns make explicit reference to issue positions held by political opponents (e.g., "my opponent, Robert Republican, will raise your taxes but I will not"), or indirect, where campaigns produce comments or statements on the same issues as their opponents without explicitly mentioning their opponents' positions (Xenos and Foot 2005).

Whether offline or on the Web, position taking and direct and indirect dialogue are variants of informing that serve as the principal ways that candidates transmit policy-relevant information about themselves to prospective voters. In offline campaigning, however, both indirect and direct issue dialogue are quite rare. In a content analysis of issue statements appearing in newspaper articles related to campaigns for U.S. Senate in 1988 through 1992, Simon (2002) found that rational-acting candidates avoided both kinds of issue dialogue whenever possible.

Models of campaign discourse indicate that in order to maximize votes, campaigns seek to highlight issues on which the candidate has a stance that is likely to appeal to the most voters. In other words, campaigns seek to focus voters' attention on issues for which the candidates' positions are likely to be widely well received. Assuming that issues favoring one candidate work to the disadvantage of other candidates and that all candidates approach issue selection strategically, one would expect candidates to discuss those issues their primary opponents do not much more frequently than issues on which opponents advance a position. According to this logic, campaigns have little incentive to engage in indirect issue dialogue. Furthermore, because mentioning an opponent publicly increases that candidate's visibility and thus works against the fundamental goal of vote maximization, campaigns generally seek to avoid direct issue dialogue (Benoit et al. 2003; Simon 2002; Zaller Forthcoming).

In the Web campaigning practice of informing, position taking is manifested in the campaign site presentation of a candidate's stance on an issue. Issue dialogue occurs when two or more campaigns within a race each present opposing candidates' positions on the same issue on their respective sites. For instance, a few days before the 2002 election in Colorado's 7th congressional district race, all four campaign sites associated with the Democratic, Republican, Reform, and Green party candidates evidenced position taking and issue dialogue. The campaign site of the Green candidate presented positions on five issues: campaign finance reform, the environment, taxes, healthcare, and national security.[28] On the Reform candidate's site were two of the same issues, campaign finance reform and healthcare, as well as several other issues: education, small businesses and farming, term limits, Social Security, and Medicare.[29] The Democratic candidate's site overlapped on taxes, education, Social Security, and Medicare, and addressed two issues not mentioned by other candidates.[30] The campaign site for the Republican candidate demonstrated significantly more issue breadth than the other three by displaying his positions on thirteen issues, including taxes, education, healthcare, and Medicare.[31]

In short, in this congressional race there was indirect issue dialogue among the campaign sites on five issues. Indirect dialogue was evident among the Green, Reform, and Republican candidates' sites on healthcare in general, and among the Republican, Democratic, and Reform candidates' sites on healthcare for seniors (Medicare) and education. There was indirect issue dialogue on taxes among the Republican, Democratic, and Green candidates' sites, and on campaign finance reform between the Green and Reform candidates' sites. Both the Reform and the Democratic campaigns engaged in direct dialogue with the Republican candidate. The Reform candidate did so by posting an analysis of his opponents that included an explicit critique of the Republican candidate's position on taxes.[32] The Democratic candidate's main campaign site included his position on abortion in the issue section, and a link from the home page to a second site (also produced by the campaign) that criticized the Republican candidate's position on abortion.[33]

As previously discussed, the predominant strategy in position taking offline has been the avoidance of issue dialogue with opponents (Simon 2002). Position taking on the Web evidences a somewhat different pattern (Xenos and Foot 2005). Although a strong majority of campaign Web sites from the 2002 election evidenced position taking, only 8 percent of campaign sites with issue position sections engaged in direct dialogue with their opponents by referencing the opponent's position on one or more issues. This rate is consistent with findings from studies of direct dialogue offline (Simon 2002). Campaign sites in 32 percent of races evidenced at least one instance of indirect issue dialogue. In races in which both major party candidates produced Web sites, position taking was even more prevalent, with indirect dialogue evident on more than 80 percent of campaign sites.

Further evidence of indirect dialogue on the Web is provided by Williams et al. (2005). In a comparative analysis of the Bush and Kerry sites prior to the 2004 presidential election, they found a strong correlation between the issues discussed on the home pages of the two campaign sites over a period of ten weeks leading up to the presidential election. The high level of position taking and indirect issue dialogue in the 2004 presidential race and in the 2002 races in which both major party candidates produced campaign Web sites indicates that the practice of informing in Web campaigning differs significantly from the ways in which informing has traditionally taken place offline. These findings indicate that the Web is a media environment in which it is noticeable if a candidate—such as an incumbent—does not engage in position taking on particular issues.

Offline, the traditional development of campaign messages tends to evolve from simple recognition and introductory messages that appear early in a campaign (like the familiar biographical advertisements), to strategic issue-related appeals later on. However, a temporally regularized form of basic campaign information presentation on the Web may alter the dynamics by which campaign messages evolve over the course of the election season in offline media. The ease with which campaign sites can be compared may force candidates to make some aspects of all of these types of communication available at all times throughout the campaign, thus diluting the agenda-setting effects created by strategic timing of paid advertising and other communications.

Furthermore, some campaigns have found that posting issue positions on their Web sites serves an agenda-setting function in relation to the news media. As the Webmaster of Jesse Ventura's 1998 gubernatorial campaign in Minnesota commented:

> We rejected that idea [that posting issue positions would alienate some prospective voters] and published all of Jesse's public policy positions on the web site. Soon after we did so, the media began moving off the wrestling theme and started treating Jesse more seriously as a candidate. One newspaper called him "Jesse 'The Wonk' Ventura," referring to the large amount of public policy information on his web site. After this information was posted, the issues pages of the site were second only to Jesse's biography in popularity. Users seemed to enter the site asking, "Who is Jesse Ventura and where does he stand on the issues?" Reporters and pundits frequently referred to and quoted from Jesse's public policy positions as stated on his web site (Madsen 1998).

Madsen's comment indicates that position taking on a campaign site may prompt journalists to report on the issues that the candidate wants to address. Having analyzed the ways that campaigns employ position taking and issue dialogue, we now turn to examine the use of convergence in the practice of informing.

Convergence

As explained in chapter 2, the technique of convergence involves the integration of the online and offline realms of production, whether through media, organizations, or activity. New media in general, and the Web in particular, can be viewed as bearing a hybridization of the affordances of older, non-digital media such as print, film, broadcast radio, and television (e.g. Manovich 2001). The incorporation of offline media is common in the

Web production technique of convergence as it is employed in relation to the practice of informing.

Brochureware (Kamarck 1999) reflects the digitization and hypertextual rendering of texts that were originally created on analog or offline media, such as type-written and photo-copied flyers. This variant of convergence has been utilized significantly in campaign sites. Another variant is providing video or audio files on a campaign site that were originally produced for dissemination on television or radio; this tactic accomplishes several things for a campaign. First, it adds diversity to the content of the site: Posting a 30-second video advertisement featuring the candidate on the campaign site allows site visitors to glean information through hearing and seeing the candidate in ways that they might not get from written texts and even still images.[34] Second, audio and video files extend what Seely, Brown, and Druguid (2000) might call the social life of these campaign informational artifacts across time and space. For instance, the archive of television and radio advertisements on Pat Buchanan's presidential campaign site in 2000 allowed site visitors to view or listen to them for many weeks after they were broadcast, and to do so from locations far beyond the geographical reach of the local or even national radio or television stations on which the ads were originally broadcast.[35]

Nearly instantaneous debate response systems, developed by presidential campaigns beginning in 2000, are yet another example of informing through convergence. The Gore and Bush campaigns recognized that some of their core audience members, especially journalists and campaign activists, would be experiencing the debate in a mixed-media environment, simultaneously using online and offline media. The campaign organizations created almost-real-time response systems (e-buttal systems) on their respective Web sites to allow those watching on television to simultaneously review campaign staffers' responses to each point and counterpoint of the debate.

The 2004 Bush and Kerry campaigns similarly employed e-buttal during debates, with even more effort invested than in the 2000 presidential campaigns. Both campaigns demonstrated the significance they placed on this strategy with the depth and rapidity (every minute or two) of updates that campaign staff posted to their respective campaign during each debate. Each campaign had anticipated the response of its opponent to each question and had prepared more numerous and more lengthy rebuttal comments than would be allowed on the televised debate. These comments were posted in a special section of the campaign site during and following each round of debate.

Finally, the practice of informing through the technique of convergence is manifested in campaign efforts to publicize the presence of the Web site in offline modes or media. Yard signs and posters bearing the campaign site URL exemplify this approach. Some of the most delightfully anachronistic examples of the blending of online information into the offline environment are banners proclaiming a campaign site URL hung on wooden kiosks at state fairs.[36] In an interesting twist on the brochureware phenomenon, some campaigns have been observed distributing printouts of pages from campaign sites at campaign events. Whether for convenience or to demonstrate tech-savvy, the offline distribution of html-formatted information—sometimes with URLs and href tags intact—illustrates the bi-directionality of convergence.

In this section we have demonstrated the varied ways that convergence is employed in informing. The integration of online and offline realms of production enables campaigns to inform across the electoral Web sphere and the rest of the electoral arena. In the next section we focus within the electoral Web sphere on the technique of linking.

Linking

Linking, or the insertion of a hypertextual element that associates two Web objects, is foundational to Web production. The form of linking of primary importance to the practice of informing is internal linking, in which objects or pages within a single site are interlinked. As a production technique associated with the practice of informing, linking is a way for campaigns to structure the information architecture of their sites, thus defining the range of possible user experiences.

A campaign's choices regarding the internal linking on their Web sites can shape users' perceptions of the informational value of the site, as well as influence users' senses of motion/navigation and control. Internal linking facilitates expansiveness in the breadth and depth of the materials, while enabling site visitors to select the type and level of information they wish to view. For example, in the issue section of Al Gore's 2000 campaign site (the most extensive site in that presidential race), information on Gore's positions on a wide range of issues was provided in three levels of detail: bullet points, paragraphs, and lengthy white papers available for downloading as Adobe PDFs. A site visitor could select the level of detail desired for information about Gore's stance on any of the issues listed. The beneficial effect of internal linking on the informational value of a site is evident when a site with multiple levels of internal links, such as the 2002 congressional campaign site for Libertarian candidate Andy Horning (IN-7), is compared to a site with no internal links, such as the one produced for fellow Libertarian congressional candidate Jim Higgins (MO-1) in 2002.[37] The internal links on Horning's site allowed visitors to easily select the informational elements they wanted to view. The lack of internal links on Higgins' site required visitors to scan a lengthy single page of text to locate the information in which they were interested.

Outlinking, or linking to Web objects posted on a different site, from the main campaign site to another site produced by the candidate or campaign may enable more extensive information—and thus improve the credibility of the candidate—while keeping the campaign site distinct from other sites in the electoral Web sphere. An example of this is when an incumbent's campaign site links to the candidate's government office site.[38] Other campaign sites link to one or more Web pages produced by the candidate outside of the political sphere. For instance, the biography page of John Graham's (D-CA-48) congressional campaign site in 2002 linked to Graham's faculty page at the University of California at Irvine, offering the campaign site visitor "more details on [Graham's] academic career."[39]

Another variant of outlinking for the purpose of informing is providing a link from a primary campaign site to a campaign-produced anti-candidate site that criticizes one's opponent. During the presidential primary campaigns of 2000, for example, the main Bradley campaign site displayed a link to an anti-Gore site called moreaboutgore.com, which was also produced by the Bradley campaign (Stromer-Galley 2000). In another instance, the front page of Mike Feeley's (D-CO-7) primary campaign site in 2002 featured a quote by a former district vice-chair of the Republican party expressing concern about his Republican opponent, Bob Beauprez, and support for Feeley. A link supplied with the quote resolved to a second site (also produced by Feeley's campaign), misleadingly labeled www.beauprezfacts .com. This site was devoted to critiquing Beauprez's stance on abortion.[40] Each of the previous examples illustrate ways in which campaigns engage in informing across two or more campaign-produced sites by linking between sites.

Outlinking can also be a way of offering site visitors information beneficial to the campaign's goals without the site producer assuming responsibility for collecting, maintaining, and displaying the information. Many
campaign sites urge visitors—many of whom presumably are supporters—
to register to vote. In 2002, about 30 percent of campaign sites facilitated
voter registration by providing external links to Web sites produced by
civic organizations or government bodies that handle voter registration.
The prevalence of this feature increased to 44 percent in 2004. Examples
include the 2002 campaign sites for Stan Matsunaka (D-CO-4) and Tom
Harkin (D-IA-Sen), which provided an array of voter registration information, including links to the voter registration form and election information section on their respective Secretary of State sites.[41]

The previously discussed documentation technique of linking to the campaign's reports on the Federal Election Commission Web site facilitates campaign site visitors' access to contributor information, without providing it
directly. This technique, then, is another type of outlinking for the purpose
of strategic informing. It can be risky for a campaign to link to an information source on another site rather than to post that information on its own
site. Campaigns have no control over the information posted on another
site; the producer of the other site may modify that information at any
time. Thus outlinking requires a calculation of risk and a release of control.

Links have both functional and symbolic values (Beaulieu 2005; Rogers
and Marres 2000). In this light, linking in the practice of informing can be
understood as a way for campaigns to provide and structure information,
but also to perform a type of hypertextuality, thus symbolically displaying
technical expertise. In other words, the dearth of both internal links and
outlinks on some campaign sites conveys both a lack of depth in their information infrastructure and an absence of Web fluency. Linking can also
be integral to coproduction, as we discuss next.

Coproduction

Coproduction, as introduced in chapter 2, is the technique of jointly producing a Web object through texts, features, or links. Within the practice
of informing, coproduction can be employed in several ways, one of which
is the joint production of Web materials by different branches of a campaign. For example, the campaign calendar for a presidential candidate
may integrate information produced by several geographically distributed
campaign offices. The use of content from an incumbent candidate's

government-produced site on a campaign site is a similar kind of coproduction in the practice of informing. In such cases, the campaign site
functions as a type of boundary object (Star 1988) through which the
candidate-promoting activities of various branches of a campaign coalesce
and are coordinated.

Another type of coproduction as part of informing takes place between
the campaign and other actors. One variant is the appropriation of content
from news producers by the campaign, a type of coproduction that we term
unilateral. Another variant occurs when a campaign teams up with one or
more individual site producers to create or distribute information about a
candidate. In the offline world, candidates have long used materials produced by other actors—such as press organizations—for their own campaign purposes. Reprinting and distributing favorable editorials or news
stories on their own letterhead is a form of coproduction. When a Web producer reproduces material previously distributed by an external organization on its own Web site, and does so without providing a Web link to
the external organization, the campaign is coproducing through appropriation as part of the practice of informing. Some campaigns have presented
scanned images of newspaper articles on their sites.[42] One reason for a
campaign to employ this seemingly retro technique may be to convey a
sense of authenticity. Another motive may be that because scanned images
represent the candidate's presence in the offline news media, they may
symbolically convey the message that the candidate's views and activities
are "newsworthy" and thus should be attended to by site visitors. Many
other campaigns simply re-key or cut and paste materials from newspapers
or newspaper Web sites, usually with a reference to the original producers
but frequently without a hyperlink to the original producer's Web site.
Adam Schiff's (D-CA-29) site in 2002 employed an unusual variant of appropriation: The campaign appears to have saved complete pages from the
Los Angeles Times Web site, and then served them through its own site.[43]

Finally, coproduction in informing is evidenced when campaign organizations contribute information about a candidate to Web sites produced by
other actors, such as government bodies or civic organizations. For instance, in each of the last several elections, Project Vote Smart has sought
responses from campaign organizations to a standard survey of issue positions. The responses from the campaign organizations are provided verba-
tim on Project Vote Smart's site. In 2000, 2002, and 2004, the Democracy

Network (DNet), produced in cooperation with the League of Women Voters, also relied on campaign organization participation for its content. Similarly, in recent elections the producers of the election section of the Washington State Secretary of State's site have offered campaigns the opportunity to provide candidate information and the URL of the campaign site on their government site.[44] Browsing such sites suggests, however, that many campaigns have not contributed the information requested by these site producers. This indicates that Web campaigning on sites not controlled by the campaign organizations is less common than Web campaigning in venues sponsored by the campaigns themselves. Whether they have found it inconvenient or strategically undesirable is unknown, but the relatively low levels of campaign participation in these coproduced sites indicate that there are tensions involved in informing. We discuss several of these tensions in the next section.

Tensions in Informing

Informing is seemingly a straightforward Web practice. However, our analysis of campaign Web sites and data from site producer interview and survey responses reveals at least six areas of tensions. The first three tensions are shared by many kinds of site producers and pertain to the accuracy, volume, and currency of the information producers are expected to create and maintain. Producing accurate content, and keeping it accurate during an evolving campaign, requires a lot of effort. As one congressional campaign site producer in 2000 explained,

I've found [managing the campaign Web site] somewhat overwhelming. We have a lot of help now, but just getting things up on the Web site, making sure they're correct when they're out there for people to see. You want to make sure they're very accurate statements because it's like a quote in a newspaper. If you do something wrong or say something wrong, people are going to use that against you. We wanted to make sure we were very accurate and very detailed as to what [the candidate's] positions were.

Second, campaign site producers also experience tension regarding the volume of information to produce or provide. Too much information (particularly when it is not well organized) may overwhelm site visitors, and too little information may leave them unsatisfied. In short, erring in either direction may reflect poorly on the candidate.

Third, campaign site producers experience the pressure of currency, a need that is further complicated by the cross-pressure of serving both first-time visitors and regular visitors. Campaign site producers must provide a site that is attractive and functional for new visitors at the same time that they are providing the features and information repeat visitors would expect. An up-to-date Web site comes at a cost. It encourages regular visits but also requires producers to generate new content continually and quickly in relation to unfolding events that are reported around the clock. Campaigns must monitor the Web environment on at least a daily basis in order to keep a campaign site current in relation to sites produced not only by other candidates but also by a wide range of other political actors including news organizations, bloggers, and advocacy groups. This continual pressure for currency demands that campaigns engage in a new kind of sociotechnical network: in effect, a rapid-response production system. Unsurprisingly, many campaigns, especially those at the House and Senate level, have opted not to engage in the currency game, a choice that is evidenced by the lack of dynamism on most campaign sites up to and including the 2004 election cycle.

The second cluster of tensions encountered by campaign site producers is more specifically related to campaign strategies regarding information and control. The first of these is a tension between two needs: the need many campaigns feel to maintain strategic ambiguity in the information provided to the public, and the need to use the Web's capacity for broad and deep information. As one campaign manager commented in 2000,

I think most of the other campaigns that I've looked at, both congressional and other campaigns in general, are using the Internet for very general things. As I said, the policy statement [on our site] is a very general policy statement, rather than a detailed plan. I think [the candidate] wants to do more plan, more detail, and then there is more risk when you do that.

Although the Web allows campaigns to disseminate many plans in great detail, campaign managers such as this one recognize that providing details decreases the ambiguity that allows many candidates to appeal to a diverse array of people.

Another control-related tension has to do with the durability and potentially long period of availability (what we might term *permanence*) of the information campaigns posted on the Web. Current estimates of the average life of a Web page on its original server range from forty-four days to one hundred days (Rein 2004; SAP AG 2004). However, the fact that a producer changes or eliminates a Web page does not guarantee that it hasn't been captured, stored, archived, or cached somewhere else by someone else. The widespread caching of pages by search engines such as Google, as well as by large Internet service providers (ISPs) such as America Online, introduce a time lag and thereby foil attempts by campaign organizations to eliminate previously posted pages.

Search engines and ISPs are not the only organizations that store and make available older Web pages. The introduction of RSS feeds (XML file formats for syndicating Web pages, known as Really Simple Syndication), particularly during the 2004 campaign, has the effect of decentralizing content management and making it nearly impossible to retract or recall information once posted. In addition, when organizations such as the Library of Congress and the Internet Archive systematically archive campaign Web sites, as was done in the 2000, 2002, and 2004 elections, campaign Web sites become a permanent part of the public record. Most campaigns have not objected to the inclusion of their sites in Web archives. Some campaigns proudly announce the inclusion of their sites in a Web archive,[45] others request that their sites not be displayed.[46] The creation of publicly accessible Web archives of campaign-produced materials is vital to the study of many aspects of contemporary politics, including scholarly, journalistic, and opposition research. Even apart from Web archives, browser caches and mirror sites make expunging Web materials difficult. Overall, the possibility of permanence on the Web may cause some campaigns to refrain from posting some kinds of information. In short, for campaign Web site producers, the desire to control information may trump the desire to disperse it.

The third control-related tension arises from the fact that generally all information provided on a public Web site is accessible to any Web user in the country (and the world). Just as businesses seek to target particular audiences with persuasive messages tailored to their interests, many campaigns seek to tailor messages to particular voter segments. In the elections between 2000 and 2004, some major party campaigns segmented their email distribution lists by the issue interests and campaign commitment level of the recipients. The number and content of messages sent to different groups varied. However, segmenting users and differentiating campaign messages is more challenging on the Web than in email. Lynn Reed, campaign manager for Bill Bradley's 2000 presidential primary campaign, elaborated this tension in an interview:

Reed: Let's take press as an example because our site handled that differently than the other sites. From the beginning we intended to handle it differently. We set up a press center for a number of reasons. Number one was cost savings. We thought that the more reporters we could get to receive press releases by email rather than fax, the more money we would save. In order to do that we sent it to the press center, which was a way that the reporters could come on online, sign up, and indicate what they wanted to receive. The company called Issue Dynamics, which was another one of the consultants and part of this team, modified an existing product of theirs so that with one push of a button the press secretary could hit both the people who were signed up by email and the people who were signed up by fax, so that it was an integrated list and not two separate lists that you must continually crosscheck against one another. That was a very key early decision and most of that was a cost saving. But from a message point of view, I knew that I wasn't going to want to put every single press release on the public site. Secondarily to that, there might be a press release that is written from a certain perspective for reporters that I might want to tweak a little bit for the general public. And it's the difference of audience, and there is a very fine art to how you write a press release for its intended audience of reporters. Probably, 80 percent of the time that was fine for the general public, but there were cases when it wasn't and I wanted to have the flexibility.

Interviewer: So it wasn't framed as journalists only, although it was as if 'all the same content appears but at a public place, and if you are a journalist it will be organized differently and is easier for you to find.' But in fact, there were some differences in the content.

Reed: Right. I didn't want the general user to feel as though he or she was excluded from this.

Interviewer: Yes. One of the reactions we had was we wondered if people will react and go, "Well, wait a second, what are they telling journalists that they are not telling us?" Did you get any feedback to that effect?

Reed: Not really. I was surprised. I'm sure we had some people sign up on the thing who in fact were not journalists, but what we had more was people who were school journalists, or people who were foreign journalists or people who were Internet only journalists, who would never have gotten the time of day from a press secretary without this. So I think it wound up being more of an advantage in that that kind of under-served niche of the press actually got treated equally (Reed 2000).

As Reed's reflections illustrate, it is more difficult on the Web than in less public and pervasive media to create and maintain distinct messages for different kinds of audiences, whether journalists versus citizens, Iowa voters versus California voters, or union members versus managers. But there are ways.

Major party presidential campaigns in the 2000 and 2004 elections, and a few congressional campaigns in 2002 and 2004, were able to strategically frame campaign site messages for some users by inviting visitors to personalize the campaign site. Site visitors could complete a Web questionnaire in which they registered themselves with the campaign, selected the issues that they considered most important, and affiliated themselves with one or more socioeconomic groups. The campaign site then employed cookies, (a packet of information sent from a server to a client computer via a browser, which transmits information back to the server), to ensure that the version of the site a registered user saw on subsequent visits foregrounded their particular interests—creating the possibility that site visitors with different demographics could receive different and potentially contradictory information from a campaign.

Finally, the dilemma of whether to be solely proactive in various aspects of informing or to also react to opponents and other critics creates another control-related tension for campaign site producers. In a 2002 survey of campaign site producers, we asked a set of questions regarding how concerned campaign site producers were about false information online. One-third responded that they were "very concerned" about inaccurate news reports online. One out of three also reported being very concerned about other political actors spreading false political rumors online to shape public opinion. And one-quarter of the site producers surveyed said they were very concerned that unqualified people give political information online.

Many campaigns feel compelled to monitor the Web environment daily to attempt to manage and respond to the information (or misinformation) that is provided about them by other political actors. The majority of campaign site producers keep close tabs on their opponents' sites. A handful of campaign site producers admitted to visiting an opponent's site several times a day; about 11 percent visited daily, and another 36 percent reported visiting their opponents' sites weekly. When a congressional campaign manager in 2000 was asked in an interview whether she thought about the prospect of campaign opponents visiting the site, she responded candidly:

We do. Honestly, there are certain things—we don't want to put down every single thing that the campaign is doing. We talk about all the major public events that we have. We're not going to write down, "[the candidate] has a meeting with these fundraisers that day, or a meeting with this person." We don't get that extensive, but I think you'll find just about everything that we're doing is usually right there.

One-third of the site producers reported having responded on their own sites to changes in the content, features, or links on an opponent's site. Some employed a strategy of posting notices on their campaign sites to make the official status of the site explicit. For instance, the front page of the 2002 campaign site for Ed Pastor (D-AZ-2) explained,

This is the only official web site of the Pastor for Arizona Committee. While other web sites might advocate Ed Pastor's election or the defeat of other candidates, and while they might contain links to this site or republish information or materials that we have made available to the general public, they are not authorized by the Pastor for Arizona Committee, nor have they been coordinated in any way with the Pastor for Arizona Committee.[47]

Informing is a familiar practice deeply embedded in the traditional mission of campaign organizations. Interestingly, one candidate in 2002 told site visitors that although financial contributions to his campaign would be appreciated, the most important contribution would be to get Internet access in order to become informed:

Regarding contributions, the most important contribution you can make to good government is to get yourself access to the INTERNET. That's where the best campaign information is available. If you can't afford the equipment, etc. ask your local elementary school to set up a Cyber Café where you and your neighbors can surf the web in the evenings. Your local public library can also help you with Internet access.[48]

The fact that the candidate made this statement on his campaign Web site begs the question of whether constituents without Internet access would see it. However, he may have made the same appeal in other media as well. The statement indicates the importance that a growing number of candidates place on the role of the Web for informing citizens.

The tendency for political campaigns to be waged largely through ever-shrinking sound bites has been demonstrated by several analyses (see, for example, Adatto 1990). The Web provides a forum within which campaigns can expand their practice of informing with an ever-increasing number of gigabytes. Furthermore, evidence indicates that some campaigns have taken advantage of the opportunity to shift their practice of informing toward providing heterogeneous types of information in various media formats with multiple structures, targeting different audiences. It is beyond the scope of this book to evaluate the quality or value of the information provided by campaigns on the Web, or to compare it to campaign information in other media. However, it is clear that the Web affords opportunities for expanded breadth and depth of information at relatively low cost, and that many campaigns are taking advantage of that affordance.

This affordance suggests a more complex model of communication than suggested by the early, linear sender/receiver models (Lasswell 1948; Shannon and Weaver 1949). These models assumed a monolithic sender, and discrete messages sent at particular points in time. In contrast, informing in the context of Web campaigning is engaged in over time by the sociotechnical network of a campaign in affiliation or differentiation from other actors. Many types of information, or messages, have multiple elements; the structure as well as the substance of those elements shapes the visitor/receiver's interpretive frame and experience of control over message exposure. Furthermore, Web archiving transforms the sender/receiver model by rendering durable a message that a sender might have intended as ephemeral.

In summary, we should not be surprised at the degree to which campaign organizations engage in informing. Although the early history of politics on the Internet suggested the potential for alternatives modes of campaigning, informing emerged as the initial and dominant practice as the prevalence of Web campaigning expanded. As we discuss further in chapter 7, the practice of informing became nearly ubiquitous in Web campaigning by 2002. All campaigns with a Web presence engaged in this practice, albeit with some variety in the specific techniques employed. There are some campaigns that only engaged in the practice of informing rather than choosing to use the Web to involve, connect, or mobilize. At the same time, although we view informing as a distinct practice, each of the other practices we consider in the following chapters also entails some aspect of informing. Involving requires the distribution of information about a campaign in order to recruit supporters to participate. Connecting entails enabling an interaction or exchange of information between site visitors and other political actors. Lastly, mobilizing involves equipping supporters to promote the candidate to others, that is, to become information disseminators on behalf of the campaign.

4   Involving

A Practice Observed: Involving

The main campaign site produced for Joe Lieberman, a Democratic presidential primary candidate in 2004, made strategic use of the practice of involving. From the front page, a site visitor could use any of several links to access the campaign's online structures for involving. A page urging visitors to "create momentum for Joe" featured a map of the United States.[49] Clicking on a state in the map led to a state-specific campaign page, framed within the main site. Each state page included photos of Lieberman with citizens of that state, a schedule of upcoming local events, and the invitation to "make a contribution from your state."[50]

   The campaign also developed an online structure for involving that invited site visitors to coproduce a photo album. The entry point was a link on the front page labeled "Dogs for Joe," featuring a headshot of a blond dog.[51] The same photo appeared on the Dogs for Joe page, labeled "Fenway the Dog." Part of the text on the page was narrated by Fenway, Lieberman's dog, and explained his support of Lieberman:

One of the reasons Joe is this dog's best man is that I can count on him to be there to protect our beaches, our forests, our parks, and all the places that are part of my natural habitat. Although his global warming bill didn't pass, I am proud of the way he refused to roll over and play dead and worked his tail off for a principle he deeply believes in. He is a fighter, and I know he'll keep at this until we cap those greenhouse gases and do what's necessary to protect the planet for litters to come.[52]

Visitors to the page were asked "Does your pet support Joe? Send a photo of your dog to info@joe2004.com and put 'Dogs for Joe' in the subject line of your email. We'll add your dog to our Dogs for Joe photo album!" The campaign's email address had an embedded mailto code that invoked the site visitor's email application to generate an auto-addressed message, and a link was provided to the album itself.

By January 2004, the photo album displayed pictures of more than eighty dogs, evidence that this involving strategy resonated well with site visitors.[53] The captions for a few photos were just the dogs' names, but many captions made tongue-in-cheek statements of support for Lieberman, such as "Casey is thoughtful but tough as nails—just like Joe!," "Woo is dreaming of Joe in the White House," and "Daphne says that if terriers could vote, Joe would win." By inviting supporters to coproduce a section of the campaign site, the campaign involved supporters in the campaign.

The Practice of Involving

Campaigns engage in the Web practice of involving when they create and provide online structures facilitating interaction between site visitors and the campaign organization. Web site features that manifest this practice include those that allow visitors to subscribe to the campaign's email list, indicate willingness to volunteer time or effort, or make a financial contribution. Involving as a campaign practice is a familiar and traditional part of electioneering. In fact, the earliest campaigns to use computer networks as part of their campaigning repertoire engaged in involving practices. However, when Web technologies were introduced, involving was not widely adopted by campaigns initially, and its growth has been more modest than that of the practice of informing. Nevertheless, involving has more recently emerged as one of the most important and essential aspects of Web campaigning, and as such, it represents a likely arena for rapid and significant expansion in the coming election cycles. At the same time, involving as a Web campaigning practice entails certain threats to traditional campaign organizations. Attempting to meet site visitors' expectations for continuous involvement, and establish and maintain technical and organizational capabilities for handling significant data management responsibilities, requires considerable resource investment and organizational restructuring.

Campaign organizations engage in the most simple and common form of the practice of involving by providing particular types of information that facilitate site visitors' abilities to contact the campaign. Campaign contact information, included on more than 80 percent of campaign sites in

2002, provides the opportunity for site visitors to initiate contact and inter-act with the campaign organization. For this reason, what is seemingly the simple provision of information is closely associated with the practice of involving, not just the practice of informing.

In its more complex forms, the Web campaigning practice of involving is manifested through online structures that enable organizations to query site visitors for information that is required by the Federal Election Com-mission for contributions and other types of data. The data most com-monly requested from a site visitor by campaigns are typically the site visitor's name, street address, and email address, as well as some indication by the site visitor of a desire to contribute time or money to the campaign effort. These more complex involving features, through which information is solicited from site visitors, were present on slightly more than half of campaign Web sites observed in 2000 and three-quarters of campaign sites in 2004.

The relatively few campaigns and other political organizations that were early adopters of the pre-Web Internet pioneered the practice of involving. In the late 1980s, several computer conferencing systems supported polit-ical activists with bulletin board services. Computer bulletin board and conferencing systems—such as The Well (Whole Earth 'Lectronic Link), PeaceNet, EcoNet, and hundreds of online community bulletin boards, as well as Usenet—included as participants candidates running for elective office (Rheingold 1993). Many of these earliest adopters of computer networking for political purposes used these early systems to engage in dis-cussions with other users of the systems and to recruit and involve partici-pants. The relatively few scholarly analyses of the early use of computer networks, as well as an examination of the popular literature of the time, suggests that involving was an especially significant practice (Shannon 1994; Downing 1989).

As the number of Internet users grew and the Web emerged, two factors contributed to a slight dampening of campaigns' adoption of the Web practice of involving. With the emergence of the graphical browser and the associated explosion in the number of Internet users, the Web became a mass medium. The online population came to bear characteristics similar to those of the general population in terms of political inclinations and en-gagement levels. Once the Web browser was widely distributed, the Web quickly became more a medium that relied on a "push" or transmission model of communication and less a medium that required or facilitated an interactive paradigm (as the pre-Web Internet did). The Web was viewed primarily as a method of one-to-many communication through computers, akin in this respect to publishing and broadcasting. In general, most Web producers during the 1990s construed site visitors more as readers and less as participants. During the same period, the percent of campaign organizations campaigning on the Web was greatly expanding. With this expansion came a level of caution and reluctance not usually associated with the earliest adopters of new technology (Rogers 1995). Thus, as Web campaigning in general diffused through the population of campaign organizations, aversion to risk reduced the proportion of campaigns willing to engage in involving. The risks associated with involving are discussed later.

As we have discussed, the practice of involving, in its simplest form, is enacted when campaign organizations provide information facilitating contacting the campaign, such as a telephone number, street address or email address. There are some structural differences from campaign to campaign in the way that this type of feature is produced. Some campaigns simply provide a textual reference with just a post office box address for the campaign.[54] Some sites provide just a street address and phone number for their physical campaign office,[55] while others provide only an email address. For instance, the 2002 campaign site for Dennis Umphress (Lib-CA-16) had a page labeled "Contact Us," which consisted of the statement, "Email general correspondence, requests for more information, or offers to volunteer to: *dmumphress@hotmail.com*" and the suggestion, "If you have a question on a specific subject please email all of the candidates for their positions," along with his opponents' email addresses.[56] Some campaigns such as Umphress's provide just a simple text email address to encourage email contact, while others provide an email address with an embedded mailto code. Still others employ a Web-based form to allow site visitors to create a database entry that is a message to the campaign; some sites refer to this as "sending a note" or "email."[57]

Along with the structures used to facilitate contact, the rhetorical framings of invitations to contact the campaigns vary widely. The mere presence of any contact information implies an invitation to contact, and many campaign sites simply present that information under a heading such as "Contact." Other campaigns post texts one or more paragraphs in length inviting input and feedback of various kinds. The 2002 campaign site for John Graham (D-CA-48) exemplified the latter. On a page labeled, "How You Can Help," a text written in the first person and signed by Graham included the following invitational paragraphs:

The single best way you can help elect the best Representative for the 48th Congressional District is to recommend to your friends that they visit this and my fellow candidates' websites. **This is crucial** [emphasis in original]. We should all cast our ballots on November 5th based on the best information available.

I'd be most pleased if you might host a coffee or other event in support of my candidacy. All I ask is that you organize about 20 48th District voters (or more) on a weeknight. I'll be glad to stop by and provide more details about my ideas. Please just call me at 949-856-1969 or email is even better at *john@graham4congress.org*.

I am very much in need of your criticisms and good ideas. Please let me hear what you think about the issues the others and I have raised regarding your federal government. Email is the best way to share your ideas with me—*ideas@graham4congress .org*.[58] (Italics in original.)

This type of invitation evokes a form of "text-based interactivity" (Endres and Warnick 2004) and constructs an interactional relationship between the site producer and visitors.

During the primary season in early 2000, we conducted a series of focus groups in which we met with citizens—potential users and coproducers of campaign Web sites—to explore the value they ascribed to different types of Web campaigning. Many of our participants saw value in being able to email the candidate and the campaign. One participant stated, "It gives you a voice back to the candidates, a very important one." Another recalled for her group the experience she had in emailing a candidate through a campaign Web site. She explained that she utilized the email option because of its ease: "They gave me an opportunity to respond to the candidate right there online, which I was more likely to do than pick up a pen or pencil and get the address and send some question or comment to him." Other participants elaborated that, for them, email served as a direct channel to the campaign, via which they could ask for clarification on an issue they had not seen covered in the press or could not find on the candidate's Web site, or convey their own issue positions.

The more complex methods of engaging in the practice of involving occur when campaign organizations collect data from campaign site visitors who provide it voluntarily and consciously. Site visitors, of course, also provide data about their navigation through a Web site without doing so explicitly or intentionally or even, perhaps, without realizing what they are doing. Site log files, for example, can be examined to determine the path individual visitors took through a particular Web site, that is, what pages were visited in what order and for how long. These data, in which site visitors are identified by an IP address only, may be useful to a campaign as it evaluates its Web strategy; however, they have little significance as involving mechanisms to the campaign organization.

Web site features and production techniques associated with the practice of involving that include data collection are generally focused on facilitating the ability of campaign organizations to accumulate financial, informational, and volunteer resources, such as campaign contributions, issue concerns, and commitments to work for the campaign. Online structures that enable these aspects of involving are designed to facilitate interaction between the campaign organization and individual site visitors. Such features include structures for site visitors to provide an email address to receive future messages from the campaign, to make electronic campaign contributions online, or to provide contact and other information related to volunteering for the campaign. Features of this type were heavily used during the 2004 election. A telephone survey conducted during November 2004 by the Pew Internet and American Life Project found that an estimated 7 million people signed up to receive email from the presidential campaigns alone, 4 million contributed to a campaign online (up from 2 million in 2000), and 4 million signed up to volunteer via campaign Web sites (Rainie, Cornfield, and Horrigan 2005).

In requesting contributions, an increasing number of campaign sites go beyond presenting a postal address to which checks could be mailed by providing an online structure to mediate electronic funds transfer. The latter allows campaigns to collect additional information from donors, including both the information required by the Federal Election Commission as well as additional data of value to the campaign. Of the sites that request contributions, most do so in a straightforward manner. Of those that provide a rationale, most highlight the need for funds to extend the campaign's message. However, one particularly creative framing of the contribution request was found on the campaign site of 2004 congressional candidate Thaddeus McCotter (R-MI-11). The "Contribute" section featured a fairly elaborate, tongue-in-cheek narrative depicting the candidate as a guitar player and the campaign as a band, and included quotes from "John, Paul, George, and Ringo" about the candidate's musical abilities.

The contribution pitch was an invitation to "join the band" of the campaign, and various types of perks were offered to contributors at different levels. The site provided a downloadable form (Adobe PDF) on which donors could indicate whether they would be "performing" as "blue grassroots" by pledging $400, "rhythm section" at $500, and so on, up to "conductors" at $5000 or more.[59]

Online structures soliciting volunteer labor for the campaign also vary significantly. The most basic type is the provision of contact information for the campaign office with a statement to the effect that the campaign needs volunteer help, accompanied by an invitation to participate. Alternatively, some campaigns provide a downloadable form to be mailed to the campaign office, on which site visitors are asked to indicate the type of volunteer labor they are able to provide.[60] To mediate this type of interaction entirely online, a Web form is required, which can be set up to either generate an email to a campaign address with the information the user has provided or to function as an interface to create an entry in a database. As an example of the latter, the 2004 campaign site for Jim Nussle (R-IA-Gov) created a Web form in order to solicit information from volunteers. The information collected via this form could have been directly entered into a campaign database record for the site visitor.[61] In this particular case, eight volunteer activities were pre-selected such that site visitors submitting the form would by default indicate interest in all eight unless they deselected or opted out of one or more of the types of volunteer help being offered. Pre-selecting response options is a way of influencing the response options submitted.

Some campaigns use online structures for volunteering to elicit other kinds of personal information from site visitors beyond their names and contact information. For example, the volunteer section on the campaign site for 2004 Democratic presidential primary candidate Dick Gephardt invited site visitors to "volunteer at the level of commitment you'd like." The Web form requested a broad array of information from site visitors, including whether they were union members (and if so, of which union), which issues concerned them, what special skills or interests they had that could be of use to the campaign, and how they found about the campaign Web site.[62] In contrast to Nussle's 2004 campaign site volunteer page, Gephardt's volunteer page had only three of seven actions pre-selected as default settings for site visitors. In comparing the volunteer sections on

Thaddeus McCotter's 2002 and 2004 campaign sites, it is apparent that McCotter's campaign learned the value of soliciting additional information in a structured format from prospective volunteers. The 2002 version of the volunteer page requested basic contact information from the site visitor, provided seven volunteer activities as options from which the visitor was invited to select as many as desired, and offered a textbox in which visitors could write comments to the campaign.[63] In contrast, the 2004 version of McCotter's volunteer page requested an additional five fields of contact information (including home phone, work phone, and county of residence), the name of the site visitor's spouse, the visitor's occupation, title, and employer. The 2004 version lacked a textbox for open-ended comments, and instead asked visitors to indicate the three issues that concerned them most, and offered an additional five volunteer activity options along with the ones provided in 2002.[64]

Both Web campaign site producers and visitors to Web sites value features associated with the practice of involving, but they do so to a lesser extent than with features associated with the practice of informing. In a survey of campaign site producers conducted after the 2002 elections, respondents were asked to rate the importance of a series of goals for their Web sites. Goals associated with the practice of involving—signing up volunteers, publicizing events, soliciting donations—were ranked as important, but they were not as important as the goals associated with the practice of informing, as discussed in chapter 3.

In a survey of Internet users we helped conduct during the 2000 campaign, relatively few had visited campaign sites, and of those who did, slightly less than one-third indicated that they looked at the volunteer sections or expressed interest in becoming involved with campaign organizations through the Web sites. However, a survey conducted by the Pew Internet and American Life project in 2004 found that 11 percent of U.S. Internet users (approximately 13 million people) reported engaging in campaign-related activities online during the 2004 election cycle. Participants in focus groups conducted in New Hampshire during the presidential primaries in 2000, few of whom had visited campaign sites prior to participating in the study, expressed interest in interacting with the candidate or campaign staff, especially through email or chat forums. They wanted to be able to indicate willingness to get more involved in the campaign through the Web site and were not surprised by the requests on the candidates' sites to contribute to the campaign or to volunteer. One participant described her reaction in this way: "I think they are going to take any opportunity to get any money or anybody to come along, so it doesn't surprise me at all that the credit card is there or the volunteers—I mean that is what it is out there for, to pull people in, to get them involved in whatever way." Some found it surprising when the candidates offered an array of ways to get involved, such as putting up lawn signs or creating an e-precinct (that is, using the Internet to organize fellow supporters within their electoral district). They found these many opportunities to get involved desirable, especially for those who may want to become more involved but are not sure how to do so.

More specifically, focus group participants wanted the opportunity to email candidates if they had a question, although they did not expect or necessarily want the candidate to respond. For example, one participant, when asked what she would like to see on a candidate site, said, "What I would like is if I had a question for a candidate, not just [this candidate], anyone, if I could put my question in there and send that off and then I could get an answer." They also wanted information on how to contact the campaign at the local level. One New Hampshire resident said, "I think there should be something on there for local contact people too—if you wanted to get in touch with somebody like in Dover or in this area, to help do something with this campaign." These respondents viewed online structures for contacting candidates and campaign staff as an important component of a campaign site. In the following sections we examine the ways that convergence, linking, and coproduction are employed in the practice of involving, but first we introduce a technique that is specific to involving: transaction.

Techniques for Involving

Transaction

Campaigns that want to catalyze and manage site visitors' involvement require online structures that allow them to obtain information provided by site visitors. By creating such online structures to facilitate Web-based interactions, campaign organizations establish a transactional relationship with site visitors. The technique of transaction mediates these relationships and is associated uniquely with the practice of involving. A transaction requires site visitors to provide information and creates an implicit, and sometimes explicit, responsibility or obligation on the part of the campaign organization to process and manage the information properly and efficiently. Creating and managing transactional relationships on the Web requires that campaign organizations adopt new tools in association with the practice of involving.

Transactional relationships are not new to campaign organizations, which have always had systems of varying sophistication for processing donations and managing volunteer relationships offline. However, transactional relationships created and managed in online environments differ from offline relationships in significant ways. For example, Web site visitors may be more sensitive to and have more concerns about engaging in online transactions with campaigns than they have in establishing relationships with campaigns in person or through other modes. Despite the fact that by the 2004 election, nearly 70 percent of Internet users had bought a product online (Pew Internet and American Life Project 2005), there was still skepticism and reluctance to engage in online commerce, perhaps especially with unknown and ephemeral organizations such as campaigns. Furthermore, online transactions via campaign sites create a need for campaign organizations to establish and publicize policies for managing these relationships. Finally, creating a transactional environment, especially one that is capable of handling financial contributions and managing a complex volunteering environment, requires a campaign to establish computerized database structures to process the transactions. For these reasons, the emergence of involving as a Web practice has been somewhat slower and less extensive than the emergence of informing, described in chapter 3.

In order to engage in the practice of involving, campaigns need to develop an underlying technical infrastructure to manage the transactional elements. This can be as simple as some automated capability for processing electronic mail or as complicated as a fully automated system for accepting regular donations from contributors via credit card or automatic bank withdrawal. These kinds of background ("back-end") processes require technical expertise. However, such technical expertise is also required to develop the front-end forms-processing infrastructure to transform the fundamentally static Web HTML environment into a dynamic transactional environment.

One of the primary ways campaigns seek to involve site visitors is through online structures that collect and manage email addresses. Although not yet a mainstream practice in congressional campaigns, it is becoming increasingly common for campaigns to purchase email addresses from outside vendors (Howard 2006; Hunter 2002). However, we focus our analysis on the collection of email addresses through campaign Web sites. Viewed through the lens of the technique of transaction, site visitors' email addresses are a resource that can be harvested and managed via the campaign site when appropriate online structures are produced and configured strategically.

One critical production decision is whether to merge email addresses collected through a campaign email list sign-up feature with addresses collected from volunteer sign-up features. Campaign email list sign-up features are often given informational labels such as "Signup for Campaign Updates" or "Subscribe to Campaign News." The risk of merging addresses from email and volunteer signup features is that those who signed up expecting to receive informational updates from the campaign may be repulsed by emailed requests to volunteer or donate. The opportunity in the merging of these addresses is that a larger number of individuals will receive requests to volunteer or donate, as Bill Bradley's 2000 campaign manager, Lynn Reed, observed in her explanation of that campaign's decision to merge addresses collected through both kinds of features:

Reed: The email lists we started building from day one. One decision that we made ahead of time that I believe wound up helping us greatly in the end was that the email list was not separate and distinct from our supporter database. It was a part of our supporter database. You didn't sign up for the email list and then separately sign up to volunteer; it was one form. What that meant for us on the backend was that you had to manage it a little bit differently. We had to build a pretty sophisticated database in order to manage that, but as the list built up, we were able to email subsets of that list very efficiently. We started building up names for twelve months before we ever needed to subdivide it and just mail to the people in the California 12th congressional district. But by the time you are ready to email people in that district, you've got a significant number of names.

Interviewer: In terms of volunteering and getting involved, do you recall how many volunteers you were able to recruit off the Web site?

Reed: We'll probably have to define what we mean by volunteer because our total database of names that we collected through the Web site was around 85,000 names. Now, people indicated that they were willing to get involved at different levels within that 85,000, but in practice, if we had your email address, we were going to at least ask you to volunteer. You might have checked off the box that said volunteer, or you might not have checked off the box that said volunteer, but if we had an email address, we were going to give you the opportunity to volunteer whether you said so or not (Reed 2000).

Reed's comments illustrate production decisions entailed in creating Web forms and database architecture to support the transaction of soliciting email addresses from site visitors, as well as strategy decisions regarding how to use the email addresses collected via the campaign site.

Email addresses are increasingly viewed as an important resource by campaigns. The growth in the number of email addresses amassed by presidential campaigns in 1996, 2000, and 2004 is quite revealing. Bob Dole's 1996 campaign collected 70,000 email addresses, and gained one-third of its volunteers (15,000 out of 45,000 total) via its campaign site (Arena 1996). At the end of the 2000 presidential primary season, the Bradley campaign had collected 85,000 email addresses through a combination of an email signup and volunteer features on its site. McCain's campaign site producer reported that 142,000 email addresses of volunteers were acquired via the Web during the 2000 primary season (Fose 2000).

In contrast, at the end of the 2004 presidential primary season, the Dean campaign had collected about 600,000 email addresses (Spagat 2004), and the Kerry campaign had about 690,000 email addresses (Harris 2004). Even though the incumbent George Bush was not yet officially campaigning in May 2004, the Bush campaign had collected about 6 million email addresses by then, including many purchased from vendors (Harris 2004). A Kerry aide contended to a reporter at that time that his campaign's email list, though smaller, was just as valuable as Bush's since it consisted solely of volunteered addresses and did not include addresses purchased from vendors (Harris 2004). By the end of the 2004 presidential election, the Kerry campaign had collected 2.7 million email addresses, mostly through the email sign-up feature on its campaign site (Faler 2004). Although the growth in the average size of presidential campaigns' email databases across election cycles may reflect the general increase in the proportion of the population with email accounts during this period, it also indicates an increasing willingness on the part of Internet users to divulge their email addresses to political actors. Furthermore, it is also a rough indicator of the increasing importance of email addresses to campaigns and the scale of database architecture needed to manage email addresses. The fact that a campaign staffer in 2004 felt the need to defend the size and sources of a campaign's email database points to the significance that had come to be attached to email addresses as a campaign resource.

The fate of email addresses collected by campaigns hinges technically on the ability to preserve a campaign's databases and migrate them across operating systems and database software applications. As a Washington Post reporter observed, "Few cared what happened, for example, to Al Gore's email list when his Democratic presidential campaign folded. But with the increasing maturation of the Internet as a political tool—and the huge sums that can be raised online—some experts said those addresses can remain valuable long after an election" (Faler 2004). However, some former campaign staff and political analysts have voiced concerns over the ethics and privacy implications of transferring database records including email addresses from a defunct campaign to a political party or other entity (Hunter 2002; Faler 2004; Spagat 2004). We discuss this further later.

Beyond collecting and managing email addresses, some campaign organizations have extended their transactional capacity to build ongoing strategic relationships with site visitors. These campaign sites include capabilities to bring together data provided intentionally and consciously by the site visitor with additional data about the site visitor. The visitor's experiences on the Web site, including the frequency of page views, may be combined with data about the site visitor obtained from outside sources, such as party registration, turnout history, contribution record, and purchasing patterns (from credit card company databases). Constituent relationship management (CRM) systems attempt to extend to the political realm the powerful marketing tools commonly found in the business community, with the goal of providing relevant information to individually identified site visitors (Howard 2005; Seiger 2003).

As campaign organizations have begun enabling transactional relationships with site visitors, some have taken explicit steps to articulate boundaries and establish terms to govern that relationship, most commonly by posting privacy policies on their Web sites. It is evident that users of candidate Web sites want clear privacy policies. Focus group participants in 2000 indicated that they were (already) weary of having their email addresses and personal information sold or otherwise transferred and then receiving unwanted solicitations. They desired explicit statements regarding the

purposes for which the information they provide Web site owners would
be used. As one participant stated, "I like the fact they say okay when you
give us this, this is how we'll use it." An online survey of Internet users
conducted by researchers at the Institute for Politics, Democracy and the
Internet in 2003 confirmed the views articulated by the focus group participants: Of survey respondents, 69 percent felt hesitant about providing
their email addresses and 89 percent felt hesitant about providing credit
card numbers to political Web sites. The reasons for their hesitation included fears about privacy, security, and unwanted email (Seiger 2003).

Campaign site producers employ a variety of strategies for articulating
and structuring the transactional relationships they establish with site
visitors. To date, a majority of them have no statement whatsoever, leaving the terms of the relationship completely unstated. In our analysis of
campaign Web sites, the proportion with a section labeled "Privacy"
addressing the campaign's use of personal information and visitors' site-
use data increased from 10 percent in 2000, to 17 percent in 2002, and
then again to 29 percent in 2004.

Among those sites that have posted an explicit policy, some were minimal and straightforward. For example, the 2002 Web site of Mary Bono
(R-CA-45) simply stated that the campaign "will not disclose your email address or any other contact information you have provided us. We will not
provide your contact information to any other organization unless you
specifically authorize us to do so."[65] Privacy policies on some other sites
acknowledged complexity in the relationship between the campaign and
site visitors: This more comprehensive approach was taken by Tom Harkin
(D-MO-Sen) in 2002. The privacy policy posted on his campaign site
acknowledged that "some" of the information provided by site visitors,
including name, address, and phone numbers, "may be shared with similar
organizations (such as county Democratic groups)."[66] The Harkin campaign
stated that information associated with contributions would be reported, as
required by law, to the Federal Election Commission, and explicitly noted
that server log information was not matched to other personal information. Still other campaigns appear to have appropriated policy and terms of
use from e-commerce or other types of sites. Larry Craig's (R-ID-Sen) 2002
campaign site used language common to commercial sites. The privacy policy was headlined as "LarryCraig.com's Promise to You, Our Customer,"
and approached the relationship with the site visitor as one might expect a

business to do with a customer.[67] The policy referenced shipping addresses, promotions, games, and storing items in a shopping cart, and was one of the few we observed that promised to notify the site visitor by email of changes to the policy. Most sites reserved the right to change the privacy policy without notification and also explicitly noted that the sites contain links to other sites that may be governed by different privacy policies.

A campaign Web site privacy policy that evolves within and across elec- tions can be problematic, as we demonstrate by comparing the privacy statements on Bush's campaign site in 1999, 2000, 2003, and 2004. As of October 1999, Bush's campaign site had no privacy policy, although it had already been soliciting email addresses and volunteers via the site for at least six months.[68] By the end of November 1999, the campaign had posted an undated privacy statement that addressed several aspects of what the campaign would and would not do with the personal information visitors voluntarily provided to the campaign via the site.[69] However, this statement did not address whether the policy was retroactive, that is, whether the current terms would also be employed in managing personal information that had been provided prior to the posting of the privacy policy.

In regard to personal information provided to the Bush campaign by a site visitor for the purpose of customizing the campaign site, the campaign's policy stated, "We will never share any of your personalization information with any third party" in November 1999. In regard to personal information provided to the campaign in conjunction with volunteer sign-up, the campaign promised it would not be shared with other organizations without the site visitor's permission. However, the campaign's statement did not specify whether email addresses collected through the site's email sign-up feature would be shared with other organizations, leaving that possibility open. The policy included the statement, "We will continue to evaluate our efforts to protect your information and will update our privacy policy whenever necessary," but did not indicate how updates would be announced and whether changes would be applied retroactively to personal information provided prior to any privacy policy updates.[70]

Bush's campaign organization redirected traffic from the campaign Web site, georgewbush.com, to the Republican National Committee Web site for most of 2001 and 2002, but began soliciting donations and email addresses for the 2004 re-election campaign via its site in June 2003. At that time, the privacy policy began:

Welcome to the temporary site for GeorgeWBush.com. An expanded privacy policy
will be available when the full Web site is launched. GeorgeWBush.com currently
enables supporters to voluntarily sign up to get involved with the effort to re-elect
President George W. Bush. GeorgeWBush.com will not collect any individual information without your knowledge.[71]

Thus, any site visitors who signed up to volunteer did so with no idea what
uses the campaign would make of the personal information they provided
the campaign in the sign-up process. In August 2003, a more detailed policy was posted that differed from the 2000 policy in a few key ways regarding the use of personal information provided by site visitors.[72] This
statement assured site visitors that the campaign would not retain the
names and email addresses supplied by visitors through site features that
enabled visitors to forward links from the site to others via a Web form,
nor use that information for any other purpose. Although the policy assured visitors that their own personal information would not be sold to
any other entity, it asserted the campaign's intention to "share your information with Republican organizations committed to re-electing President
Bush ... and the Republican ticket," such as the Republican National
Committee, Republican state party organizations and local Republican
groups.[73] By the eve of the 2004 presidential primaries, the Bush campaign
site privacy policy had provided opt-out mechanisms whereby volunteers
recruited through the site could decline to have personal information provided transferred to other entities.

As the 2004 presidential election got underway, not only was the
campaign's assurance from 2000 that personal information would not be
shared with third parties absent from the site, but the Bush campaign had
reserved to itself the authority to disseminate the email addresses and other
personal information of site visitors in any way that served the Republican
party. The policy did not mention whether email addresses collected during the 2000 election or earlier in 2003 would now be subject to the new,
more liberal clauses. The policy concluded with the campaign's assertion of
its right to revise or update the privacy policy at any time: "While we do
not intend to make any changes to this policy we do reserve the right to
do so. If any changes to this privacy policy are made the date that the
revised or updated policy is posted to GeorgeWBush.com will appear at
the bottom of the page." The original date of posting, August 18, 2003,
did not change over the period of the 2004 election, so it seems these terms

served the Bush campaign's needs adequately. Whether they served citizens well is a subject for future research.

Our purpose in comparing the various statements made by Bush's campaign organization between 1999 and 2004 is to illustrate the ways in which the online structures and policies undergirding transactions between campaigns and site visitors have implications beyond a particular election, and the ways they may change over time. Databases of personal information supplied by site visitors to Bush's campaign in 2000 under particular terms of use fell into a murky morass during the interim period between elections. Although not explicitly addressed by the campaign's policy in 2003, these databases were most likely migrated into the 2004 re-election campaign's information architecture—under significantly different terms of use.

In sum, the technique of transaction on campaign Web sites establishes the terms of the relationship between the campaign organization and site visitors. This technique is generally employed in ways that enable the campaign organization to assume responsibility for managing the details of the relationship and thus retain control over the data necessary for such management. Decisions entailed in the configuration of transactional on-line structures have significant implications for site visitors, particularly in regard to privacy, and for a campaign's capacity to share informational resources across the campaign organization and migrate such resources across elections. Next, we turn our attention to the use of convergence in the practice of involving.

Convergence

The technique of convergence, or the integration of the offline and online realms, is employed in the Web campaigning practice of involving in several ways. Convergence in involving can be as simple as using a Web site to solicit mail-in donations of contributions to an offline postal address, or as sophisticated as a donor database with a Web interface that allows supporters to self-enroll by entering their names, addresses, credit card numbers, or even bank account information for automated monthly contributions to a campaign. In this section, we analyze five distinct types of online structures reflecting the technique of convergence as it is employed by campaigns in the practice of involving.

The first is the provision on a campaign Web site of documents intended for distribution, such as posters or flyers. Formatted to be easy to download and print, these documents are designed for offline distribution: The campaign site functions as an online repository and dissemination structure for them. For example, as we discuss in chapter 6, flyers and posters may be intended by some campaign site producers as mobilizing tools, as when they encourage supporters to distribute them to others on behalf of the campaign. Here, our focus is on the way that posting distributable documents on a campaign site can foster a sense of belonging among supporters in relation to the campaign. Such documents can come to symbolize supporters' association with the campaign. Max Fose, campaign Web producer for presidential candidate John McCain in 2000, explained how the online provision of flyers strengthened bonds between supporters and the campaign:

When we started [providing flyers on the site], John McCain came to the headquarters and said, "I'm sick of signing those flyers" because everyone would print them out and go to these rallies. It was a way we could tell that this was working because they were showing up to these rallies with these flyers that were nothing more than Uncle Sam saying, "Vote John McCain." They had a connection to the campaign—that's what it did (Fose 2000).

Fose's account demonstrates that one way supporters enact their affiliation with a campaign is by printing out a flyer and bringing it to a campaign event to be autographed by the candidate.

A second variant of convergence for involving is seen in the calendar feature found on many sites in each election. Campaigns that post a prospective calendar of campaign-sponsored events enable interested site visitors to learn about and make plans to attend in-person gatherings, which may increase their involvement with the campaign. About one-third of campaign sites provided a calendar in 2004; about the same proportion of campaign sites employed this feature in 2002. For example, the 2004 campaign site for Democratic presidential primary candidate, Carol Moseley-Braun, provided a calendar of offline campaign events, such as the candidate forums, fundraisers, and television programs, in which she planned to participate. This site also included a related feature that manifested convergence in the involving practice: an Adobe PDF sign-in sheet template for organizers to download and use "for gathering information at events for Carol supporters."[74]

Citizens look to the Web to provide them with information about candidates. But they also expect to find ways to contact or interact with candidates—an expectation they may not have when learning about candidates in other media. Focus group participants during the presidential primaries in 2000 expressed interest in using a campaign Web site to find out where the candidate would be, when the next debate would be, and when the candidate would next be in their area. One participant said he would use a candidate Web site to learn the following things about a candidate: "How he did in the recent debate, or where he's gonna be the next time, or where he's booked—you know, if he has an interview on Dateline." Some participants criticized one of the candidate Web sites they saw because its schedule of events was not up-to-date.

Of course not all interested site visitors are supporters of the candidate; the downside to calendars is that they provide the opposition with lists of events to disrupt. A comment from a site producer surveyed in 2002 illustrates this dilemma: "We initially posted an event calendar, but found that our opponent used it to find out where we would be, and then showed up at the same places. We took down the calendar after a month or so." This tension is discussed in more detail later.

The third variant of convergence we consider in association with the practice of involving is the quasi-self-organizing "Meetup" phenomenon that emerged as a facet of Web campaigning during the 2004 presidential primary campaigns. Campaign-focused Meetups were enabled by the Web service provided by a company called Meetup.com, which bills itself as "[helping] people find others who share their interest or cause, and form lasting, influential, local community groups that regularly meet face-to-face."[75] Meetup.com, the brainchild of Scott Heiferman, was launched in June 2002, as "the first easy-to-use service that allowed people to participate in and organize local gatherings about things they care about."[76] The service is topic-neutral; the topical focus of any Meetup event is up to its organizers. However, Meetup staff initiated some events, and thus deserve credit for the first electoral campaign Meetup.

The introduction of Meetup as a convergence tool in Web campaigning was somewhat serendipitous, but the appropriation of Meetup was strategic for the practice of involving. On March 5, 2003, nearly 500 people gathered at the Essex Lounge in Manhattan in the hope that Democratic presidential primary candidate Howard Dean would appear. The gathering had been initiated by Meetup's executives, not by campaign staff, and organized on Meetup.com. Over 400 people had signed up in advance on Meetup.com to indicate their intent to attend the gathering. Much to the delight of those gathered, Dean showed up. Soon afterward, Dean's campaign negotiated an agreement with Meetup's management to receive the email addresses of those drawn to the campaign through MeetUp.com in exchange for a monthly fee (Hemingway 2003). By the end of 2003, approximately 150,000 Web-using Dean supporters had indicated their interest in the campaign by signing up on Meetup.com, contributing significantly to Dean's ascent (Overfelt 2003; Wikipedia 2005). Most of the other Democratic presidential primary campaigns developed Meetup followings as well during 2003 and 2004, as did many congressional candidates in 2004.

When a campaign contracted with Meetup.com, the Meetup site producers created a campaign-specific page, to which the campaign site linked.[77] Linking to a campaign-focused page on Meetup.com facilitates involvement in the campaign by enabling face-to-face gatherings of supporters; it also enables voter-to-voter connections outside of or with loose ties to the campaign itself—a phenomenon we discuss further in chapter 5. Meetups enable mobilization as well by facilitating supporters in becoming advocates for the campaign, as we discuss in chapter 6.

A fourth variant of convergence is the use of the Web for coordinating offline volunteer work. Jesse Ventura's (Ref-MN-Gov) 1998 campaign demonstrated this variant by making extensive use of the Web as a mechanism for distributed labor by campaign volunteers. As Webmaster Phil Madsen described in a brief reflection on the campaign, establishing a Web-based data entry system enabled the cash-strapped campaign to efficiently digitize contact information collected from thousands of people at the Minnesota State Fair:

Five thousand people completed volunteer forms at Jesse's State Fair booth. Many requested bumper stickers and lawn signs. With little time left before election day, no computers in the office, and no money to hire a data entry service, we turned to the Internet. We set up a private web site for data entry. The form fields on the data entry site matched the fields on the printed State Fair form. A Jesse Net appeal for data entry volunteers was answered by over 70 people. After asking them to complete a minor administrative action online, 48 serious and reliable volunteers remained, which we named the Data Entry Team.

We divided the paper forms into packets of 100+ and mailed one packet to each DE Team member. Working from home, DE Team members went to our private web site and entered the data there. We downloaded that data into our database and printed mailing labels. Within days, we had bumper stickers and fundraising letters on the way to the 5,000 new supporters we met at the State Fair. Except for postage to mail the DE Team packets and copying the printed forms for backup in case they were lost, the total cost of the data entry operation was $0 (Madsen 1998).

Web campaigning enables the distribution of some kinds of volunteer activities across time and space, but other kinds of campaign work still entail tasks that are most efficiently done by gathering people in a particular geographic location. The final type of convergence that we discuss in relation to involving is the provision of location maps of brick-and-mortar campaign offices on campaign Web sites. A campaign office location map is a type of virtual tool that facilitates involving supporters in offline volunteer activities such as preparing mailings and telephoning potential voters. For instance, the 2000 campaign site for congressional candidate Thomas Tancredo (R-CO-6) linked to a map providing the user with exact directions to the campaign headquarters in Littleton: Once on the volunteer page of the site, potential volunteers could click a link labeled "Campaign Headquarters" to retrieve this map.[78] The map was generated by Mapquest.com, an online company that offers a free mapping service to Web users, deriving its revenue by selling advertisements on its site. To create the map a campaign site producer entered the office street address on Mapquest.com, and then embedded a link to the URL of the resulting map in the text on the campaign's volunteer page. The use of such maps on campaign sites makes it easy for potential volunteers to locate campaign offices, and thus reduces a barrier to involvement.

Linking

The technique of linking is relevant to the practice of involving in at least two ways. First, the Web allows for the production of hyperlink-based database interfaces that greatly facilitate the practice of involving. These interfaces and the underlying databases reduce the transaction costs of opportunities for involvement for both campaigns and citizens. Campaigns can recruit more broadly and manage greater amounts of transactions less expensively. Conversely, citizens can get involved in campaigns with less effort, and do so more quickly and more specifically in accordance with their interests and abilities. For instance, a sixty-four-year-old, unemployed woman who attended the Meetup meeting of 2004 presidential candidate Wesley Clark's supporters in Honolulu, Hawaii, was quoted as explaining that her involvement in Meetup was "to learn more about Clark and to find out what I can do besides send money I cannot afford to give to help get him elected" (Williams 2004).

Second, outlinking facilitates the practice of involving using links between multiple sites produced by the campaign within a particular election cycle. As we explained in chapter 2, a growing number of campaigns have established a Web presence that extends beyond the primary or main campaign site and includes multiple Web sites all produced by the campaign. John McCain's 2000 presidential primary campaign may have been the first to produce a multisite Web presence: mccain2000.com and mccaininteractive.com.[79] Given the difficulties in comprehensively identifying the universe of the main campaign-produced sites for any election, estimating the prevalence of campaigns with multiple sites is more difficult still. However, we identified several congressional campaigns in 2000, 2002, and 2004 that each produced two sites. By the 2004 presidential primary season, the phenomenon had become commonplace. The Web presence of eight of the nine Democratic presidential primary campaigns in 2004 included three or more sites each, and two campaigns, Dean's and Kerry's, included at least seven sites each.[80]

The creation of a multisite Web presence facilitates involving because with each site a campaign produces, it creates another virtual door through which curious site visitors may enter and become involved with the campaign. For example, a Web user surfing for Internet resources on the topic of leadership integrity in the autumn of 2003 could have happened upon the URL www.leadingwithintegrity.com without foreknowledge of the Lieberman presidential campaign's sponsorship of the site. The site promoted the candidate through the lens of leadership integrity and served as an entry point into the rest of the campaign's Web presence. A link to the primary campaign site, joe2004.com, was prominently posted on the home page of www.leadingwithintegrity.com, along with an invitation for visitors to get involved in the campaign, through attending a local campaign event, signing up for campaign email, or contributing to the campaign.[81] However, most outlinks from a campaign site are to sites produced by other actors, and thus do not generally manifest the practice of involving.

Coproduction

Since involving characterizes the practice of gathering supporters and resources for a particular campaign, uses of the technique of coproduction
are somewhat limited in comparison with the other practices. However,
there are at least four types of coproduction employed in involving: (1) online structures produced with the help of vendors; (2) online structures,
campaign donor information, and other transaction records incorporated
from a previous campaign or provided to a campaign by the party with
which it is affiliated; (3) polls and graphical features coproduced through
user actions; and (4) discussion forums. In this section we discuss the affordances of each type of coproduction for the practice of involving.

It is not unusual for the online structures that mediate the transactions
associated with involving to be coproduced by online transaction support
service vendors (such as E-contributor or Paypal) or organizations specializing in database management systems. Such organizations usually provide
transaction or database management services as contractors. These arrangements are sometimes indicated by "powered by" notices on the front page
of the campaign site, giving credit for back-end technology and support to a
vendor. Meetup.com and Mapquest.com, discussed previously as enabling
various kinds convergence-related involving, are other types of vendors
with which campaigns coproduce online structures for involving. We do
not classify vendors as political actors in the same sense that parties, news
producers, and advocacy groups are because many online service vendors
provide services to competing candidates. We therefore consider vendor-
based coproduction to be associated with the practice of involving but not
associated with the Web practice of connecting, which encompasses the act
of providing bridges between site visitors and other political actors.

However, just as some political consultancy firms tend to work with either Democratic or Republican candidates, some technology service providers work primarily or even exclusively with candidates associated with
a particular party. In an ethnographic study of a community of Web site
designers who specialize in political Web sites and other technology consultants based in Washington, D.C., Howard (2006) found partisan patterns in vendor-client relationships. He also documented the competitive
strategies of various campaign and party organizations to cultivate and
sustain technological expertise and information resources. These findings
indicate that although coproduction in the context of involving is usually

at a technical or structural level, rather than at the content level, it can still be politically consequential. Coproduction in involving can reflect the political economy of a campaign in that major party candidates in competitive national races are more likely to have higher campaign receipts and to receive more attention and support from their respective parties (Kahn and Kenney 1999; Westlye 1991), and thus they may be more likely to contract with professional—perhaps partisan—vendors to coproduce online structures. Our survey of site producers in 2002 provides a rough indicator in this vein: Although 21 percent of the site producers responsible for Republican or Democratic campaign sites reported that they were consultants paid by the campaign, none of the campaign site producers for campaigns affiliated with other parties were paid consultants.

A second variant of coproduction is seen across election cycles in campaigns for candidates that run for office multiple times. This is consistent with the traditional strategy employed by candidates who intend to run again and who therefore maintain lists of supporters and, particularly, donors compiled in a previous election. A successful candidate in at least three races, Thomas Tancredo (R-CO-6), recycled much of the campaign site he used in 2000 in his run for re-election in 2002, including the volunteer page.[82] Although Tancredo's 2004 campaign site had a distinctly different appearance and new information features and structural elements, the information fields on the volunteer form remained mostly the same.[83] By using the same fields on the volunteer Web form across three elections, Tancredo would have been able to build a database of contact, contribution, and volunteer interest information over three election cycles. Any candidate considering a second run for public office, whether incumbent or challenger, has good reasons for preserving the online structures for involving that were developed for a particular election. Functional online structures are investments that can provide greater returns over time, both due to the greater economic efficiency of re-use and to the information resources accumulated via these structures. It remains to be determined whether Web users perceive campaigns' re-use of online structures or entire campaign sites as desirable attributes of stability and consistency or as a lack of innovation and currency.

Third, an opinion poll can function as a coproduced feature for involving on a campaign site if the results are posted on the site. The site for Charles Laws, previously referenced, included an opinion poll in which site visitors could respond to survey questions and view results. Similarly, the campaign site for Steve Udall (D-AZ-1) offered site visitors the opportunity to participate in the "Udall 2002 Poll."[84] John Sophocleus' (Lib-AL-Gov) 2002 site featured a poll on the question, "Who is best qualified to lead Alabama to economic prosperity?" Respondents could choose "a professional politician, a professional economist, other, or nobody/not sure" and view poll results displayed on a page produced by the Web hosting company Homestead.com.[85]

Like polls, graphical features that can be shaped by site visitors' actions are a variant of coproduction within the practice of involving. After losing the Iowa primary, Dean's campaign added a feature called the "One Million Dollar Comeback Bat" to the front page of its main site. An outline of an upright baseball bat was framed with text urging visitors to contribute toward the campaign's goal of raising an additional million dollars, along with a link to a Web form for online donations. Text within the bat stated the amount of funds received toward the goal and the number of contributors to date, and the coloration of the bat visually depicted the proportion of funds received toward the goal.[86] After $1.4 million had been donated in a seven-day period, the bat was fully colored, and the text "Home Run!" was added to the graphic.[87] During the general election, graphics mimicking the Dean bat were observed on other campaign Web sites. In mid-October 2004, Richard Romero (D-NM-1) played to local culinary culture by employing a chile pepper graphic framed by text urging supporters to "keep the heat on" his Republican opponent by "filling the chile pepper" with ten thousand dollars "by Tuesday."[88] These kinds of coproduced graphical features tacitly invite site visitors to make repeat visits to the site to check on their progress. Such features also convey the implicit message that the campaign itself is coproduced.

Lastly, discussion forums can be built using any of several applications, such as Internet Relay Chat tools for synchronous discussion, or message boards and multiauthored Web logs (blogs) for asynchronous exchanges. Discussion forums were extraordinarily rare on campaign Web sites prior to 2004. Stromer-Galley (2000) provides several reasons for campaigns' reluctance to enable discussion on their sites, centering on their concerns about losing control. The concerns expressed by Bradley's campaign manager, Lynn Reed, illustrate the perspective of many campaigns in this regard:

Interviewer: Let me ask you about bulletin boards. Have you thought at all about putting up either a citizen bulletin board or an event that Bradley would attend?

Reed: I was a major roadblock in the way of people who wanted to do that stuff.

Interviewer: Were there people on the campaign who wanted to do that?

Reed: There were people on the campaign who wanted to do it. There were some Silicon Valley advisors who wanted us to do it. My opinion is that although that stuff makes sense in a commercial setting, although that stuff makes sense on CNN.com, although it makes sense on whatever good government/democracy site you're running, it's not right for a candidate site. The number one rule for political communication is to be on message. And you don't know what people are going to say, and you are giving a forum for your opponents to come and say bad things about you. You're giving a forum for these same nut cases that we were just talking about to come and say bad things about you. And even if by some way you could restrict it to the people who actually support you—I'm not necessarily going to be on message. The reason to be on message is to try and convince undecided voters, and it's against the most fundamental rule of political communication.

Interviewer: It's too risky?

Reed: Yes. I believe that in the long run I will lose that fight.

Interviewer: Really, why?

Reed: Because I think the tide over ten or twenty years will shift to where people expect that, and younger people in particular expect it.

Interviewer: And they expect it because ... ?

Reed: It's just part of what the Internet is supposed to be about (Reed 2000).

Reed was not alone in avoiding the use of discussion features on campaign sites. The opportunity to view visitor comments in any form was present on fewer than 3 percent of campaign sites in 2002. One example of a candidate who risked online discussion was Charles Laws (Gr-NV-Gov). His site was organized as a multiple-author discussion forum, with site visitors invited to submit new topics or comment on existing topics.[89]

Another approach to involving through the provision of opportunities to participate in discussion forums occurs with blogs. A blog, although similar in some respects to a message board application, is distinct from the older style discussion forums. Blogs have a recognizable form, organized generally by date of posting, and they provide a more-or-less-standard interface for visitors to access, review, and, in some cases, add postings. Although introduced as a feature on a candidate site in 2000,[90] blogs were on very few campaign sites in 2000 or 2002. Most were single-authored by the candidate or, more likely, a campaign staffer, and were largely used to report the candidate's daily campaign activities. Some candidates, starting with Tara Sue Grubb (Lib-NC-6) in 2002, built their entire Web sites as a blog.

During the lead up to 2004 presidential primaries, the campaign blog emerged as a central element in campaign Web sites. Starting with the Dean campaign, which launched its read-only blog in March 2003[91] and a fully participatory blog three months later, other presidential campaigns followed suit, notably the Kerry, Gore, and Edwards organizations. Our analysis of postings to the Dean campaign blog between July 2003 and February 2004 indicate that more than 40,000 different accounts were used to post more than 600,000 messages. The success of Dean's collaboratively authored blog, in terms of providing opportunities for many individuals to become involved with the campaign through posting messages, appears to have stimulated other campaign organizations to follow suit and provide similar opportunities for supporters to become involved.

Single-authored campaign blogs reflect the practice of involving in that the typical blog pattern of frequent, relatively brief, descriptive posts may help site visitors gain a candidate's or campaign staffer's selective and strategically constructed perspective on the daily life of the campaign, and thus cultivate a sense of familiarity and affinity with the candidate. Allowing unmoderated discussion on a campaign site can be detrimental to the campaign's effort to remain focused on a strategically determined message. However, discussion forums can also be tools employed in the technique of coproduction within the practice of involving.

Multiauthored blogs and other kinds of discussion forums on campaign sites have a cultivating function similar to single-authored blogs, but they reflect the technique of coproduction as well. Collaborative authoring of a blog by campaign staff and site visitors involves site visitors—whether opponents, inquirers, or supporters—in the process of agenda-setting and the framing of issues. This can generate valuable information for campaigns about the concerns' of potential voters, but the release of control can also create problems, as we will discuss in chapter 5. In many of the focus groups conducted in New Hampshire in 2000, participants spent time explaining the challenges they believed campaigns that created online discussion forums faced. Participants identified five obstacles: (1) the increased cost of designing a site that allows discussion versus one that does not; (2) the need for a dedicated staff member to manage email responses or a discussion forum; (3) content accountability; (4) antagonistic use of the discussion forum by non-supporters; and (5) the scale and volume of traffic such interactive opportunities might generate. Such challenges are the focus of the next section.

Tensions in Involving

The Web practice of involving creates both opportunities and tensions for campaigns. The opportunities are related to the extended reach of the campaign to potential supporters via the Web, but they are also related to the means by which transactions between supporters and campaigns are mediated. Offline, traditional campaign strategies for involving can be characterized as facilitating informational and sometimes financial transactions that take place at particular points in time. Each transaction is often discrete from any others. Besides money, the most valuable resources given by supporters to a campaign are their names and addresses. In offline involving, campaigns may take whatever volunteer effort and money is offered at a particular time; a volunteer's or contributor's name, street address, and phone number may or may not be recorded to enable future contact or involvement. On the Web, the transactions that are foundational to the campaign practice of involving routinely entail the recording of these data. Many other kinds of information such as email addresses, credit card numbers, and permission to make automatic monthly withdrawals, may be requested and recorded as well.

Web-based transactions are also more easily traceable and repeatable. Web technologies afford campaigns expanded opportunities to aggregate information, which enables the cultivation of relationships to increase the likelihood of transactions that, in turn, bring in greater resources. From a user's perspective, Web-based involving on the part of campaigns can seem entangling. To the extent that information mediates power and control, the campaign Web practice of informing effects a shift of power and control to the Web user, while the practice of involving effects a power-and-control shift to the site producer (Neuman 1991). Although the Web provides enhanced tools for campaigns to cultivate ongoing relationships with supporters throughout an election season and across election cycles, these increased opportunities also entail tensions for campaigns. More extensive networks of campaign supporters, more frequent points of contact with supporters, and more intense forms of interaction with supporters— all enabled by the Web's affordances—increase both the stakes and the

risks of involving for campaigns. In the remainder of this section we analyze four tensions campaigns face in this regard.

The first tension can be characterized as expectation management: Many
involving features provided on a campaign site create an expectation on
the part of site visitors. If site visitors are invited to sign up for email
updates, some will draw negative conclusions about the campaign if no
email updates are sent. If a campaign email address is posted on a site, focus
group participants in 2000 indicated that visitors who write to that address
expect that someone within the campaign (ideally the candidate) will read
and respond to messages sent to that address. Likewise, discussion forums
such as message boards or blogs require management and perhaps modera-
tion. If volunteers are solicited, then those who agree to help will expect
to be contacted by the campaign. A strong response to a request for volunteers can overwhelm a small campaign organization, and attempting to distribute volunteer labor over time can be difficult. As anyone who has
coordinated volunteer help can attest, the free labor is appreciated but the
process of managing volunteers requires a significant amount of time and
energy.

A second tension concerns sustaining involvement through the course of
a lengthy electoral campaign without overwhelming supporters or over-
loading staff. There will always be some portion of campaign "junkies" on
one end of the spectrum who eagerly anticipate several emails a day from
the campaign, and antisocial or simply info-swamped supporters on the
other end who get irritated by a weekly campaign email update even
though they requested it. But finding the balance between fulfilling the
majority of supporters' expectations for periodic updates and other forms
of contact from the campaign, and not annoying them with too-frequent
or lengthy emails or phone calls can be difficult. The volunteer sign-up
page on Dick Gephardt's 2004 presidential campaign site reflected this
tension. Site visitors were offered the opportunity to sign up for "instant
updates with the latest news about Dick Gephardt," but that option
required the visitor to indicate assent to the statement, "I realize that this
may mean one or more emails every day."[92] Since the production of each
email update or other form of contact requires time and energy by the candidate or campaign staff, another kind of balance must be found between
this and other campaign activities.

Along with the tension of sustaining involvement throughout an election season without overwhelming supporters or staff, a related challenge

for most candidates who hope to run again is sustaining involvement across elections. Those candidates that have recruited a substantial number of supporters are loathe to lose their attention and support. An increasing number of candidates attempt to maintain supporters' interest in them as political actors, whether or not they have succeeded in becoming elected officials, by maintaining an ongoing Web presence after the electoral period. Such sites are part of the pattern of the "permanent campaign" (Blumenthal 1980), or what we suggest, in chapter 8, could be thought of as the continuous campaign. Though there are many campaign sites that remain on the Web, unchanged, after the election, an increasing number of once-and-future candidates, including both office holders and those who were unsuccessful but anticipate a future campaign, are maintaining an active Web presence in between campaign seasons. The focus on these sites is typically the candidate's issue positions or political activities post-election. In the case of incumbents, this presence is distinct from their official governmental Web site. For example, Congressman Sherwood Boehlert (R-NY-23) maintains an active site between campaigns, informing supporters of activities and soliciting contributions.[93]

Perhaps the ex-candidate who has maintained the most active permanent campaign site to date is John Kerry. Since his defeat in the presidential election of 2004, he has continued to update his campaign site regularly and use it for purposes beyond what a future Senate campaign site might entail, including fundraising for the Democratic party.[94] A continuous campaign site enables a once-and-future candidate to sustain supporters' involvement across elections and, in some cases, across different offices.

The final tension regarding involving is the management of data resources across elections. Although Web applications and databases enable the accumulation and preservation of the data resources generated through the Web practice of involving over time, this practice engenders several critical questions, such as:

(1) Who owns the information resources accumulated by a campaign?

(2) How are these resources maintained and migrated across ever-changing technological platforms?

(3) How are these resources re-purposed and/or distributed in a subsequent political campaign?

(4) Who decides, and how are such decisions communicated to the supporters, if at all?

These questions indicate the importance of anticipatory planning for campaigns engaged in the Web practice of involving, and the significance of comprehensive and explicit privacy policies on campaign sites to earn the trust of site visitors (Howard 2005; Seiger 2003).

In summary, the vast majority of campaign organizations engage in the practice of involving by providing contact information or establishing transactional relationships with site visitors. By 2004, the prevalence of involving rivaled the prevalence of informing. However, more complex forms of involving, in which campaign organizations obtain information or data provided explicitly and consciously by site visitors, remain less common. The lower incidence of these facets of involving can be explained, in part, by their distinctiveness, in particular, the necessity for campaign organizations to establish a transactional relationship with site visitors. This requirement dictates a distinct set of skills and a commitment of resources at a different scale than those necessitated by the practice of informing.

Most generally, adaptation of this practice requires campaign organizations to be able to request, accept, and process data provided by site visitors, requiring that they create and manage a transactional relationship with site visitors. There are two implications of this requirement. First, the technical expertise demanded by the practice of involving is considerably different than that required to simply produce and distribute information on the Web. Second, the practice of involving necessitates an entanglement of the campaign organization with site visitors far beyond the familiar push or broadcast pattern found with the practice of informing.

These factors are exhibited in the tensions associated with the practice of involving, and they explain in part why these practices are not more widespread. While the practice of informing requires campaigns to, at a minimum, adjust traditionally produced print and broadcast materials and content to the Web environment, the practice of involving requires campaign organizations to transform systems and operational procedures to the Web environment. In some respects, this is similar to the tension between "art" and "code" discussed by Kotamraju (2004). The transformation of content requires resources associated with design and mark-up (art), while the transformation of operations requires resources associated with programming and systems (code). The Web-producing community, as described by Howard (2006), required several cycles for this set of skills and talents to emerge.

The decision to simply have a campaign Web site in any given electoral cycle reflects a commitment to the practice of informing. Having made such a decision, campaign organizations could, and in many cases did, make a one-time investment of campaign resources—time, money, and attention—to create the site. It was often the case that a relative or intern or other low-level campaign staff person who happened to be familiar with HTML assumed responsibility for developing and maintaining (or not maintaining) the Web site. The very simplistic sites, which made use of basic HTML, did not require the campaign organizations to commit beyond this simple initial investment. However, among those campaigns that engaged in the practice of involving, the commitment was of a very different level. More complex code requires more resources and attention and more decisions by those at higher levels of the campaign organization, and obligates a campaign to a continuous involvement with their Web site. Rather than a one-time consideration, a campaign organization that practiced involving made a commitment to devote resources to the Web site throughout the campaign period.

This set of decisions associated with the practice of involving contrasts sharply to those entailed in the practice of informing, as demonstrated in the previous chapter. However, the focus of both informing and involving is the dyadic relationship between the campaign and site visitors. In contrast, the practices of connecting and mobilizing to which we now turn our attention entail site visitors' interactions with other political actors.

5 Connecting

A Practice Observed: Connecting

A 2000 House candidate, Bonnie Bucqueroux (Green-MI-8) constructed a Web site featuring a wide array of opportunities for visitors to connect with other political actors. In many respects, the Bucqueroux site foreshadowed the Dean 2004 presidential primary campaign Web presence as a "hub and resource" for supporters (Bucqueroux 2000). Four features in particular stand out: the use of a blog as a surface for communicating with supporters, the provision of a forum to which others could contribute comments, the extensive collection of links to other political actors, and the inclusion of a page connecting other political actors to tools for what she termed "cyber-campaigning."

"Bonnie B's Campaignblog" was one of the first, if not the first, blog posted by a candidate for federal office. The blog was mentioned in her announcement of the launch of the campaign site on August 30, 2000, in which she stated, "'Blogging' is the new online rage that allows Bucqueroux to share insights and ideas immediately."[95] All of the posts on the blog were from the candidate. A total of nine posts were made between September 22, 2000 and October 26, 2000, describing a series of campaign events and the candidate's attempts to be included in televised debates featuring the major party candidates.[96] The blog used software provided by Blogger, then in its second year of operation. The forum called "Sound Off!" on the Bucqueroux site, invited site visitors to "Say hello, wish us well, or tell us what you think about a specific issue." A total of twenty-three comments were published on the site between August 20, 2000 and November 13, 2000. About a third of the comments were comments on the Web site, but many others were substantive discussion of issues or the campaign. Not all were complimentary. One commenter, for example, engaged the campaign on the issue of the value of the Green party itself:

Thursday, October 26 at 04:04 AM:

Jim Smith from Lansing wrote:

I think that you are a waste of time. You and the rest of your Green party people are going to be sorry for the next four years if you cost good people like Al Gore and Debbie Stabenow the important elections because you are simply trendy liberals. Maybe Al Gore isn't perfect, nor is Debbie, but they sure as hell are a lot better than Bush and Abraham. At least they'll take the time to listen to common sensible people.[97]

Critical comments like this evidence that the forum, though sponsored by the campaign, was an open discussion space.

The Bucqueroux site provided a list of "links that matter," directing site visitors to a topically sorted list of more than one hundred external Web sites.[98] The campaign grouped links under eight subheadings: The Greens, Other Michigan Friends, Other Friends, Political Web Sites, International, Worth A Look, Alternative Press, and Progressive Organizations. Site visitors were invited to send the campaign email with additional links to be added. Interestingly, Bucqueroux did not provide links to her opponents' Web sites. She reflected in an interview that she had considered it, but "just didn't think that in some ways their sites were worth it. I know that I certainly would not be in danger of getting a reciprocal [link]" (Bucqueroux 2000).

Bucqueroux's list of outlinks was one of the most extensive collections of links on any 2000 campaign Web site. Visitors could, if they chose, use her site as a kind of political portal. The scope of the links on Bucqueroux's site prefigured the Dean campaign's use of links in the 2004 presidential primary. Both campaigns offered site visitors connections, via hyperlinks, to many types of political actors—and a large number of actors of each type. A campaign's willingness to provide links suggests a conception of a campaign site as a portal or resource, a view shared by relatively few campaigns in 2000.

In addition to connecting site visitors to other political actors, the Bucqueroux campaign also structured its site as a resource for other campaigns seeking to employ the Internet for political purposes. To this end, the Web site included a page titled "Why we are running a cyber-campaign" that included links to several tools being used on the site.[99] These tools supported search, translation, blogging, and polling. The discussion of Web campaigning focused on the campaign's use of the Web to "level the playing field" with major party candidates who had vastly greater resources. Again, similar to the Dean campaign, the Bucqueroux campaign was self-reflective about its use of the Web, and saw itself as participating in a new mode of campaigning, which they hoped would transform politics and engage citizens.

The Practice of Connecting

The third of four Web campaigning practices we analyze is connecting. Campaign organizations engage in connecting when they provide bridges on or to the Web between two (or more) political actors. Whereas the aim of involving is cultivating site visitors' relationships with the campaign, the aim of connecting is to facilitate site visitors' interaction with other political actors. In this chapter, we explicate two types of bridges—cognitive and transversal—and examine the tendency of campaign organizations to engage in the practice of connecting through the techniques of association, coproduction, convergence, and linking. We conclude our discussion of connecting as a Web practice by exploring reasons campaigns seek to connect to other political actors, as well as reasons why they might avoid connecting.

Campaign organizations provide bridges between two (or more) political actors in a variety of contexts. Campaigns frequently engage in connecting practices in the offline realm. Distributing a printed brochure listing endorsements is a means of providing a connection between the endorsing actor and the recipient of the brochure. Similarly, reproducing and distributing news articles about the campaign provides a bridge between the recipients of the materials and the press organization. On the Web, similar bridges are created through a campaign's provision of information that references another political actor via text or images, sometimes employing a form of intertextuality by referencing or incorporating text authored by another into the campaign's text (Mitra 1999). We describe these types of connections as cognitive bridges because they invoke cognitive processes to make the connections between the actors.

A second type of connecting occurs when campaigns create transversal bridges that incorporate and go beyond cognitive bridges by facilitating movement and a shift of attention from the connecting actor to the "connected to" actor. In the offline realm, a campaign might create a transversal bridge by participating in an event sponsored by a supporting organization. For example, when a candidate attends a rally at a union hall, the campaign has provided the structure (attending the event) enabling a connection to be made between attendees and the union. Similarly, locating a campaign office adjacent to the offices of a political party provides a transversal bridge for the visitors between the campaign and the party. On the Web, transversal bridges are created through hyperlinks, which enable users to direct their browsers to move from one place (Web site) to another in cyberspace (Saco 2002). To illustrate the distinction between cognitive and transversal bridges, consider a campaign distributing a statement containing endorsements of its candidate by other political actors. Whether in a paper brochure or on the Web, it enables a cognitive connection between the campaign and the endorsers. When a hyperlink to an endorser's site is embedded in a statement of endorsement on a campaign site, a transversal bridge is created which—if clicked—in effect, transports a user to the endorser's site.

On the Web, campaigns have developed the practice of connecting site visitors to others through cognitive and transversal bridges by employing each of the three techniques introduced in chapter 2, as well as one additional technique. Copying, abstracting, and headlining content produced by another actor (such as news articles about the campaign) on a campaign site are some variants of coproduction for the purpose of connecting. Transversal bridges are uniquely enabled by the Web through hyperlinks, and the technique of linking is used in the Web practice of connecting in several ways. Convergence is important in connecting because it enables campaigns to establish either cognitive or transversal bridges with political actors whose primary identity or historical significance is associated with their offline presence.

The fourth technique employed in the practice of connecting is association—through statements of a candidate's affiliations with other actors such as civic or religious organizations, or through comparisons by which candidates differentiate themselves from opponents. In the remainder of the chapter we describe the range of ways each technique is used within the Web practice of connecting, provide several indicators of the level to which campaigns engage in connecting within the electoral Web sphere, and discuss the reasons for and against greater use of linking in the Web practice of connecting from the perspective of site producers.

Techniques for Connecting

Association

We begin our exploration of the practice of connecting by examining the technique of association. Strategic association is integral to connecting, whether offline or on the Web, and it is often incorporated within or along-side the other Web production techniques of coproduction, convergence, and linking. Association with, or dissociation from, other political actors is part of the process of image creation and management for a campaign (McLeod, Kosicki, and McLeod 1994; Selnow 1998). We describe several examples of campaigns using the technique of association to connect Web site visitors to other political actors, and then we assess the frequency with which campaigns engage in this practice.

A campaign may associate itself with other political actors by directly referencing others in the content of particular texts or images on its Web site. For instance, association may be manifested through explicit state-ments of affiliation with a political party or civic organization. Posting endorsements on a campaign site, whether from individual citizens, advo-cacy groups, or other officials, is another variant of the association tech-nique. One congressional campaign site producer in 2000 explained the value of endorsements in the following way:

There are some key issues that people pay attention to, so, for example, if the Sierra Club endorses somebody, and they have a link to their endorsed candidates, that's really important. If you're a dues-paying member of an organization … Unions have done it for years, not through the Internet. I'm a dues-paying member of what-ever union and I get something in the mail that says, "Here are the candidates we've screened and endorsed." It means something.

Public statements in support of a candidate, posted on a campaign site, cre-ate cognitive bridges that frame how a site visitor views both the candidate and the endorser.

One of the campaign sites that had endorsements in 2002 belonged to a Green Party candidate, Ray Tricomo (Gr-MN-Sen). His campaign used the affordances of the Web to post not only the names of individual sup-porters, but also links to statements of support that some individuals had written about him.[100] At the top of the endorsement page on Tricomo's site was an invitation to contribute an endorsement by emailing Eric, the campaign's manager for "media relations and literature distribution" and Webmaster, as follows: "If you would like your name added to this list please email Eric. Individuals interested in submitting a written endorse-ment for Ray Tricomo should also email Eric." The word "email" was en-coded as a mailto in the HTML both times it appeared, to make it easy for a site visitor to contribute an endorsement. By inviting site visitors to submit endorsements, the campaign enabled site visitors to coproduce its endorsement feature with the campaign, as we will discuss in greater detail later.

When a campaign references texts produced by another political actor on its own site, such as an advocacy group's mission statement or an opponent's speech, it may be honing its own image by either aligning or differentiating itself from that actor. A campaign site reference to the candidate's opponent, such as through comparison of issue positions, is often to differentiate—for example, to say, "I have a better economic plan than my opponent." References may, however, sometimes be an attempt to align, for example, "I am as committed to the environment as my opponent." Both rhetorical strategies employ the technique of creating an association between the candidate and another political actor for the Web site visitor, whether that association is positive or negative in nature. The 2004 campaign site for Elizabeth Rogers (D-AZ-5) drew explicit comparisons between the issue positions of Rogers and her Republican opponent, incumbent J. D. Hayworth. A section on Rogers' site called "Hayworth in his Own Words" featured detailed comparisons of the two candidates' positions on five issues. In one comparison, the Rogers campaign posted a scanned image of a letter received from Hayworth on congressional stationery by a Rogers' campaign volunteer in June 2004, in response to a letter protesting the leak of the name of CIA operative Valerie Plume.[101] Rogers' campaign annotated five elements of Hayworth's digitized letter and wrote a commentary critiquing each element. The commentary included outlinks to nine government documents and news articles from an array of sources.

Campaign-produced parody of the opponent is another form (though an indirect one) of comparative association for the purpose of differentiation. A few campaigns in the U.S. elections in 2000 and 2002 created parodic Web sites about their opponents. For example, Spencer Abraham's (R-MI-Sen) 2000 campaign produced the "Liberal Debbie" site parodying his opponent, Debbie Stabenow.[102] In 2002 Ohio gubernatorial candidate Jim Hagan's campaign's Web presence included both a non-humorous site criticizing his opponent Bob Taft, firetaft.com, and a parodic site, taftquack.com, in addition to the main Hagan campaign site.[103] The Hagan campaign announced the launch of taftquack.com in late August and linked to the parody site from the front page of its main site.[104] About a month after the parody site was created, the Hagan campaign attempted to draw more traffic to it through the mobilization practice of encouraging site visitors to "please send this link to 10 people, and remember to keep checking back for the latest commercials and updates."[105] The parody site was updated several times during the campaign season, and contained press releases from the Hagan campaign and links to the volunteer sign up and donation features of Hagan's main site.[106] It also hosted an archive of parodic animated "Internet ads" and billboards that employed the Taft-Quack theme, which allowed Web visitors to view and re-view them any time (an example of offline convergence, as we explain later).[107]

The Bush-Cheney campaign in 2004 produced several digital parodies of presidential challenger John Kerry. The parodies were a series of animations archived in a section of the main Bush-Cheney site labeled the "Kerry Media Center," linked to from the home page.[108] Each animation parodied Kerry in a different way. For example, one depicted him as a "flip-flopper" boxing against himself. Another mocked his wealth via an interactive "Journeys With John" game, in which a Web user could "travel" with Kerry, selecting which of his multi-million dollar homes to visit, whether to take a private jet or a yacht, etc.

Association is a fairly common technique among campaigns that engage in the practice of connecting. In our observations of campaign Web sites produced by candidates running for U.S. Congress or state governor in 2002, we found that 43 percent provided at least a cognitive bridge to a political party. One out of four campaigns posted endorsements by other political actors on its site, and one out of five referenced civic or advocacy groups explicitly or aligned its position on at least one issue with another political actor. Eleven percent of candidates compared their issue stances with those held by a political actor other than their opponents, and 6 percent engaged in direct comparison on the Web with their opponents' issue positions. Having sketched the use of association in connecting, we now examine the technique of convergence.

Convergence

Convergence is the blending of the online and offline realms. One aspect is the reciprocal integration of the Web and other media environments—that is, the integration of other media into the Web environment and the integration of the Web into other media environments. As a site producer surveyed in 2002 explained, "Web sites are a great way for voters to get an inside look at candidates in a new medium. It also forces the candidates to combine the print and TV medium into one: the Web." By 2004, it had become commonplace to see campaign billboards, flyers, and television commercials with URLs promoting Web sites. However, as we explained in chapter 2, our conceptualization of connecting through the technique of convergence extends beyond media integration. Through the technique of convergence, a campaign creates a structure that enables or encourages a user to engage with another actor in the offline world. When campaigns engage in connecting through the technique of convergence, they are attempting to shift a site visitor's orientation or attention to another actor offline, or to encourage some kind of action on the part of a site visitor with or in relation to some other actor in the offline world. Convergence may be employed in ways that primarily or solely advance the practice of connecting. When campaign sites display photos of the candidate interacting with supporters offline, it is the equivalent, perhaps, to kissing virtual babies online. However, the use of the convergence technique in the practice of connecting sometimes manifests also in the practice of mobilizing, as we discuss in chapter 6. In other words, sometimes the object of a connecting activity in which convergence is employed is mobilization: enabling supporters to become advocates for the candidate.

Convergence may be employed directly or indirectly by a campaign. For instance, direct convergence between online and offline actors or realms is apparent when a campaign site posts the street address of another actor, such as a government office. In contrast, we would consider the following online structure to be an example of indirect convergence: a campaign encouraging a site visitor to take online action (for instance, make a donation) on behalf of or in relation to an online actor (for example, a 527 group) in order for that online actor to take action offline (such as run a pro-candidate ad on cable TV). In this section we focus on the range of ways that convergence is employed by campaigns directly in the practice of connecting, making note of instances in which the convergence technique is serving both connecting and mobilizing purposes. We focus on the practice of mobilizing in chapter 6.

Campaigns are experimenting with various strategies for convergence. We found several variants of this technique employed in the campaign practice of connecting across the 2000, 2002, and 2004 elections. One variant of connecting through convergence was the posting of digital photographs from campaign events. Photographs of a candidate with supporters function to shape the image of the candidate through association. However, such photographs also serve a convergence function, acting as proxies that allow site visitors to interpolate themselves in the place of the supporters featured with the candidate. Moreover, photos of supporters enjoying each other's company at campaign events can function to increase the sense of affinity Web site visitors have with other supporters of the campaign, as they can see themselves among people who share some of their characteristics in the images on a campaign site, and thus synthesize the experience of an offline event with an online representation. As a campaign Web producer for a congressional candidate in 2000 explained, "One of the things we do is take digital pictures of some of the campaign activities and tell people, 'Hey, log onto our Web site, and you can see your picture up on the site.' That's been very helpful to people."

A second variant of connecting through convergence is manifested on the calendar feature found on many sites in each election. Although most campaign site calendars focused on campaign events, and thus were associated with the practice of involving, some campaign site calendars displayed events sponsored by political actors other than the campaign, such as news producers or advocacy groups. This allowed connections between site visitors and the sponsoring groups, connections that were expected to take place offline. The "Schedule Highlights" section of the campaign site produced by Pat Buchanan, the Reform party candidate for president in 2000, exemplified this calendaring strategy.[109] The events listed on the site in late October included scheduled appearances over the coming week by Buchanan or his running mate, Ezola Foster, on talk radio, on cable and network television programs, at town hall meetings, on university campuses, and at a dinner with a pro-life organization. Details for finding the sponsoring organizations were provided for most of the events listed.

Comparison of the calendars provided online by the Bush presidential campaign at different points in the 2000 and 2004 elections provides an interesting window into the development of calendaring as a convergence technique associated with the practice of connecting across election cycles. On December 16, 1999, the only calendar element on the Bush site was a small section on the front page labeled "Schedule," under which was listed a single event, "CNN Larry King Live—Thursday 12/16 (check local listings for viewing information)." In this way, the campaign facilitated an offline connection to a press organization. One month later, on January 14, 2000, just two weeks before the first primary election in New Hampshire, the schedule feature was no longer on the front page (and the date at the top of the page was January 6, 2000, indicating that the front page of the site had not been updated for eight days). On February 15, 2000, the front page displayed the current date and included an announcement at the top of the page of three future events: a debate to be carried live by CNN the evening of February 15, a 90-minute "One-on-One with Governor Bush" to be broadcast on South Carolina television stations (and on the Web) on February 17, and the South Carolina primary on February 19. These events served to connect site visitors to both press organizations and those actors responsible for conducting the primary election. No other schedule or calendar feature was present on the site. The front page on March 2, 2000, announced another debate to be broadcast that night and included a "Primary/Caucus Calendar" feature that listed the dates of upcoming primary elections. And on March 9, 2000, two days after Bush's "Super Tuesday" sweep of eight states, a "special edition" of the campaign site mentioned only one prospective event: "There are 316 days, 14 hours, 45 minutes and 27 seconds until the end of the Clinton/Gore era!"

During the general election season in the autumn of 2000, the Bush campaign continued to make only minimal use of a Web calendar. By mid-August, a "Calendar" page had been added to the site, linked from the front page, but throughout August and September, the only event listed on the calendar was the election on November 7.[110] From mid-August through the election itself, media events featuring Bush were announced on the front page of the site. But only in October did the campaign begin to actively maintain its calendar, and even then, the only events posted on October 4 were upcoming nationally televised presidential and vice-presidential debates.[111] By the end of October, there was a noticeable shift in the campaign's Web calendar strategy toward enabling site visitors to connect with the campaign by learning about upcoming events in which they could participate in ways other than viewing.[112] A headline text on the calendar page on October 21 explained, "Welcome to georgewbush .com's calendar of events! Below you will find information on national events. If you wish to look at your local calendar, visit your state site! State sites can be accessed via the state drop down menu in the left hand toolbar of this page." The "national events" listed included a "'W Stands for

Women' Bus Tour" in which John McCain's wife Cindy joined Laura Bush and Barbara Bush in a campaign tour of Wisconsin, and a "Barnstorm for Reform" in which an unspecified set of governors campaigned in several states on behalf of Bush. However, no detailed information was provided about when and where supporters could participate in these events. And by October 31, a week before the election, Bush's Web calendar was blank again except for the announcement of the election date.

In contrast, during Bush's second run for the presidency in 2004, his campaign made substantial use of its Web calendar, though mostly when engaged in the practice of involving rather than the practice of connecting. In mid-December 2003, the front page had a section titled "Events Calendar" with the subtitle, "Show your support at events in your area," indicating the campaign's hope that the calendar would be used by supporters to learn about events in which they could participate.[113] In mid-January 2004, as the Democratic primaries were heating up, a "live chat" event with Bush and Cheney was listed as part of "Bush's positive agenda" on the site's Web calendar.[114]

By mid-February, the Bush campaign was making more strategic use of its Web calendar.[115] Ten events scheduled in five states—where the presidential race was expected to be closely contested in the general election—were listed for the upcoming week, including four "organizational meetings," regional "trainings," and other gatherings of supporters, with no mention of whether Bush or Cheney would attend. Details and contact information were provided for each event.[116] In addition, the calendar page included a sophisticated search menu that allowed a site visitor to search for events by state and date range. These calendar features reflect the practice of involving as well as connecting.

Most significantly, the campaign had enabled coproduction of the calendar by adding a feature inviting supporters to complete a Web form to add their events to the calendar database.[117] The Web calendar was maintained actively (in collaboration with supporters) throughout the rest of the 2004 election season. The development of the Bush campaign's Web calendar between the 2000 and 2004 elections evidences the growing awareness of the potential of Web calendaring for cultivating supporters and connecting them with other political actors. In particular, the ability of supporters to add events to the database, while serving as an online structure supporting mobilizing for the host of the event, enabled the campaign organization to facilitate the ability of site visitors to establish connections with political actors not formally affiliated with the campaign organization.

A third variant of the convergence technique is the provision on a campaign site of offline contact information for other political actors. In 2000 and 2004, most presidential campaign sites and many of the House, Senate, and gubernatorial candidates in each election employed this variant of convergence, connecting site visitors to other actors, such as political parties, voter registration organizations, or broadcast or print news producers, by providing street addresses and phone numbers. In some cases, the use of this variant of convergence corresponded with the technique of association, that is, offline contact information for another actor, such as a political party, was provided to establish the candidate's alignment with or divergence from that actor. However, this type of convergence was also employed for other reasons, such as enabling site visitors to register to vote or to express their support of the candidate in online or offline forums.

Finally, in chapter 4 we introduced campaigns' use of meetups to cultivate supporters as part of the practice of involving. However, meetups are also tools for connecting in that meetups enable supporters to meet one another in person. From a campaign's perspective, facilitating a sense of community and solidarity between supporters while cultivating supporters' sense of affiliation with the campaign is strategic. The fact that in 2004 some politically engaged citizens used meetups as a dating arena (Beaucar Vlahos 2003) was not counter-productive to campaigns' aims.

Coproduction

The third technique associated with the practice of connecting is the coproduction of content. Coproduction, as explained in chapter 2, is most simply defined as the joint production of Web objects, and thus of Web spheres. In this section, we discuss two ways in which campaign Web sites engage in coproduction for connecting, through the provision of forums to which site visitors can contribute and through appropriating materials produced by others.

Forums to which site visitors can contribute content—including message boards, chatrooms, and blogs—enable contributors to connect with each other through the technique of coproduction. The reluctance of candidates to create opportunities for interactive discussion on their Web sites, documented by Stromer-Galley (2000) in the 1998 election, appeared to have abated somewhat by 2004. As we discussed in chapter 4, the campaign blog emerged as a central element in campaign Web sites during the 2004 presidential primary election. The success of the blog, in terms of providing opportunities for many individuals to connect online with other supporters, appears to have stimulated other campaign organizations to follow suit and provide similar opportunities for supporters to connect with each other. These efforts in 2004 were preceded by some early, somewhat faltering attempts to provide similar opportunities for connecting. For instance, the 2000 campaign site of congressional hopeful Pam Ellison (Ind-MN-4) featured a message board where site visitors exchanged comments with each other and on which the candidate participated actively.[118] Richard Clear, a congressional candidate in Washington's 2000 primary election (R-WA-5), coproduced a discussion space linked from his campaign site through an outside vendor, which noticeably did not display either the campaign colors or logo. Furthermore, would-be participants were required to register with the partnering site to post messages to the discussion board, which may have discouraged use.[119] Overall, however, opportunities for connection through discussion forums on campaign sites were extremely limited prior to 2004, and they remained relatively infrequent through the 2004 election, growing from one percent in 2000 to 14 percent in 2004.

A second approach to coproduction for the purpose of connecting builds on campaigns' well-established tradition of appropriating materials produced by other actors. As we explained in chapter 3, campaigns engage in unilateral coproduction by re-presenting news articles on their sites. Some campaign sites also appropriate materials originally produced by political parties, nongovernmental organizations, and government agencies. Campaigns' reuse of other actors' materials has the effect of providing a connecting bridge between the site visitor and the coproducing actor, framing the site visitor's perceptions of both the candidate and the coproducing actor.

There are several strategies campaigns take when coproducing materials, some of which are more collaborative than others. In our view, providing opportunity for the original producer to maintain control over its own content is more collaborative; the absence of such opportunity is less collaborative and can reflect unilateral coproduction. The four variants we have identified, ranging from least to most collaborative, are full-text copying, abstracting, headlining, and syndicating.

The first variant of appropriation, which we introduced in chapter 3, occurs when a Web producer reproduces in full text on its Web site material previously distributed by an external organization, and does so without providing a Web link to the external organization. For example, the 2002 Web site for Tim Hutchinson (R-AR-Sen) included a link to "Endorsements" on its front page.[120] That link resolved to another page listing endorsements by a number of advocacy groups and press organizations, each with "click here for details" beneath the name of the organization. These links all resolved to pages purporting to be accurate and full representations of press releases or editorials from the endorsing organization, with the appropriated content below the standard header found on other pages within the Hutchinson campaign site.[121]

Some campaigns have discovered the copyright implications of full-text appropriation the hard way, particularly in regard to news articles. One congressional campaign manager in 2000 explained:

> We've made some mistakes. For instance, there have been some newspaper stories that came out, and of course, some of us who are personally online and communicate with our relatives and friends, we've learned how to cut and paste and send stories. So we cut and pasted a story from the [local newspaper] giving them full credit and everything. We thought, well, this is cool. I asked [the campaign Webmaster] to do that, and a few days later, we got a very irate email from the publisher's office of the [newspaper] saying that we're in violation of copyright laws. In hindsight, it makes perfect sense. It was dumb to do that, because the [newspaper] wants people to go to their Web site, so if they can read the story on our Web site, they're not going to link to the [newspaper's site] and the [newspaper] will let you put anything on there you want, as long as it's done as a link to their Web site.

This campaign manager regretted having directed his Webmaster to post the copied text of a news article on the campaign site, and wondered aloud later in the interview if that kind of misstep could cost a candidate the election.

A related variant of appropriating is abstracting, enacted when a Web site producer posts on its Web site brief descriptions or short excerpts—essentially, abstracts—of materials produced by other organizations, and provides a Web link to a page produced by the other organization. The Web site produced by the 2002 campaign of Dave Chandler (Gr-CO-7) provided excerpts from selected news stories and editorials, with links to pages on the sites maintained by the original producers that presumably contained the full text of the original materials.[122] While the original producer cannot control the abstracted portion of the content, it remains in control of the full or expanded view.

The third variant of coproduction is headlining, which occurs when a campaign organization creates a headline or title of materials produced by other organizations, and provides a Web link to a page on the original producer's site. For example, headlines, source citations, and links to news stories produced by press organizations were provided by the Web site produced in 2002 for candidate Anna Eshoo (D-CA-14).[123] In this example, the campaign organization was faithful to the original producer in its choice of headlines, and the original producer controlled all but the wording and placement of the headline or title. Any visitor interested in viewing the body of the content was provided with a link to a Web site controlled by the original producer of the information. The campaign manager and Webmaster of a Republican congressional campaign in 2000, interviewed together, described the affordances of headlining for their campaign:

Manager: I think when you look at the Web site and you go through it, you understand not only where [the candidate] stands on the issues, but also who's come out to back him. Also, they come out of it seeing what the campaign is up to. We regularly put up our press releases and links to different articles that are in the paper, and they get to see all of that. I think the big thing is they come away knowing who he is, and with a good understanding of his candidacy. That's the big thing. In this area, [the candidate's] stand on the issues is pretty much where everybody else is. That's the biggest thing they'll come away with from looking at it. It's not just another Republican who's running for office; they'll see the differences, where he differs from some other people in the party. They'll realize that he is more of an independent-minded person.

Interviewer: Do you have any particular kinds of articles that you want to make sure that people are seeing, or are you, literally, linking to everything you can find?

Manager: Most of the articles you'll find on the race, I think you'll find out [on the site]. If our opponent has a big fundraiser, we're not going to link to that, but the main thing you'll find is good articles talking about us, updates on what's going on with the campaign, and general articles about the race itself.

Webmaster: We want to make sure that people don't think that this race has been decided or anything like that. We want people to know that there's a lot of energy involved in the race, there's a lot of attention on the race. We want people to know that they can get involved. This isn't something out in the middle of nowhere; this is right in their laps.

These campaign staffers' comments underscore the functions that headlining can perform for campaigns. Headlining provides site visitors with information about the candidate from a presumably objective journalistic perspective. When headlining is done frequently on a campaign site, it connotes energy and dynamism on the site and in the campaign itself. Headlining also enables the campaign to implicitly ascribe significance to the race by highlighting the attention journalists are paying to the race.

In our analysis of 2002 campaign Web sites, we found that more than 40 percent of campaigns appropriated materials originally produced by press organizations. Of those, more than half re-presented the content by copying and pasting full texts without providing links. About a quarter abstracted the material, and less than a fifth provided headlines with links to the original material.

Finally, connecting through the technique of coproduction is enacted when campaign organizations distribute through syndication content that has been produced by other actors. In syndication, a campaign displays content created by some other actor on its site, and, depending on the specific arrangement made with the producing entity, controls the framing, frequency of updating, and other aspects of the content. The content itself remains under the control of the syndicator. The emergence and easy availability of software and systems supporting RSS (Really Simple Syndication) feeds in the self-publishing, blog environment creates the opportunity for candidates to employ syndication within their practice of connecting. For instance, the RSS feed created by the Bush-Cheney campaign in 2004 was subscribed to by some Republican candidates running for other offices, such as Tom Buford (R-KY-6).[124] A creative instance of syndication was the use of music by Robert Hoyt on the campaign site of Nanette Garrett, a Green party gubernatorial candidate in Georgia in 2002.[125] Garrett syndicated the audio files for five of the songs from Hoyt's CD "As American As You," and provided a link to Hoyt's site through which the CD could be purchased. Other instances in which campaign organizations seek to affiliate themselves with another political actor by syndicating content produced by that actor include the use of a syndicated feed from a nongovernmental organization or political party. A campaign organization's choice to draw attention to the syndicating producer signals the practice of connecting.

It should be noted that within the context of Web campaigning, not all syndication features instantiate the practice of connecting. In essence, the technique whereby a producer syndicates content produced by a third party and presents it to site visitors potentiates a relationship between site visitors and the third party. However, unless the producer of the syndicated content is clearly identified, there is no bridge between the site visitor and the syndication source, and thus this type of syndication does not manifest the practice of connecting in the context of Web campaigning. To illustrate, the 2000 campaign for candidate Jim Rogan (R-CA-27) contracted with content provider moreover.com to provide news headlines for Rogan's campaign site. On Rogan's site, the moreover.com name was not made readily available by the campaign and could only be obtained by evaluating the source code of the page.[126] In view of the lack of textual evidence suggesting that the campaign sought to explicitly affiliate itself with moreover.com, this was an example of the practice of informing, but not connecting.

Connecting by definition involves three actors: a particular site producer, a visitor to that producer's site, and a third actor. Thus, specificity is important in situating a particular campaign as a subject engaged in connecting. The provision of tools by campaign organizations for distributing their own content to other site producers, as many presidential campaigns did in the 2004 primary and general elections, does not invoke the practice of connecting, rather the practice of mobilizing. In such cases the syndicating campaign uses the Web to turn supporters (in this case, the campaign offering the syndicated content) into advocates, by syndicating the campaign's content to be hosted on supporters' own sites and thus be viewed by visitors to those sites. It should be noted that the online structure of a content feed offered by a campaign and disseminated via another actor's site manifests the practice of connecting on the part of the political actor who receives and hosts the campaign's content feed. Some 2004 House and Senate candidates, such as Tom Buford, and to a more limited extent other down-ballot campaigns, did just that. They provided online structures facilitating the Web practice of connecting for site visitors to other political actors by hosting content feeds from one of the presidential campaign sites.

In sum, discussion forums and the appropriation of content produced by other actors are the primary ways that coproduction is employed in the practice of connecting. As we have demonstrated in this section, the creation of transversal links to other actors' sites is central to several forms of coproduction. In the next section we focus on other ways that linking facilitates connecting.

Linking

The fourth technique we examine in the context of connecting is linking. Within the context of Web campaigning, we define the technique of linking as creating a transversal bridge for a user. A transversal bridge, as discussed previously, enables a user to move to a site produced by another actor. Although a transversal bridge is purposive, it is content-neutral—that is, the bridge could be intended by the producer to promote affiliation, differentiation, or even opposition. By creating outlinks from campaign Web sites to Web sites produced by others, campaigns help create an electoral Web sphere within which citizens and others who use the Web can engage in various political actions. Thus, linking can be considered a form of coproduction; what is being coproduced via links is not usually a campaign site but the electoral Web sphere as a whole.

Kamarck (1999) reported that in 1998, 51 percent of campaign Web sites provided outlinks to at least one site produced by a different type of political actor. In 2002 we found that three-quarters (76 percent) of campaign sites linked to other actors. Of these outlinking campaign sites, nearly all (84 percent) linked to sites produced by at least one of the following types of political actors: civic or advocacy groups, government bodies, press organizations, or political parties. An analysis of the number of types of political actors' sites to which candidate Web sites linked indicates that 25 percent of the sites examined provided links to three or four types of actors' sites, and 35 percent provided links to one of the four types of political actors' sites. The mean number of site types linked to by all candidates was 1.67. The extent of outlinking was stable during the course of the 2002 election season; our data indicate that only 10 percent of the candidate sites examined exhibited a change in linking behavior over a three-month analysis period.

We concur with the observation by Rogers and Marres (2000) that "to link is to recognize. . . . Similarly, non-linking is a form of non-recognition, or, more radically, is an act of silencing through non-recognition" (pp. 16–17). We contend that the presence or absence of links to other site types indicates recognition or non-recognition by campaigns of other political actors. While 84 percent of the sites included a link to at least one type of political Web site, the observation of variance in the number of types of political Web sites suggests the presence of different Web strategies. Further evidence of this finding is provided by the presence of variance in the types of political Web sites to which outlinks were provided.

Finally, our findings from 2002 provide a hint of strategic linking with the observation of shifts during the campaign on the part of a few sites in the types of outlinks provided. We calculated a change in outlinking pattern as a shift from presence to absence, or a shift from absence to presence, for each of the four types of outlinked political Web sites examined. Just over 10 percent of candidate Web sites had changes in linking practices during the course of the campaign. Very few sites added or deleted outlinks to either political party or government sites. Just over 4 percent of the candidate Web sites observed changed linking practices to civic/advocacy sites, and just over 8 percent of the sites changed practices related to press sites.

Daniel Mongiardo's (D-KY-Sen) 2004 campaign site was a model of linking for the purpose of connecting site visitors to other actors. Along with links to the Web sites of forty-five local newspapers and television stations, Mongiardo's site provided links to more than fifteen party, government, NGO, and citizen sites.[127] One of the links, to a discussion forum on Kentucky politics, was framed with a specific invitation to "join the blog about politics in Kentucky," furthering coproduction of the Web sphere in the context of connecting.

Whereas Mongiardo's site linked only to actors that were inherently political, some campaigns link to actors that cannot be considered political (such as hobby associations) for the purpose of image shaping. But by doing so, campaigns create a transversal bridge by which political significance may be ascribed to the linked-to actor. Occasionally, candidates create links to the Web sites produced by their opponents; we found that about three percent of campaign Web sites included such links in 2002. For example, the 2002 campaign site for John Graham (D-CA-48) had a section labeled "Compare Candidates," from which the site provided outlinks to the congressional site of Graham's incumbent Republican opponent (an incumbent whose campaign for re-election did not produce a campaign site), and to VoteSmart.org, a non-partisan civic site that facilitates candidate comparison. Graham's Libertarian opponent did not produce a campaign site, and this fact was noted on Graham's site. The links were framed by two invitational statements: "I urge you to take a look at my fellow candidates' websites as well. I hope they also provide a similar path to mine," and "For more information on [my opponent's] voting record, several independent evaluations of his service, and the sources of his campaign financing please visit http://votesmart.org".[128] In addition, Graham provided a summary of the differences between his stance and his Republican opponent's stance on five issues. A different approach was taken by New Jersey Senate candidate Murray Sabrin during the 2000 primary race. The Sabrin site included a graphic link with the text, "Look how scary America can be if Corzine is elected: Visit his site then come back to Murray's." Clicking on the graphic launched the Corzine Web site in a frame, under a link to "RETURN TO MURRAYSABRIN.COM."[129]

The 2004 campaign site for Elizabeth Rogers (D-AZ-5) outlinked not only to the live version of her Republican opponent JD Hayworth's site but also to a publicly-displayed archival impression of the opponent's site, in order to demonstrate that the opponent had purged his site of references to the Iraq war.[130] Throughout 2003 (and into 2004), Hayworth had made numerous statements in support of the Iraq war, some of which were made on his campaign site or reported in news articles linked-to from his campaign site. On Friday, August 20, 2004, the Arizona Republic ran an editorial endorsing Hayworth and asserting that "Hayworth has been a staunch ally of the administration on Iraq and the war on terrorism. The defense of this country is an issue on which Hayworth is passionate." On August 23, Rogers noted on her campaign site that over the weekend of August 21–22 all references to Hayworth's 2003 press releases and magazine articles advocating the Iraq war had been deleted from his campaign site. She substantiated her argument by providing a link to Hayworth's campaign site live on the Web, a screenshot of the Hayworth site taken by the Rogers' campaign on August 23 showing that all 2003 news items had been removed, and along with a link to what was probably the most recent archival impression of the press page on the Hayworth site publicly available at that time, on the Internet Archive's Wayback Machine. The archival impression had been created on December 6, 2003, and as Rogers asserted, it included several press releases and commentaries authored by Hayworth explaining his support for the war.[131]

To the extent that campaigns engage in linking, most do so unilaterally; in other words, most of the sites to which a campaign site links do not link to the campaign site. This technique of creating nonreciprocal links was demonstrated on Tom Flynn's congressional campaign site in 2000 on a page called "Political Searchers," which enabled visitors to search a database of campaign Web sites and a database of contributors to federal campaigns, as well as to follow links to several other political actors (including political professionals and political portals).[132]

There is sometimes a form of reciprocity between campaign sites and sites produced by other actors, such as news organizations, citizens, or portals. When a candidate site links to the endorsement page on a press site, and the press site in turn includes a link to a candidate site in an endorsement of the candidate, we consider these links to be reciprocal links. However, if a campaign links to an article on a press site and the press site links to the candidate site in a portal-style list, it seems more plausible to consider this as what could be termed a "co-link" rather than a reciprocal link.

One manifestation of reciprocal links involving candidate sites is the phenomenon of Web rings. A Web ring is a set of three or more sites that interlink. Within an electoral context, Web rings help a campaign establish themselves in relation to other actors. For example, in 2002, some minor party candidates created Web rings among their sites and the sites produced by their party. One example of this was the Web ring between Green Party candidates in Massachusetts in 2002, which also included links to the national and state-level Green Party sites.

Moving far beyond the Web ring, the Dean presidential primary campaign in 2004 expanded the technique of linking considerably not only by employing a large number of links but also by qualitatively reshaping the linking process. The campaign took a dynamic approach to establishing transversal bridges. The campaign managed its linking actively, and thus the outlinks on the campaign's sites evolved considerably between 2003 and 2004. By the end of January 2004, the front page of the Dean campaign's blog site linked to over 375 different Web sites produced by entities other than the campaign.[133] This was by far the highest number of outlinks on any campaign site we had observed. Transversal bridges were made between the campaign Web headquarters, individual supporters, and independently managed local affiliates, and were sustained throughout the primary election cycle.

Having discussed the importance of the linking technique in the practice of connecting, we need to note that not every link indicates connecting. Clearly, candidates create links for purposes other than associating with or differentiating from other actors. A page within a campaign site is likely to contain links to other pages within the same site or within other sites produced by the campaign, as well as to Web pages that are part of a candidate's Web presence beyond the current campaign (such as an incumbent's office site, personal site, or campaign site from a previous election). Since links may be created for a range of purposes within Web campaigning— and since any link may serve more than one purpose—the number of outlinks on a page or a site alone is not an adequate measure of the linking technique within the practice of connecting. Links need to be interpreted and linked-to sites examined in order to analyze the relevance of particular links to the practice of connecting.

Tensions in Connecting

The practice of connecting, as engaged through the techniques of association, coproduction, convergence, and linking, creates both opportunities and tensions for campaign organizations. In this section, we contrast the opportunities with the tensions. We identify four primary opportunities associated with the Web campaigning practice of connecting: shaping candidate identity, establishing candidate credibility, building community, and extending resources.

Identity shaping is an attempt by the campaign organization to establish who the candidate is and why the candidate is seeking the particular office. Identity shaping, of course, is part of any campaign, and campaigns have a well-established set of techniques to facilitate its accomplishment in the offline realm. Both on and off the Web, candidates seek, as part of their identity-shaping process, to affiliate themselves with some certain political actors and define themselves in opposition to other political actors. Though we find that candidates are likely to provide only cognitive bridges to those actors from whom they seek to differentiate themselves and to generally refrain from providing a transversal bridge, it is also the case that the Web is used increasingly by campaigns to provide contrast and comparison. Transversal bridges in the form of links are more likely to target the sites of actors with whom the candidate is seeking to affiliate. However, we found some exceptions to this trend, evidenced in the three percent of campaign sites that linked to opponents in 2002. One respondent to our 2002 survey of site producers explained: "Not only did we link to the opponents' Web sites, we also included their names in our key words so that our site would pop up when searches were done for our opponents. We felt

that comparing us to our opponents would be beneficial to our campaign."
As comparison of candidates online becomes more common on civic and
advocacy group sites in an electoral Web sphere, it is possible that more
campaign sites will link to their opponents' sites in order to control and
to try to frame the ways that undecided voters are likely to make comparisons. Campaigns may also view connecting as part of a process of establishing credibility for the campaign beyond the shaping of the personal
identity of the candidate. The desire to build credibility may be one reason
why campaigns associated with minor parties have engaged in more extensive linking than do major party campaigns. This tendency may also explain our observation that challengers are more likely to link to civic and
advocacy groups, political parties, and press organizations than are incumbents. Closely associated with the process of establishing credibility is
the attempt to build community through connections. Providing links to
actors that do not specifically support or oppose the campaign (including
government sites, civic groups, or other non-political organizations) has
the potential to be perceived as a public service. This could be viewed as
creating a sense of community and identification and thus building social
capital (Putnam 2000; Barber 1984). This approach was particularly and
dramatically evident in our observations of the New York City primary
election for Mayor in 2001, where the candidates' Web sites were transformed into gateways to public service groups and charities in the immediate aftermath of the terrorist attacks of September 11 (Foot and Schneider
2004).

Finally, we see campaigns' engagement in the practice of connecting via
the Web as a strategy for resource extension. In view of the scarce, dependent, or asymmetrical resources in most races, some campaigns use the apparatus of other political actors to further their objectives. This may be part
of the explanation for the tendency of candidates who are more likely to be
short on resources to connect to other actors than are candidates who are
more likely to have extensive resources. In general, candidates from third
parties, candidates for House seats, challengers, and candidates in less competitive races were more likely to engage in the Web practice of connecting
than candidates from major parties or those running for Senate seats,
incumbents, or candidates in highly competitive races.

Overall, we found that relatively few campaign organizations engage extensively in the practice of connecting. With some significant exceptions,

including the Dean campaign in 2004 and others cited in this chapter, very few campaign organizations that we observed during the three election cycles set themselves up as a "hub or resource" (Bucqueroux 2000) to connect site vistors to the electoral Web sphere. We suggest that the extent of connecting is relatively low for several reasons, including the desire to maintain control of campaign messages and site traffic, concerns about the repurposing of materials by opponents or even supporters, concerns about legal issues, and a general aversion on the part of campaigns to risky behavior.

As we have discussed previously, a primary objective of the traditional campaign organization is to maintain control over its message. However, this objective extends to attempting to control the messages of other actors such as press organizations. Establishing connections to other actors, in both offline and Web campaigning, risks losing control over the message of the campaign. Other political actors may, at any time, become less desirable associations for campaigns and even may require campaigns to formally renounce their association. Campaigns have, for example, returned donated funds to actors with whom it wishes to disassociate. By referencing other actors in the content of particular texts or images on its Web site, the campaign is exposing itself to the risk that the desired association will cease to be a positive one, as events outside the control of the campaign—such as indictments or financial scandals in which the associated actor becomes involved—may cause the association to become negative.

More broadly, connecting through the techniques of coproduction and linking is also a risky proposition for campaigns. Linking to another actor exposes site visitors to the messages produced by that other actor. To the extent that those messages are not positive ones for the campaign, the value of establishing a connection is called into question. Though campaigns may try to frame the interpretation of the messages produced by the linked-to actor (either figuratively through the text used to characterize the transversal link, or literally with HTML code that frames the linked-to message) it is not clear how successful such framing is in the Web environment.

Furthermore, the messages or content to which links are provided may change after the campaign has created the link or after a campaign has co-produced the message. Consider, for example, the experience of the campaign for Maria Cantwell (D-WA-Sen) in 2000. The Cantwell campaign had determined that it would be strategic to display a photograph of its opponent, Slade Gorton (R-WA-Sen) on its Web site with a satirical textual frame. Perhaps for fear of running afoul of ethical considerations associated with copyright and plagiarism, the campaign chose to display the photograph through an image link in which the provider of the photograph remained the Gorton site, rather than copying the image file and serving it from the Cantwell site. The Gorton site promptly changed the underlying image on its own site, while retaining the original file name, thus causing the Cantwell campaign Web site to display an image other than the one it had intended to show its site visitors (Connelly 2000).[134] Both Cantwell and Gorton posted personal responses to the incident on their respective sites. Gorton, trying to downplay the photo's significance, wrote "Maria, it's yours."[135] Cantwell portrayed Gorton as technologically un-savvy, and concluded her response with the following assertion: "Linking to other files on the Internet is a practice as old as the Web, and is endorsed by some of the most knowledgeable people working on the Internet today, including World Wide Web founder, Tim Berners-Lee. In a statement regarding the fundamental nature of the Web, found on the World Wide Web Consortium Web site, Berners-Lee wrote on the subject of linking: 'Its universality is essential: ... a hypertext link can point to anything, be it personal, local or global.'"[136] Cantwell's response, although accurate technically, glossed over the ethical concerns syndication can evoke when another site producer's content is framed critically.

In addition to concerns over losing control of messages by establishing connections to other actors, campaigns may also find the practice of connecting threatening because they risk losing the attention of visitors to their site. Campaigns compete with other actors for attention. Having captured that attention, they may question the desirability of giving it away by linking to a Web site produced by another actor. "We wanted our site to stand on its own, not be a thoroughfare," said one producer. The Webmaster for Jesse Ventura's (Ref-MN-Gov) 1998 campaign—credited by some as the first win an election based on a Web campaigning strategy (Madsen 1998)—noted in his post-campaign reflections that the decision to not provide links to any other Web sites was a strategic one: "Early on, Jesse decided the web site would be operated like a cul-de-sac and not a crossroads. The site would not be a place for people to arrive at and then exit via links we provide. Once people entered our site, we wanted them to

stay and look around. No links to external web sites were provided"
(Madsen 1998). This comment reflects the notion that choosing not to out-
link is a method of shaping, if not controlling, site visitors' behavior.

When asked about linking to an opponent's site, a site producer in 2002
commented: "The last thing you want people to do is leave your site to go
find out what lies your opponent is telling about your candidate. If you
want to do comparisons, either do them on your own site or use a popup
window (use sparingly) to link them to a non-partisan site." Tensions were
also expressed about the prospect of linking from an incumbent's candidate site to his or her office site. When a congressional deputy campaign
manager in 2000 was asked why the campaign site did not link to the incumbent candidate's U.S. House site, he said: "We just wanted to keep it
separate because we didn't want to get into any possible ethical questions.
I'm sure that we could technically link it. I think we could technically link
it from the campaign to the official Web site. We don't want to get into any
ethical question." These statements reflect campaigns' desires both to avoid
ethical ambiguity in Web campaigning and to maintain site "stickiness"
(Lewin 2003). The notion of stickiness in a Web site includes features that
encourage site visitors to return to a site as well as attempts to keep visitors
from leaving a site. It is predicated on the basis that the attention of site
visitors, once captured by a specific site, is too valuable to give away to another site via a link.

Of greater concern is the view that connecting to other political actors,
especially through transversal links, gives rise to the possibility that the material ultimately viewed by site visitors clicking on the link will not be the
same as was intended when the connection was created. Though few
instantiations of the practice of connecting go as far awry as Vice President
Cheney's attempt to connect debate viewers to factcheck.org, as discussed
in the introduction to chapter 1, the uncertainty created by a link seems
sufficient to discourage its implementation in some cases.

Similarly, the practice of connecting through coproduction, and even
through the technique of linking, can place campaign organizations on
somewhat uncertain legal terrain. Some campaigns may be wary of copyright infringement, either on their own part or on the part of those organizations to which they connect. Connecting to organizations whose tax
status prevents political activity could lead to questions and allegations
threatening the independence of those organizations. The possibility of

providing links to organizations that may be registered as lobbyists for foreign governments is another legal barrier.

Overall, then, a significant reason for not connecting, especially through the technique of linking, is that it is perceived by some campaign organizations as risky. Campaigns are inherently risk-averse organizations (Selnow 1998). This risk-aversive behavior is particularly applicable to environments in which the opportunities for rewards are perceived as low. As one Web producer told us during the 2000 campaign, "We're not sure we can win the election based on what we do on the Web, but we know we can lose it if we blow it on the Web." Given the lack of perceived rewards—especially prior to 2004—campaigns were, in general, cautious in their experimentation with connecting. The presidential primary campaign of Howard Dean seemed to have changed this calculus. The online component of the Dean campaign was created as a distributed Web presence. One part of the Dean campaign coproduced presence, the fordean.org network of sites, included a single site that connected more than 500 discussion groups, state and local Dean action coordinators, and Dean supporter Web sites.[137] This extensive use of connecting as a Web practice set a new standard for Web campaigning that was, in part, emulated by other organizations in the 2004 campaign. We should anticipate more emulation in future campaign cycles. The rewards associated with connecting, including establishing credibility, building community and social capital, and, in particular, extending scarce resources, seem to have outweighed the risks of losing the attention of site visitors and sharing control of the campaign message. Most importantly, the practice of connecting, as described in this chapter, often includes involving, mobilizing, or both. The interrelationship between connecting and mobilizing, as well as the techniques through which campaign organizations instantiate mobilizing via connecting, is the focus of the next chapter.

6 Mobilizing

A Practice Observed: Mobilizing

The Web presence of John Kerry's presidential campaign in 2004 manifested an elaborate strategy for equipping supporters to promote the candidate to others. By mid-June 2004, a section labeled "Online Headquarters" had been created, focusing visitors' attention on seven features that the campaign hoped supporters would use in advocating on behalf of Kerry.[138] Through a feature called the "Media Corps," site visitors were invited to become part of a "group of committed supporters who want to bring John Kerry's message home to local media markets." The campaign promised, "if you can contribute five to ten minutes a week—and your creativity and energy—we'll supply you with all the information you need to become one of our Online Advocates." This feature included an extensive set of materials (beginning with an "Assignment for the Week"), links to relevant news articles, tips on contacting local television and radio stations, talking points to use in communicating about the campaign, and style guides for writing letters to editors.[139] One aim of the Media Corps was to build a shared sense of group identity and purpose between members—in other words, to build a community of advocates. This was evidenced in two ways: in the campaign's use of the first person plural tense to describe the corps ("We are a group of committed supporters ..."); and in the sign-up form for the Media Corps, which included the requirement that recruits agree to allow their contact information to be shared with other members of the Media Corps.[140]

Another mobilizing feature in Kerry's Online Headquarters urged supporters to participate in "online networking groups" and explained:

Friendster (http://www.friendster.com), Tribe (http://www.tribe.net), and Ryze (http://www.ryze.com) are great places to reach out and build your network of supporters for

John Kerry. Create your profile, download a picture, post information about your support for Kerry and upcoming events. By providing information, links to the website, issues, and updates more people will learn about John Kerry and get more involved in the campaign.

A related feature encouraged visitors to promote Kerry by posting on blogs and in discussion forums, and provided links to twenty of them:

"Blogs" and Forums allow you to make comments about articles and have discussions with other people across the country. Start by visiting the Kerry Blog and Online Forum; then use the list available by clicking below to join some of the largest and most diverse sites on the Internet. People supporting each campaign are talking about the issues and the candidates so be sure to sign up for the daily updates from the campaign when you pledge to take online action![141]

Kerry supporters were also urged to "Register for and Promote MeetUp On-line." In this feature, the campaign site producers explained,

"MeetUps are a great way to find other people in your area who support John Kerry and are taking action on and offline. Use the tools available on the MeetUp page to make your MeetUp as informative and effective as possible. Promote MeetUp online and help grow the grassroots base of Kerry's team by encouraging people to register."[142]

Links were provided to Kerry's Meetup page, and, ironically, to a PDF "Organizer Toolkit" that appeared to have been originally designed for offline use but was subsequently posted on Kerry's site.[143] By soliciting Meetup initiatives through the action features in the Online Headquarters section, the Kerry campaign was trying to capitalize on the catalyst that Meetup provided the Dean campaign during the year leading up to the presidential primaries. A participant in an August 2003 "Meetup for Dean" event in Albany, New York, was one of many who linked from a blog to the Meetup page on Dean's campaign site. The day after a Meetup gathering he described it as an online structure that not only facilitated involvement but also engendered mobilization. In describing the people he had met through Meetup, he wrote, "This is grass-roots volunteerism, not centrally organized. These are the kinds of people who will go to caucuses, write letters, canvass for voters, take people to the polls. All over the country."[144] The Kerry campaign sought to cultivate the "power of many" that the Dean campaign tapped into through Meetup (Crumlish 2004).

A fourth feature in Kerry's Online Headquarters was an invitation to "Add Your Kerry Site to a 'Web ring.'" The rationale provided was that "unofficial Kerry websites are popping up all over the web and one of the best ways to make sure yours is seen is to link to other sites that support John Kerry. Visit http://dir.webring.com/rw to find out more."[145] By enabling supporters to easily register their sites along with other supporters' sites in a directory run by a non-campaign entity, the campaign increased the visibility of supporters' sites at the same time that it avoided both the labor of creating its own directory and the potential liabilities of outlinking from the campaign site to sites purporting to be produced by supporters.

The Online Headquarters also challenged supporters to take an "online action pledge" in which they could commit to any of nine actions to promote the campaign online, using the structures provided by the campaign: "As an active online supporter for John Kerry, I will join with other Kerry online activists to spread John's message and build support across the internet. I pledge to take the following online actions for John Kerry ..."[146] Action commitments included the following: "Email my friends and family to let them know what is going on at the Campaign," "Post information and comments on the Kerry Blog and Forum two or more times per week," "Post information and comments on outside Blogs and Forums two or more times per week," and "Join a Networking Group and promote John Kerry and Kerry Events." However, the action commitment to "Attend a Kerry2004 MeetUp" also included a link to the terms at meetup.com with the caveat, "Kerry MeetUp is the place for our grassroots supporters to get together and make a difference. By checking this box, you are agreeing to MeetUp's Terms and Conditions."

The Practice of Mobilizing

In the context of Web campaigning, we define the practice of mobilizing as using the Web to persuade and equip campaign supporters to promote the candidate to others, both online and offline. By allowing themselves to be mobilized via the Web to engage in candidate promotion, supporters participate in coproducing the campaign along with the candidate and campaign staff. While campaigns have much to gain from mobilizing supporters via the Web, the Kerry campaign's caveat about Meetup's terms and conditions, described previously, highlights the fear of losing control with which all campaigns wrestle. The caveat points to the fundamental tension in mobilizing: Online structures that facilitate promotion of a candidate can also be employed and appropriated (or misappropriated) in unintended ways.

The term "mobilization" is used frequently in studies of politics and technology to refer to an actor's attempts to get another individual or group to take a particular action (Crumlish 2004; Earl and Schussman 2002; Gibson, Rommele, and Ward 2004; Lusoli, Ward, and Gibson 2002). Schier (2000) defines mobilization as catalyzing any of an array of actions within and across relatively large, heterogeneous groups (such as political parties). He contrasts this notion of mobilization with activation, which he specifies is evoking a particular action by a particular segment or narrowly defined group of people, usually elites. However, neither Schier's concept of mobilization nor his concept of activation address the dynamic in which a political actor catalyzes supporters to attempt to persuade others through personal advocacy. This two-step process is the focus of our concept of mobilization. In this chapter, we examine how campaigns use the Web to enable supporters to become advocates.

For an electoral campaign, the aim of mobilizing is to expand the campaign exponentially by motivating and equipping supporters to promote the candidate within supporters' social networks and spheres of influence, such as neighborhoods, workplaces, organizational settings, and local media markets. The fundamental logic is that if supporters are galvanized to promote the candidate, the promotional messages they author and distribute will reach more potential voters (and especially potential supporters) than will the campaign's messages. In addition, these supporter-authored messages will be perceived as more credible and thus more persuasive than those authored by the campaign. However, when supporters do distribute promotional messages produced by campaigns, an additional layer of credibility is added, thus making the campaign's promotional messages more effective.

This concept of mobilizing as helping supporters become advocates is resonant with Barber's functions of political talk in "strong" democracies, that is, democracies in which citizens actively participate. The hope of campaigns engaging in mobilizing is that supporters who attempt to advocate for the campaign will have a positive influence on the opinions or attitudes of others toward the candidate. The fear is that the influence will be negative. Mobilizing builds conceptually and technically on each of the three Web campaigning practices we have analyzed so far. It centers on the retransmission of information—outside the watchful eye of the campaign organization—about a candidate by involved supporters to others with whom they are connected in some way, whether online or offline.

The essence of mobilizing as a practice of Web campaigning is extending a campaign through supporters who make use of promotional resources provided via the campaign site. The entire practice of mobilizing can be understood as enabling supporters to coproduce the campaign within the electoral Web sphere and offline. Although technically very simple, the campaign site produced in 2004 by a congressional Green party candidate, Van Presley (MN-8), illustrated the foundational logic of mobilizing. One page of the site featured an electronic document designed to resemble a leaflet, with dotted lines signaling where to cut between sections with scissors once the document had been downloaded and printed. The Web page introducing the document began with the text: "What can one person do? A lot! For as Margaret Mead said: 'Never doubt that a small group of thoughtful, committed citizens can change the world, indeed it's the only thing that ever has.' To start with, you can copy & print the leaflet text below, photocopy it, and hand it out to your friends & associates!"[147]

The mobilizing logic also appeared on the page on Presley's site that requested donations to the campaign, in the text: "Take the Power of TWO Pledge! Please get the commitment of TWO others to contribute, and then, ask them to continue the chain! The only language understood by the Powers-That-Be is the Language of Power. That means Grassroots Power: Spread the word by Powers of Two! 'Politics begins in personal relationships.'—William Greider."[148] Although rudimentary, Presley's site illustrates the core principle of mobilizing: persuading and equipping supporters to promote the candidate to others.

The use of Internet technologies in the practice of mobilizing by political actors preceded the advent of the Web. As early as 1988, organizations like Amnesty International used computer conferencing systems to send "action alerts" mobilizing activists to contact public officials concerning specific human rights abuses (International FidoNet Association 1989). Early Web-based mobilizing was visible during Jesse Ventura's campaign for Minnesota governor in 1998, which featured extensive tools allowing supporters to mobilize and involve others (Raney 1998; Madsen 1998). Presidential campaigns in 2000 and 2004 innovated further. Republican presidential primary candidate John McCain expanded the mobilizing practice by stimulating creation of many other sites promoting McCain, and by organizing a Web-directed phone bank. During the general election campaign, both Bush and Gore provided well-developed toolkits facilitating mobilization by supporters. These developments were pulled together and then significantly magnified during the Dean presidential primary campaign for the 2004 Democratic nomination. Among other mobilizing features, the Dean campaign greatly expanded the use of the Web for coordination of offline gatherings of campaign supporters and interested citizens, and the widespread creation of locally produced Web sites to foster participation. Some of these strategies served as models for both the Bush and Kerry presidential campaigns during the 2004 general election, as we will see later.

Campaigns that engage in mobilizing on the Web are angling for the attention of Web users who are supportive of the campaign and willing to help promote it. Campaign mobilizing via the Web can be very strategic in view of the characteristics of campaign site visitors. The Institute for Politics, Democracy, and the Internet (IPDI) found that visitors to campaign Web sites were much more likely to be civically engaged and to be opinion leaders within their social networks than the general population of Internet users or the public at large (Institute for Politics, Democracy, and the Internet 2004). Through national surveys conducted during the 2004 primary season, IPDI identified as "Online Political Citizens" (OPCs) about 7 percent of the U.S. population. OPCs were defined as those Internet users who visited a campaign Web site between October and December 2003 and who participated in at least two of the following online political activities: (1) contributed online to a candidate or political organization, (2) received political email, (3) forwarded or sent political email, (4) visited or posted comments on a political blog, (5) participated in a political chat room, or (6) visited a news Web site for news about politics and campaigns (Institute for Politics, Democracy, and the Internet 2004, p. 15–16). By December 2003, 57 percent of OPCs had signed up for email from campaign or political party sites, and 87 percent reported receiving email from one or more of these entities. Two-thirds of OPCs who received email from campaign or party organizations subsequently forwarded it to someone else. One out of four OPCs reported having viewed or posted comments on political blogs or visited political discussion groups.

IPDI researchers also found that most people who had visited campaign sites fit the profile of those whom survey researchers from RoperASW have termed "Influentials" (Keller and Berry 2003), that is, opinion leaders who are involved in political and civic activities. As IPDI researchers explained, "People who sell political ideas covet the support of 'Influentials' whose endorsement is more valuable than the average voter's. Not only are Influentials more likely to donate money, volunteer time, and write letters to the media, but they will persuade others and bring them along to the polls" (Institute for Politics, Democracy, and the Internet 2004, p. 13). Sixty-nine percent of OPCs qualified as Influentials, in contrast to 13 percent of the Internet-using population and 10 percent of the general population. The IPDI report concludes, "it is clear that candidates ... who wish to reach the people who influence everyone else must look to the Internet. They will find there a high concentration of public opinion leaders and political activists" (Institute for Politics, Democracy, and the Internet 2004, p. 10). Mobilizing supporters through Web campaigning is highly strategic, since OPCs are far more likely than the general population to write or call a local, state, or federal elected official; attend a political rally, speech, or protest; or voice their opinions through a letter to a newspaper editor or a call to a radio or television show.

Any online structure that helps a site visitor promote the candidate to others instantiates the practice of mobilizing. Facilitating the creation and dissemination of letters to newspaper editors is one type of mobilizing feature.[149] A second is the provision of materials on the campaign site intended for offline distribution, such as flyers and posters.[150] As we discussed in chapter 4, features that enable offline distribution can serve to both deepen a supporter's sense of affiliation and involvement with a campaign and engender the promotion of a candidate to others—that is, mobilize. Another mobilizing feature is the provision of "e-paraphernalia" such as graphics, screensavers, or digital wallpaper with the campaign logo, to be used on a campaign supporter's computer or Web site.[151] The 2004 Bush campaign site had an extensive array of e-paraphernalia, including screensavers, digital wallpaper, Web banners, and Web buttons. In the "Wallpaper" section, site visitors could select from among eight issue-themed options, each available in two sizes, under the heading "GeorgeWBush .com computer backgrounds not only show your support for our President Bush but the issue that is most important to you!"[152] E-postcards and related features that enable a site visitor to email a page URL from the campaign site to one or more friends are also mobilizing tools.[153] These features, and others that instantiate mobilizing, are akin to the more advanced features discussed in chapter 4. Mobilizing builds on involving, since advocates must first affiliate with the campaign as supporters.

Techniques for Mobilizing

We turn now to an analysis of how the techniques of convergence, coproduction, and linking are employed in the practice of mobilizing. We then introduce a technique that is particularly salient for mobilizing: empowerment. Empowerment in the context of mobilizing can be understood as the provision of online structures that especially facilitate site visitors to engage in political actions that are, seemingly, beyond the control of the campaign and without the campaign's knowledge. Although a campaign's intent in employing the technique of empowerment may be to increase promotion of the candidate, the online structure created by the campaign through the empowerment technique can be appropriated in a variety of ways by site visitors, including those creating parodies and distributing critiques of the candidate. It is important to note that since the practice of connecting bridges site users with other political actors, all of the features and techniques employed in mobilizing are also associated with connecting, but not all connecting is mobilizing.

A mobilizing feature may evidence one production technique on one campaign site and a different technique on another site, depending on how the feature is configured. For instance, in each election an increasing number of campaign sites has had an e-postcard feature with a text box for site visitors to add their own comments to the page URL that would be emailed to the recipient. As such, this feature reflects the technique of linking in that it enables the dissemination of URLs that are part of the campaign site. However, a campaign that uses the e-postcard feature to harvest the email addresses of recipients, or to post the comments of the sender on the campaign site, employs the e-postcard feature in the technique of coproduction as well as the technique of linking.

Convergence

Since many of the actions that campaigns want supporters to take on behalf of the candidate must take place offline, the practice of mobilizing makes robust use of the technique of convergence. We examine five types of convergence through which mobilizing is enacted. The first type is the provision of materials for offline distribution. As noted earlier, many campaign Web sites produced in 1996 and 1998 were dubbed brochureware because the sites so closely resembled traditional campaign brochures. When campaigns post electronic versions of brochures, flyers, or other documents promoting the candidate on their sites and encourage visitors to download and distribute these documents, they create an online structure for catalyzing the distribution of documents offline. A more technically advanced variant employed by some campaigns is posting audio or video files on the campaign site and urging supporters to purchase time on local radio or television stations to play the advertisements. Ralph Nader's presidential campaign site in 2000 employed both variants of this type of convergence. The site featured a wide range of documents for downloading and distribu- tion, including flyers, yard signs, and bumper stickers, as well as audio and video commercials for which supporters were asked to sponsor radio and television airings.[154] During the 2004 presidential primaries, Carol Moseley-Braun's site had an interesting array of materials formatted for easy printing and offline distribution, including her biography, resume, and issue positions, as well as a window sign and other promotional materials.[155]

In a second variant of convergence for mobilizing, campaigns use their sites to equip supporters to produce their own material for distribution in offline media, sometimes providing supporters with tips and suggested messages for interacting with local newspaper editors and talk radio hosts. Some campaigns provided letter templates and talking points for supporters to personalize. A particularly interesting and early example of this type of convergence came from the Reform party's presidential candidate in 2000, Pat Buchanan. The Buchanan campaign's efforts to have the Reform party candidate take part in the presidential debates in the autumn of 2000 employed convergence extensively. To enable supporters to contact political actors, the campaign site offered talking points and gave contact information for national television networks and the Commission on Presidential Debates. Site visitors were also encouraged to call talk radio programs and write letters to newspaper editors in support of Buchanan's participation in the debates.[156]

This type of convergence was employed increasingly in the 2002 and 2004 elections as well, with greater technical and strategic sophistication on the part of campaigns. The most basic online structures simply encouraged supporters to contact media outlets or provided a list of email addresses for regional newspapers. One such site listed 18 email addresses and urged supporters to either email a local editor individually or address the same message to all the editors: "You can email your thoughts to all of [the editors] at once! Just simply copy the following list of email addresses and then paste the entire list into the 'To:' field of your email browser."[157] Greater technical and strategic sophistication was evident on campaign sites that had location-searchable databases of local newspaper editors and media contacts. For instance, the 2004 campaign site for Jim Nussle (R-IA-1) featured a radio show look-up tool. Site visitors were asked to "enter your zip code below to find out what talk radio shows are in your area and their contact info. Give them a call and tell them who you think should be your next Congressman."[158] Nussle's site also exemplifies the growing number of campaigns in each election that enabled site visitors to send letters to editors by providing draft letter texts, creating a Web form on which a site visitor could compose a letter, selecting a newspaper or editor from a menu of names, and emailing via the campaign site.[159] This latter strategy allowed campaigns to collect the names and email addresses of supporters willing to write on behalf of the campaign and, for that matter, the texts of the letters written by supporters.

In addition to illustrating technically sophisticated implementations of the media interaction type of convergence, the Nussle site also illustrates the ways in which campaign organizations are seeking to obtain, and presumably use, information from their most ardent supporters. The Nussle campaign site producers required visitors to enter not just a city or zip code, but also to provide personal information before gaining access to the database of news editors. Incidentally, no privacy policy on the site explained what the campaign would do with the personal information provided.

Another implementation of this feature was found on Patty Murray's (D-WA-Sen) campaign site in 2004, which included a well-developed feature enabling visitors to send letters of support to local newspaper editors via the site, but did so in the context of a detailed privacy policy.[160] The campaign sought to motivate visitors to write a letter by sponsoring a monthly contest: "Remember, we choose one Letter to the Editor each month to highlight on our website. The winner receives a Patty Murray T-shirt!" Each month's winning letter was posted on the site, thus serving as an endorsement and model for would-be letter writers.[161]

The Bush and Kerry 2004 presidential campaigns went even farther in directing (as well as tracking) site visitors' engagement with offline media. Beginning in June 2004, Kerry's site recruited supporters to join the campaign's Media Corps, creating a distinctive identity and community experience for these supporters-turned-advocates that may have helped to attract other Corps members and sustain their engagement during the election season.[162] They received regular assignments via email with talking points to express in various media. The site allowed Media Corps members to report back to the campaign the completion of each assignment and to recruit other supporters into their own Media Corps teams, thus multiplying their efforts.

A third type of convergence is the use of campaign Web sites to organize phone banks, through which supporters select or are assigned a set of names (with phone numbers) to call in order to promote the candidate and request votes. John McCain's presidential primary campaign in 2000 was the first to initiate a Web-based phone bank. Supporters across the country volunteered to telephone voters in Iowa and New Hampshire in the weeks before the primaries in those states, and then received contact information for the voters they were assigned to call.[163] Max Fose, campaign manager for McCain, explained in an interview:

I thought, let's take traditional, grassroots organizing campaign activities and put them on the Internet—see if we could put them on the Internet to save the campaign money. Going into New Hampshire, we took a list of voters, put them up on the Internet, sent an email to our supporters and said, "We need you to contact ten voters in New Hampshire, make ID calls and ask them if they're going to vote for John McCain. We need you to do this from your home, at your expense, on your time, from all across the country." We had people from California, Arizona, Florida, calling into New Hampshire and IDing voters. We did a very limited test in New Hampshire ... and it worked. It was all automated. Someone could go to our site, request a list, and the list was on their screen. If they didn't have two phone lines, they just disconnected, made the calls, went back and reconnected, and tabulated the calls: this person is voting for John McCain, this person is not, or undecided. If they were voting for McCain, we asked for their email address, so we could do a get-out-the-vote email and a get-out-the-vote phone call. They hit cement and automatically went in and tagged your database. Two days before the election, we just pulled up everyone voting for John McCain and made sure they got a note ... Going into New Hampshire, we had just over 60,000 people signed up [as general volunteers], and we had 1,925 people signed up to do [the phone bank]. When the campaign ended, we had over 9,000 people doing these calls. One thing we did was to get people to make more calls. We said, "If you make one hundred calls, we'll give you a hat." We sent I-don't-know-how-many hats out. It got to the point where we were behind in sending them out: "I made my hundred calls, where's my hat?" (Fose 2000).

The McCain campaign's Web-based phone-bank system was one of several online strategies that mobilized large numbers of supporters to advocate for McCain both locally and across the country.

In the 2004 presidential race, phone banks and letter-writing movements were among the mobilizing activities for which online structures were provided through several of the primary and general election campaign sites. In early January, Dean's site facilitated supporters in writing letters to undecided voters in New Hampshire. During the autumn, Kerry supporters could initiate and register a phone-bank event via the campaign site for a particular time and date and issue email invitations to participate to friends. In addition to registering the event with the campaign and thus using the online structure provided by the campaign to issue email invitations and track responses, the initiator of any campaign event could choose to have the event listed publicly on Kerry's campaign site calendar so that others could participate. Phone-bank initiators were urged to list the event publicly: "More than 2 million people are part of the JohnKerry.com activist base. You can invite these amazing Americans to your phone bank and track RSVPs through JohnKerry.com." Concern for the event hosts' privacy was evidenced in the campaign's provision that all events listed publicly on the site would be displayed by whatever the hosts entered as their general locales (neighborhood or intersection), rather than by the hosts' personal addresses. Would-be attendees who were not invited personally by the hosts could indicate their interest to the hosts via the campaign site.[164]

A fourth variant of convergence was the use of the Web to organize house parties in which supporters would invite friends to gatherings in their homes to promote and discuss the candidate. Guests were invited to share their views on the candidate, sign up to volunteer for the campaign, and make a contribution to the campaign. Nader's 2000 presidential campaign was one of pioneers of this type of convergence, providing detailed instructions in a house party kit that included the specific email address to which lists of invitees, attendees, and contributors were to be sent.[165] Nonpresidential candidates also used the Web to catalyze house parties; examples were Laura Wells, a 2002 candidate for controller in California,[166] and three 2004 Ohio House candidates, Charlie Morrison (R-OH-15), Charles Sanders (D-OH-2), and Greg Harris (D-OH-1).[167] Morrison's instructions to house party hosts are representative of the low-tech approach many candidates used:

As a house party sponsor, your job is to invite a group of interested people to meet the candidate one-on-one and discuss, in your home, the issues relevant to the attendees. These meetings should be set up now and continue until interest drops or until time prevents the campaign from participating. The house party sponsor supplies refreshments for their guests. A typical house party might last 1–2 hours at most. If you volunteer for this, you will work with the candidate and the scheduler beforehand. You will have access to the candidate, Charlie Morrison, and all members of the Charlie Morrison for Congress Committee. As a sponsor, YOU can have the candidate in YOUR house to answer all of your friends' questions. You can be a central figure in the election process! Please Email us if you have any questions about setting up a house party.[168]

In election cycles prior to 2004, the online structures for house parties in previous elections ranged from simply the suggestion that supporters host gatherings in their homes to promote the candidate, to the provision of a downloadable kit of attendee registration forms and campaign materials to distribute, to the more advanced structure of a Web interface for event registration and the mailing of a campaign video to each supporter who registered as a party host. In comparison with previous election cycles, the 2004 Kerry and Bush campaigns' online structures for this type of convergence were much more robust. They employed Web forms for organizing house parties that were backed by Web-accessible database systems for registering events, attendees, volunteer commitments, and contributions in association with the host's volunteer activity records. These systems also allowed site visitors to RSVP for a house party or other campaign event online, thereby providing their contact information to the campaign.

House parties and other supporter-led events, while potentially powerful catalysts for the campaign, can create legal liabilities for any campaign. Again, the Kerry site posted a disclaimer reflecting these concerns. A notice on the event-planning page of the site cautioned:

Federal law prohibits contributions to John Kerry's general election account. Any fundraising at a John Kerry House Party shall be conducted solely on behalf of John Kerry Victory 2004, the DNC or John Kerry GELAC, and must comply with the prohibitions, limitations, and reporting requirements of federal campaign finance law. John Kerry is not responsible for the content of communications written by House Party hosts or guests.[169]

This notice is another indicator of the control-related tensions inherent in Web campaigning.

The fifth type of convergence in the practice of mobilizing entailed the use of the Web to coordinate the movement of bodies at strategic times (such as the final days before the election) into strategic places (such as swing neighborhoods and states) to promote the candidate and get out the vote. Nearly all of the 2004 presidential primary contenders employed this type of convergence on their sites prior to the Iowa and New Hampshire primaries. Edwards's site had a page, "On The Road For Edwards," that urged supporters to travel to New Hampshire or South Carolina. To reduce barriers for those who would be willing to fly to New Hampshire, the Edwards' site offered housing and transportation: "Sign up for John in January! Come to New Hampshire in January to help Get Out The Vote for John Edwards. Please join Team New Hampshire for the week or weekend before the primary to help with our Get Out The Vote (GOTV) efforts to ensure Senator Edwards is successful on election night, January 27th. We will provide housing and in-state transportation for all of our Edwards supporters. You will be part of history and the first step on Senator Edwards' road to the White House."[170] Howard Dean's site also featured a "NH Rideboard" on which site visitors could request rides or offer rides to others who wanted to drive to New Hampshire in the weeks before the primary.[171] Similarly, in the final days of the 2004 general election, the Bush campaign site provided an online structure to facilitate supporters in organizing friends to participate in neighborhood walks to help get out the vote.[172] Rather than just urging supporters to remind people to vote, the Bush campaign modeled mobilizing by encouraging supporters to invite friends to go door-to-door asking people to vote.

The use of the Web to organize the on-the-ground movements of supporters was also evident on many congressional sites, particularly in the days before the general election. However, some began much earlier, such as House candidate Greg Harris (D-OH-1). By June 2004, his campaign site provided an online coordination structure for supporters willing to participate in mobilizing on the ground by canvassing neighborhoods, attending community festivals, and marching in local parades on behalf of the campaign. With the statement, "We respect everyone's time and special skills and hope to provide opportunities that are both fun and fulfilling for everyone," Harris' campaign site sought to engage supporters in forms of mobilization that would be both influential and enjoyable.[173]

Coproduction

As we explained previously, all of a campaign's mobilizing activity can be viewed as facilitating the coproduction of the campaign. As supporters advocate for the candidate, they not only extend, but also shape the campaign. More specifically, however, the Web production technique of coproduction was distinctly employed in mobilizing via the Web in at least four ways. RSS feeds and other forms of syndication (discussed in chapter 5 in association with the use of coproduction for connecting) also provide online structure for mobilizing. RSS feeds enable supporters to retransmit campaign messages to Web users who visit supporters' sites rather than candidates' sites. Thus RSS feeds provide tools to individuals seeking to promote the candidate and thus multiply a campaign's potential Web audience.

A second way coproduction is employed in mobilizing is through the display and dissemination of an individual's endorsement (message of support) to members of the endorser's social network. The volunteer page on Thaddeus McCotter's (R-MI-11) 2004 site evidenced this form of coproduction. In a section soliciting endorsements, site visitors were asked to check any of three response options. The first option granted the campaign permission to use the site visitor's name as an endorser of the candidate. The names of a few endorsers were displayed on another page of the site, but it was not clear whether they had been collected via the site.[174] The second response option was a text box in which a message of endorsement could be written by the visitor and recorded by the campaign via the site. The third option was similar to an e-postcard in that it invited visitors to send their endorsement statement to five friends via email messages generated by the campaign site.[175]

Site visitors' provision of others' names and email addresses through various features on a campaign site is a third variant of coproduction. A rudimentary method for campaigns to collect the names and email addresses of site visitors' friends was the provision of contact tables (in PDF, Microsoft Word or Excel documents), which visitors were asked to complete and return to the campaign. This method was employed by several sites in 2002 and 2004, as illustrated by the "sign-in sheet" posted on Carol Moseley-Braun's site to be downloaded, printed and used by supporters at campaign events.[176] A considerably more sophisticated approach was taken by Inez Tenenbaum's (D-SC-Sen) 2004 campaign, which attempted to capture email addresses stored on supporters' local PCs. On a page labeled "Build A Buzz for Inez Online," instructions were provided on how to export a selection of addresses from Microsoft Outlook or other email clients to send to the campaign:

We've made it as easy as possible for supporters to contribute lists of their friends, family and others using the tools below. Your names are protected by our privacy policy. Each new person will receive an introductory email that encourages their participation but allows them to opt out, or stop receiving campaign news. If they choose to continue, they will receive our twice monthly I-Mail with current campaign news, invitations to events in their locale as well as information on other topics they indicate they are interested in.[177]

As alternatives to exporting from email client contact lists, Tenenbaum's site provided an Excel template in which names and contact information could be entered and then sent to the campaign. The site also suggested an email message containing the campaign site URL for supporters to send to others.[178]

E-postcards and other features that allow a visitor to email a link from a campaign site to someone in their social network are also used to build a campaign's contact database. A typical example of a send-link feature was present on the 2002 site for Joe Turnham (D-AL-3). It had a Web form with text boxes for five email addresses with the editable text: "I am emailing you to let you know about the Joe Turnham for Congress website! Joe is running for Congress in the 3rd Congressional District. His site is very informative, and will allow you to catch up on the current events. Please visit Joe Turnham's site at http://www.joeturnham.com."[179] Each time a site visitor sent an e-postcard or link to someone, the recipient's name and email address could have been collected by the campaign site. Klotz (2005) termed the use of campaign-authored texts by site visitors in such features as "plagiarized participation" because they invited visitors to send messages that appear to be written by supporters but were in fact written by the campaign. The benefit for campaigns is clear. Through these types of features, site visitors multiply contacts for a campaign at the same time that they advocate for the candidate with people they know. Features that generate campaign email from site visitors to personal acquaintances are also strategic for mobilizing because coproduced email has greater credibility and is read more often than email that is sent solely from political campaigns (Institute for Politics, Democracy, and the Internet 2004).

The third way coproduction has been employed in mobilizing is in encouraging the interlinking of the campaign Web site with supporter Web sites. To do this, the campaign Web site facilitates supporters in creating their own Web sites in collaboration with the campaign to promote the candidate and then interlinks supporter-produced sites with campaign-produced sites. This technique was pushed into new territory during the Dean 2004 presidential primary campaign through the creation of the fordean.org constellation of Web sites. As we discussed in chapter 5, the fordean.org network was a potent vehicle for connecting supporters with each other. But it also enabled the Dean campaign to create the most extensive Web presence of any campaign to date, exponentially multiplying the entry points to the campaign's Web presence. It facilitated supporters in creating sites designed to inform others about the candidate and in getting them involved in the campaign. The campaign developed syndicated graphics to place on supporter-produced sites, most famously the "Dean Bat" indicating progress toward the fundraising goal of the day.[180] Other graphical elements, with suggestions for linking to various parts of the Dean Web presence, described in the next section as backlinks, were also made available to those creating their own sites. Supporter-produced sites that lack inlinks to the campaign site accomplish less for the campaign than those that have them. Dean's campaign not only succeeded in catalyzing a very large number of inlinking supporter sites, it also employed an unconventional strategy of outlinking to hundreds of supporter sites from its campaign-produced sites.[181] The fact that only 2 percent of all congressional campaign sites in 2002 outlinked to even one supporter's site underscores how radically different the Dean presidential primary campaign's strategy during 2003 and early 2004 was in this regard. We examine the role of linking in mobilizing more closely in the following section.

Linking

Campaigns' uses of the technique of linking in mobilizing can be understood as a subset or particular strand of their uses of linking in connecting. The difference is that in mobilizing, the purpose of linking is to provide or

catalyze transversal bridges between supporters who visit the site and other
actors with whom supporters can interact to promote the campaign. Campaigns employ linking for mobilization in three distinct ways: by disseminating links in email messages, by providing outlinks to party sites and
other types of sites that provide mobilizing structures, and by fostering
campaign-oriented linking on the part of supporters.

As we have demonstrated, campaigns collect email addresses through
their sites via a range of features. The use of email to disseminate links
for mobilization is widespread; the email messages campaigns send to supporters often include requests for users to go to other actors' sites, such as
press, party, or civic group sites, and engage in a political action. The kinds
of actions typically encouraged include responding to an online opinion
poll involving the candidate, donating to the party, and posting pro-
candidate messages in discussion forums. Email messages of this type often
include links that function as transversal bridges to enable a user to move
from within the campaign's email message to another actor's site to take
action, along with a link to the campaign site. Wiese and Gronbeck (2005)
found that presidential campaigns in 2004 used email to disseminate links
to newly posted campaign site features such as fund-raising updates and
digital advertisements. In addition, campaigns ask email recipients to forward particular email messages, as Williams and Trammell (2005) demonstrate in their analysis of the email messages sent by the Bush and Kerry
campaigns in the autumn of 2004. They found that both campaigns used
text to encourage recipients to forward some email messages to others. In
addition, both employed technical mechanisms such as icons or fields that
enabled recipients to forward an email message to friends or media outlets;
these emails also relayed to the campaign the addresses to which the message was forwarded. Interestingly, the Bush campaign used both textual
encouragement and technical mechanisms for email forwarding more frequently than did the Kerry campaign.

Thirty-four percent of campaigns in 2002 provided links to at least one
party organization on their sites. One reason for campaigns to link to
parties is for the purpose of affiliation. Another is to encourage campaign
site visitors to become more engaged in the political process by making
use of the online structure for mobilization developed on those sites.
Nearly all of the presidential campaigns in 2000 and 2004 linked to party
sites with a rhetorical frame that suggested this purpose, as did some con-

gressional candidates in each election. In 2002, Katherine Harris's (R-FL-13) site provided links to seven party organizations at the county, state, and national levels.[182] More than six months before the 2004 election, Kay Granger's (R-TX-8) campaign site linked to the site of a task force funded by the Republican National Committee (RNC) called the Strategic Taskforce to Organize and Mobilize People (STOMP).[183] STOMP described itself as "a nationwide network of dedicated volunteers who have committed to assisting Republicans in competitive areas." The STOMP site provided several kinds of online structures to enable people to join the network and recruit others to join, as well as to travel to strategic regions around the country to volunteer for the RNC in key races.

Similarly, Kerry's 2004 campaign site linked to the "ePatriots" fundraising program page on the Democratic National Committee's (DNC) Web site. In the text around this link, site visitors were assumed to already have recruited others to donate to the Kerry campaign and were urged to promote donating to the DNC as well:

Join the DNC's ePatriot program and you can track your contributions in the same way you do through your Volunteer Center account, but for the Democratic Party. A strong Democratic Party is critical to the Kerry-Edwards campaign and other Democrats during this election. These funds will help make sure that our party has enough resources to fund critical field programs like voter registration and get-out-the vote efforts.[184]

A third way campaigns employ linking in conjunction with mobilizing is by encouraging and equipping supporters to create campaign-oriented links themselves, either to the campaign-produced sites or to other sites produced by supporters. One relatively common strategy was to provide campaign graphics and code on the campaign site for visitors to download and post on their own sites, thus creating backlinks to the campaign site. This strategy emerged in 2000 and was evident on several congressional sites in 2002, such as Mary Bono's (R-CA-45).[185] Laura Wells, a 2004 candidate for California's controller office, suggested to site visitors, "If you know anyone who hosts or manages a website, see if they would like to link to [this site]."[186] The front page of Joe Lieberman's 2004 presidential campaign urged visitors to add a "Joe 2004 Link to Your Website" and offered two sizes of graphics to use as labels that were embedded with link-to code for www.joe2004.com.[187] Moreover, when campaigns encourage or facilitate linking sites the supporters themselves have produced to campaign-oriented Web rings, the campaigns are attempting to persuade supporters to use linking to promote the campaign. The Web ring directory site to which the Kerry campaign directed supporters featured an "Election 2004" box on the front page that linked to Web ring registries for Bush, Nader, and Kucinich as well as to that of Kerry.[188] As of October 13, 2004, the Kerry Web ring registry included 133 sites.[189] It appears that the Kerry campaign site producers' promotion of the Web ring registry may have been at least somewhat effective in prompting supporters to register their sites; on that same date in October 2004, the Nader ring had four sites and the Bush ring had thirty-two sites.[190]

Empowerment

The technique of empowerment in relation to mobilizing cuts across all of the other production techniques discussed in this chapter. For many people, any ability to be engaged in coproducing the political Web is empowering (Trippi 2004). J. B. Lawton, a Kerry supporter in Ohio interviewed by a reporter for the Washington Post in May 2004, reads papers from around the state and blogs his political views. When he receives several responses to a posting, he is assured that "at least I know someone's reading it." Seeking to catalyze others to get involved in the electoral process, he suggested letters to the editor that other people could write, either critiquing coverage or suggesting other points about the election. He offered tips for potential correspondents, including this one:

Defy stereotypes. Liberals get (mis)characterized as effete, godless intellectuals who are out of touch with mainstream values. When appropriate, try some rhetorical ju-jitsu by citing unexpected sources. For example, the Bible—and religion in general, for that matter—is a valuable resource that the Left underutilizes ... It would be great if every single day in every Ohio paper there was a letter that was either pro-Kerry or anti-Bush (Harris 2004).

When asked by the reporter how he felt about his political blogging and protests, he replied, "I feel empowered—instead of just shouting at my television set, I can actually do something about it" (Harris 2004).

The essence of empowerment is the provision of tools that enable site visitors to take actions on their own, independently of the campaign, without the campaign tracking, managing, or even necessarily knowing about the actions. Empowerment as part of the mobilizing practice of Web campaigning is clearly a production technique in that it entails particular design and programming choices. It should be understood as a meta-technique that site producers can employ—or not—in conjunction with choices entailed in linking, coproduction, or convergence. In other words, while the technique of empowerment is manifested through each of the other three, some variants of these three techniques can also be employed in mobilizing apart from the use of empowerment. The use of the empowerment technique within and across the other three techniques may make it possible for a campaign to become a grassroots movement. It has the potential to release creative energy within site visitors and spark synergies between them. At the same time, online structures reflecting the technique of empowerment also have the capacity to be appropriated in ways that run counter to the campaign's purpose of promoting a candidate and amassing resources (both informational and financial) for that purpose. Empowerment as a technique for mobilizing requires trust on the part of campaigns—in their supporters, in their opponents, and in the democratic process itself.

Perhaps the most significant instance of innovation in Web campaigning employing the technique of empowerment took place during McCain's 2000 campaign, four years before Dean's bid for the Democratic nomination. Max Fose, McCain's campaign manager, described it in an interview:

Fose: What we did was make a very unique, back-end system that we developed. For lack of a better term, I could assign you to be a Webmaster, and give you control over Page California. So I gave you the whole California page and the ability to contact everybody in California via email; basically it was access to the database. So it wasn't Max Fose sending out a message to California—it was Max Fose, California state chairman. "Here's what's going on in California. I've updated the page," and it brought people into the campaign in droves because they had ownership. It wasn't only California, but then we broke it into 50 different regions. I bet we had over 50 people in California, updating the page, so then it turned into not being Max Fose, state chairman, but Max Fose, county chairman, or Max Fose, street chairman. I would send out an email, and you'd see the number counted—142,000—but then you'd see emails that went out to seven people, emails that went out to one hundred people. There was one message from this guy in California that said he needed fax machines for his John McCain office, which was in the garage of his house. He sent me a message back saying, "Max, we got five fax machines—you need any?" There are tangible results with it, and it's all done through the Internet, without phone calls and without handshaking, at first, where we organized.

Interviewer: In terms of the person who would have access to the Web site, the database, were these people that you knew? Were they people within the organization? You couldn't just trust anyone.

Fose: We did, though. Nine times out of ten, it was somebody who was originally hired by the campaign, a volunteer who we had trusted to do this. But a lot of times, it literally was from sending out an email. I'd get an email from somebody saying, "There's nobody in my state. Who's the organizer in my state?" and I'd respond, "We don't have anybody." "Well, I'll do it." "OK."

Interviewer: Here's the key; here you go.

Fose: Right. You just kind of watched them. Whenever the page was updated, a page throughout the whole site, I got an email saying, "page x, y, z, click through" and I'd click through and look at it and make sure it wasn't anything ...

Interviewer: Did you ever have to go back and modify anything that someone else had done?

Fose: No, we were very lucky. The other very important place where we did this was the colleges. We said, "OK, you go to ASU. You have an ASU page." Then they started competing. They'd go and look at other people's stuff and say, "Oh, I can do that better." Then they'd send out an email: "I've just updated a page. Look at this cool new graphic." It was a way for the colleges and the university people to communicate (Fose 2000).

Knowingly or not, Fose and the rest of the McCain campaign created online structures that appealed to and released the creative energy of not only opinion leaders in various spheres but also "movement entrepreneurs," as Earl and Schussman (2002) term those who catalyze sociopolitical action among others.

The leading presidential candidates since the 2000 primaries, and a growing number of congressional candidates, have employed at least some of the principles and production elements of empowerment that the McCain campaign pioneered. The 2004 Web site for Jim Nussle (R-IA-1) featured an "e-Captain" sign-up that was pitched as, "Help Jim by becoming a political electronic entrepreneur."[191]

Bush's campaign employed the same model via the "Virtual Precinct" section it introduced on the site in July 2004, including a "Team Leader Sign Up" and a feature to facilitate team leaders in recruiting other team leaders. The Action Center on Bush's site sought to convey a sense of empowerment to volunteers both rhetorically and via the tools it offered: "Take action and join the most important part of the 2004 election: the grassroots team to re-elect President Bush. Our action center gives you the tools to join the Bush team and help spread President Bush's positive message to your friends, family and your community."[192] Clicking on "Become a Bush Volunteer" resolved to a page entitled "Bush Team Leader Signup" and the following text:

As a Bush Team Leader, you will be a central part of President Bush's leadership. President Bush will be counting on you to accomplish up to six important tasks:

- Recruit 5 Other Bush Team Leaders
- Host a Block Party
- Sign Up 10 Friends to Receive Bush Email Updates
- Help Turn Out the Vote for President Bush
- Write Letters to the Editor and Call into Talk Radio Shows
- Volunteer for the President at Local Events[193]

Would-be team leaders were required to provide first and last names and street and email addresses. Providing one's phone number, Instant Messenger handle, and email format preference were optional. Recruits were asked to indicate issues of interest to them and to select all that applied from a list of twenty-six socioeconomic groups termed "coalition groups," such as Arab-Americans, Catholics, educators, investors, sportsmen, and veterans.

Finally, Gary McLeod's (Republican & Constitution-SC-6) 2004 site also employed empowerment in its attempt to appeal to those who are entrepreneurial both financially and politically. One option offered to site visitors was to become a campaign "affiliate" by getting a campaign Web site to raise funds for the campaign. The campaign provided a financial incentive for this affiliation:

If you live in the United States, please consider helping us raise money for the campaign by becoming an affiliate FREE. Sorry, we cannot accept donations or affiliates from other countries. You will earn 10 percent of the resulting donations 2 levels deep and receive a web site just like this one. Your new web site will be created for you when you complete the affiliate application.[194]

Ironically, the "Terms and Conditions" at the bottom of the Web form on which a would-be affiliate was asked to provide personal information (including full name, contact information, and tax identification number) read: "'We The People' already have too many rules and regulations coming from government, so you won't find any more here."

Many of the features we have discussed in association with mobilizing throughout this chapter can manifest empowerment. The provision of e-paraphernalia and materials for offline distribution generally reflect the technique of empowerment, as do online structures for sending links and e-postcards, Web forms for letters to editors, syndicated graphics, and RSS feeds. By producing these kinds of features, campaigns invite site visitors

to take actions in relation to others and trust that the intent of most will
be to promote the campaign. Any one of these features can also be appropriated by site users with non-promotional intentions. E-postcards from
one campaign site can be sent satirically by an opponent to friends. A site's
local newspaper contact look-up feature can be employed by the mischie-
vous to spam the newspaper. Campaign RSS feeds can be framed mockingly
on someone else's site.

On the other hand, any of these features can also be designed in ways
that attempt to use social or technical mechanisms to monitor, manage,
or in some way control what site visitors do with them. The "Online Headquarters" on Kerry's 2004 site described in the opening of this chapter did
not live long on the public Web. Some time during the summer these features were put behind a login screen preventing all but registered volunteers from accessing them. By autumn 2004, the Online Headquarters had
become the Online Volunteer Center:

Welcome to the Online Volunteer Center. The success of our campaign depends
on having a strong and active group of supporters like you. The Online Volunteer
Center provides you with tools that allow you to become an active part of our
campaign. Once you have an account, you can plan events, raise money, recruit
new volunteers, and more. You will also get your own personal Kerry web site. You
can track all of your actions to see your progress. Click here to get a volunteer center
account![195]

On the "Raise Funds" page,[196] supporters were provided with a tool
that generated a fundraising email to send to friends: "Your friends will be
pointed to your personal fundraising page where they contribute. You will
be able to track contributions." Put another way, volunteers had easy access
to information about the campaign contributions of people to whom they
sent a fundraising email. One can be sure that whatever a volunteer could
track, the campaign did track, and this allowed the Kerry campaign to
monitor users—and uses of the online structure—and, at least to some
degree, to manage both.

At the bottom of most pages in the Online Volunteer Center on Kerry's
campaign site was a statement that functioned to establish the terms of use
of the mobilizing features from the campaign's perspective. A site visitor
completing the campaign Web form to host an event, fundraise, or participate in some other way in promoting the campaign was presented with the
following text just above the request submit button.

I am volunteering my time and efforts for the campaign, but am not otherwise authorized to act on its behalf, or to hold myself out as a campaign official. I will comply with federal campaign finance law at all times.

I will not raise any funds that do not comply with federal limits, prohibitions and reporting requirements. When spending my personal funds, I will comply with all applicable limits and reporting requirements.[197]

Site visitors who did not agree with these terms had the option of not submitting the form but not of amending the terms. The terms reveal the campaign's discomfort with or concerns about mobilizing in general and empowerment in particular. Through these terms, the campaign sought to indemnify itself from potential liabilities caused by whoever might use the online structures provided.

Tensions in Mobilizing

The techniques described previously are used to create online structures that encourage and equip a site visitor to promote the candidate to others. The practice of mobilizing via campaign sites, especially in the Dean 2004 campaign, reflects a significant shift away from the previous notion of campaign Web sites as primarily informational, like a digital yard sign or an electronic billboard. The presence of mobilizing features on a campaign site reflects a campaign's perception of its Web presence as not just an information display, but also a catalytic resource hub through which entrepreneurial supporters (political influentials) can take action and thereby increase the extensity and intensity of the campaign as a sociotechnical network.

Another indicator of change in this regard was the citing of Keller and Berry's (2003) book *The Influentials* by Bush's campaign manager Ken Mehlman as one of his favorite texts "to explain the challenge of political communication in a world crowded by the proliferation of cable networks, talk shows and Web sites" (Harris 2004). According to Harris, Mehlman anticipated that online influentials would be "indispensable filters and promoters of the attitudes and arguments that [would] frame the choices voters make." Harris observed that the Bush campaign had adopted a mobilizing strategy that Harris termed "echo politics." By May the Bush campaign had reportedly collected about 6 million email addresses, including some purchased from lists, and had 420,000 volunteers signed up electronically, through whom the campaign was creating an echo of Bush's message from the neighborhood up. The Bush campaign also equipped supporters to promote Bush on local radio talk shows by distributing talking points and lists of talk shows for each metropolitan area as well as tips for getting on the air via the campaign site and email. In addition, the Bush site provided links that enabled supporters to email local newspaper editors directly (Harris 2004). Although by that time Kerry was the clear winner of the Democratic presidential primaries, he had not yet been officially nominated, and his Web campaign strategy lagged Bush's in regard to mobilization. As of May 2004, the Kerry site lacked several of the mobilizing features that were evident on the Bush site at the time, such as the letter-to-the-editor feature. That feature, along with many others, had been added to the Kerry site by July 2004; from that point on the Bush and Kerry sites were fairly similar in regard to their mobilizing potential.

As with each of the practices analyzed in previous chapters, there are several tensions particularly relevant to mobilizing that shape or constrain the appropriation of this Web campaigning practice. First, mobilizing requires conceptualizing (or reconceptualizing) the Web as a shared (that is, coproduced) medium. The overwhelmingly predominant view of the Web among campaigns through the 2000 election was of a static venue that allowed relatively cheap broadcast or billboard-style information dissemination. But mobilizing is not compatible with this view of the Web.

Second, mobilizing requires careful management of supporters' expectations on the part of campaigns. On one hand, campaigns need to motivate supporters to become advocates, and many do so by making entrepreneurial appeals. On the other hand, to optimize the impact of volunteers' activity, campaigns need ways to monitor individuals' activity sufficiently to be able to coordinate and leverage it.

Third, mobilizing walks a tightrope in relation to the segmentation of voters. Identification of distinct socioeconomic groups is useful to campaigns in targeting likely voters, and each individual volunteer has a different sphere of influence in relation to various segments. However, segmentation taken too far can alienate would-be volunteers by casting the candidate as less than genuine. It is tough to get individual supporters passionate about advocating for a candidate who has only general appeal; it is also difficult to mobilize a diverse base to advocate for a candidate who advances an amalgamation of special interests. Gore's site in 2000 employed specialized messages for twenty-four segments of the voting population; Bush's site in 2004 did the same for twenty-six segments of the population. Mobilizing also has the potential to contribute to tension between what Schier (2000) terms the activation of narrowly segmented elites and broad-based mobilization. Schier argues that activation is more effective in current political conditions in the U.S., although he rues the consequences of this for democracy. Given the nature of how information flows on the Web, with very few sites attracting many visitors and many sites attracting few visitors, it may be impossible for Web-based mobilizing by electoral campaigns to be anything but activating, similar to the way issue and interest groups routinely target specific (and often elite) segments of the population to evoke particular political actions.

The final and overarching tension for campaigns engaged in mobilizing concerns control: How much can be released, and how much can actually be retained? Campaigns cannot force supporters to use the online structures they provide and become advocates for the campaign. Nor can they force any site visitor to use the online structures in the ways they have intended them to be used. Ultimately, campaign organizations have to realize that they cannot force site visitors to take action or control the actions visitors take. Campaigns that engage in mobilization on the Web will have concluded that the benefits of desired and anticipated actions outweigh the risks associated with inaction and undesired actions.

Mobilization requires the integration of informing, involving, and connecting. It entails the provision of online structures that enable informed and involved supporters to connect with other actors for the purpose of promoting the candidate. A handful of campaigns in each election, and the major party presidential campaigns in 2000 and 2004 in particular, have developed innovative ways of enabling mobilization through online structures. This practice, with its many variants, could significantly reshape electoral politics if implemented broadly. Depending on the ways each production technique is employed and on the particular online structures created, mobilizing structures have the potential to multiply campaigns' human and financial resources. Having completed our analysis of how campaigning practices take shape on the Web, we focus in the next chapter on variances in the appropriation of Web practices and on reasons why Web practices are employed differentially across campaigns.

7   Explaining the Adoption of Web Campaigning Practices

The extent to which each Web campaigning practice has been employed across campaigns varies widely. There are also significant differences between various kinds of campaign organizations in the prevalence of each practice. In this chapter, we explore the impact of three broad types of factors on the variance in Web campaigning we have observed, examining, in turn, characteristics of Web producers, aspects of political campaigns, and the dynamics of the Web environment. We conclude our exploration of factors that explain the adoption of Web campaigning practices by focusing on a fourth factor, the impact of engaging in one practice on the tendency to engage in the others. By triangulating data presented across the book, we formalize and test the model of the interrelationships between the four Web campaigning practices that we have been developing throughout this study.

To set the stage for this analysis, we first briefly summarize an overall assessment of the extent to which informing, involving, connecting, and mobilizing were adopted across the House, Senate, and gubernatorial campaign Web sites we analyzed in 2002. Following this summary, we will turn to an extended discussion of the impact that each of these four types of factors has on the adoption of Web campaigning practices.

Since campaigns' practices are inscribed in particular Web site features, we measured the overall prevalence of Web campaigning practices through clusters of features that correspond conceptually and functionally with each practice. For the purposes of this analysis, we included as indicators of the practice of informing: the provision of a candidate biography, issue positions, campaign news, and candidate speeches. Involving was measured by the presence of information about donating to the campaign, a campaign calendar, the ability to sign up to volunteer for the campaign,

Table 7.1

Prevalence of Web Campaigning Practices on U.S. Campaign Web Sites, 1998–2004

Practice	Feature	1998	2000	2002	2004
Informing	Biography	90%	89%	92%	98%
	Issue Positions	88%	75%	90%	85%
	Campaign News	49%	52%	73%	
	Position Substantiation			86%	
	Speech Texts	20%	13%	8%	10%
	Campaign Ads	8%	6%	19%	
Connecting	Link to Any Other Site	51%		76%	
	Party Affiliation	54%		43%	
	Endorsements	49%		26%	51%
	Link to Political Site		49%		
	Link to Government Site	16%		39%	
	Link to Party Site	36%		34%	
	Voter Registration	11%	20%	31%	39%
	Link to Civic/Advocacy Group Site			30%	
	Link to Press Site			24%	
	Position Alignments			15%	
	Position Comparison to Opponent		12%	6%	
	Link to Local Site			11%	
	Position Comparison to Other			11%	
	Link to Portal Site			7%	
	Comparison Section			5%	19%
	Link to Citizen Site			2%	
	Link to Opponent Site		1%	1%	
Involving	Donation Information	71%	75%	80%	92%
	Contact Information Other than Email			83%	96%
	Email Address			81%	
	Volunteer Sign-up	55%	68%	69%	78%
	Email List Sign-up	16%	44%	41%	68%
	Photos of Campaign Events			42%	
	Campaign Calendar			34%	42%
	Visitor Comments		1%	2%	14%
	Online Polls		7%	5%	
	Online Events			0%	
Mobilizing	Offline Distribution of Materials			4%	17%
	Send Links			10%	9%
	Electronic Paraphernalia	9%		9%	8%
	Send Letters to Editors	7%	7%	4%	25%

Note on sources: Data presented for 1998 is drawn from Kamarck (1999), Democracy Online Project (n.d.), and Harpham (1999). See Appendix for discussion of data for 2000, 2002, and 2004.

and the possibility of receiving email from the campaign. The practice of connecting was indicated through the prevalence of two types of information that provide cognitive bridges for a site visitor to other actors (endorsements and position comparison to an opponent), and four types of outlinks (to government sites, party sites, civic and advocacy group sites, and press sites). The extent to which campaigns engaged in the practice of mobilizing was measured by the prevalence of four features: online structures that supported sending letters to editors of publications, sending links as email from the campaign site to others, the availability of online material produced for offline dissemination, and downloadable electronic paraphernalia.

The frequency with which each of these features were found on sites in 2002 is presented in table 7.1, along with frequencies for several other features and different election cycles (see Appendix for the operational definitions of the features assessed in this study). In general, we find an increasing prevalence across almost all features from 1998 to 2004. The features associated with informing remain very prevalent, while the features associated with other practices grow substantially. Our mapping of practices to features for this analysis is neither exhaustive nor mutually exclusive. We certainly recognize that other features could have been identified or associated with the practices under review and that some of the features could arguably be indicators of practices other than those we have suggested; however, our mapping captures the essence of each practice under examination.

The number of features from each of the clusters previously described that were present on a campaign Web site indicated the extent to which a specific campaign engaged in that practice. Campaigns whose Web sites had none of the features in a practice cluster were determined to have not adopted the practice. Campaigns that produced Web sites including any of the features in a cluster, but missing two or more were labeled as emergent adopters of the practice. Those campaigns with Web sites including all or all but one of the cluster features were determined to be established in their use of the practice. As illustrated in table 7.2, we find that informing was the practice in which the greatest number of campaign organizations engaged, and which campaigns adopted most extensively. Among the campaign sites examined in 2002, informing was an established practice on two out of three and an emergent practice on nearly all of the remaining

Table 7.2
Adoption of Web Campaigning Practices by Campaign Organizations, 2002

	Percent of Campaigns			
Practice	Not Adopted	Emerging	Established	N
Informing	1%	32%	67%	589
Involving	12%	42%	47%	1044
Connecting	28%	70%	2%	429
Mobilizing	78%	20%	2%	515

sites. Involving was established on 47 percent of the sites and emergent on 42 percent. Connecting was much more likely than mobilizing to be an emergent practice. However, virtually none of the campaigns had established either connecting or mobilizing as practices. These overall findings bring together the disparate discussions of these practices in chapters 3–6 and indicate the relative density of informing and involving and the relative scarcity of connecting and mobilizing.

Throughout the preceding chapters we have discussed the possible roles that user expectations regarding campaign sites, concerns about control, and other tensions, play in shaping what campaigns produce on the Web. We now turn to our analysis of the relationship between the adoption of Web campaigning practices and three other factors—seeking to ascertain more about why Web campaigning took the shape it did between 2002 and 2004. We first discuss the impact of characteristics of campaign Web producers, including the professional norms and expectations common to many campaign Webmasters and the individual Webmasters' experiences, skills, and values. Next, we consider the impact of two aspects—constituency and race—associated with elements of each specific campaign and with campaigns in general as sociotechnical organizations. In the last section of the chapter, we explore ways in which the dynamics of the Web environment might influence campaigns' Web practices, through the structuring influence of the emerging genre of campaign Web sites and the tendency toward symmetry between various kinds of campaigns.

Web Producers in a Social-professional Context

Whether working collectively or relatively autonomously, individuals, ultimately, are the producers of campaign Web sites. These Web producers bring with them a wide array of previous experiences and expectations about the medium in which they now choose to work. Some identify themselves as professional Web producers who happen to be working on political campaigns, and some see themselves as professional campaign operatives who happen to be working as Web producers. Others are volunteers, and still others are candidates themselves. In this section, we explore the impact of the production context surrounding campaign Webmasters. This context is shaped by the professional norms and expectations of the community of campaign site producers, as well as by the specific experiences, goals, and values of individual campaign Webmasters.

The community of professional campaign site producers that has developed during the past ten years is bound by a set of common assumptions, goals, and ideology. Richly described by Howard (2006), political consultants specializing in information technology share a sense of identity with each other that sets them apart from other political professionals, including those professionals specializing in old media (such as broadcasting) and in the traditional political fields of fundraising, polling, and field operations. These technology practitioners have a common set of assumptions about the ills of American democracy and a shared faith in the curative powers of their craft. As one consultant interviewed by Howard explained, "We're all like-minded in thinking that technology can play a role in politics, that's what makes it a community. It's not about your particular issue or your particular party. We have a shared interest in utilizing technology for everybody's greater good" (John Phillips, quoted by Howard 2006, p. 43). Another consultant focused on the commonalities across the community: "What defines our community is a common language, a common interest and a common pursuit. We share the language of the Internet, a professional vernacular, and a common set of basic experiences" (Phil Noble, quoted by Howard 2006, p. 43).

One way in which the professional norms and expectations of political Web producers shape the behavior of individuals is through the emergence of a best practices zeitgeist. An important sponsor of the effort to shape this community during the late 1990s and early 2000s was the Pew Charitable Trusts. The Trusts provided grants to "improve campaigns through the use of the Internet" to institutions such as George Washington University (GWU) and the University of Pennsylvania (as noted in the preface, the Trusts provided much of the funding to support the present work as well).

One of the outgrowths of this foundation's funding stream was the Democracy Online Project (DOP) at GWU, later recast as the Institute for Politics, Democracy, and the Internet (IPDI). In the autumn of 1999, the DOP published its first primer, the first of a number of such reports outlining best practices for online campaigning (Democracy Online Project 1999). Revised editions of the primer were published in 2000 and 2002. The third edition, expanded to thirty-six pages from the original twenty-one, had focused the set of best practices on seven specific recommendations based on democratic ideals, feedback from campaign site users, and basic principles of Web site design. These suggestions were to:

(1) make Web sites accessible to all,

(2) document issue positions,

(3) exhibit community ties through links,

(4) post and follow a privacy policy,

(5) describe rules governing Web campaigning and use of the Internet and demonstrate compliance thereto,

(6) contrast issue positions to others' positions, and

(7) provide opportunities for interactivity and communication with the campaign.

Our findings in table 7.1 demonstrate that the DOP/IPDI best practices set a higher bar than most campaigns reached in 2000, 2002, or 2004. However, through widespread distribution of these primers, and through participation and engagement with the growing community of professional Web producers, the DOP and, subsequently, the IPDI established standards for those interested in developing good Web sites.

To encourage adoption of these best practices, GWU's Graduate School of Political Management started giving annual Golden Dot Awards to political Web producers in 1998. In their original incarnation, Golden Dot Awards were awarded for substance and content, innovation, interactivity, and public accountability. Specific criteria were provided for judging Web sites in each category. For instance, the award for substance and content included the following criteria:

(1) Depth of content: What do the prose, graphics, indices, and links of the Web site have to say? How detailed is the information available on or through the Web site?

(2) Validation: Are the main claims of the Web site substantiated by information and evidence?

(3) Breadth: Are all aspects of the campaign included, or at least referenced?

(4) Rhetoric: Visitors to the site should be provided with given reasons and motivations to support the campaign.

(5) Performance: In as much as it is possible to observe, does the site practice what the campaign slogan preaches?

(6) Currency: Is the Web site kept up-to-date? Does the Web site contain a "news-ticker" of current, breaking campaign events? Is what's "NEW!" really newsworthy?

(7) Accuracy: How carefully have the contents been prepared? Is the archive complete?

(8) Message Coherence: To what extent does the site have an overall theme or message? Does each page of the site "stay on message?" (Graduate School of Political Management 1998).

By establishing detailed criteria for awards, DOP/IPDI benchmarked particular Web production techniques and helped to create a professional context within which Web producers operated. In later years, criteria for the awards were modified to reflect the shifting expectations of both Web producers and users and any innovations in Web technologies, as well as further developments in Web-based campaigning. Criteria for awards given to producers responsible for campaign sites during the 2004 elections emphasized responsiveness to "news developments or other changes in the campaign environment;" the integration of online and offline campaign activities; responsiveness to "questions from citizens, journalists, and other political activists;" disclosure of "financial, personnel, and public activity data about the organization sponsoring the campaign" (including "explanations of how the campaign operates and makes decisions"); the inclusion of a privacy policy; the presentation of features "that facilitate access by groups of citizens with special needs, including multiple languages where relevant, options that facilitate access by individuals with disabilities, and access by individuals with low computational capacity or speed" (Institute for Politics, Democracy, and the Internet 2004).

The community of professional political consultants itself has also recognized excellence in Web design and implementation through a program of awards and recognition. In 1999, the American Association of Political Consultants (AAPC), which had been giving Pollie awards in more than fifty traditional political communication categories—such as print, direct mail, fundraising, collateral and outdoor material, television, and newspaper and radio—added a technology category with three awards: the best candidate Web site, the best organization Web site, and the best initiative Web site (American Association of Political Consultants 1999). By 2004, the AAPC had made 138 awards, with twenty-six in the "Internet" category. Among the awards were best use of the Web for volunteer recruitment and management, for fundraising, persuasion, and for negative or contrast information (American Association of Political Consultants 2005). Professional Web producers in the political community value awards like the Golden Dots and the Pollies and frequently trumpet them on their own Web sites as testimony to their professional qualifications.[198]

Beyond awards and recognition, the political community recognized Web campaigning as an important component of professional practice in the late 1990s. In 1997, a Web site highlighting the "Political Site of the Day" was started by the Internet consulting firm Kessler Freedman, Inc., and this remains available at aboutpolitics.com. Jonah Seiger and Shabbir Safdar, co-founders of Mindshare Internet Campaigns and pioneers in Web campaigning, established a bi-weekly Web and email newsletter, "Campaign Web Review," to assess the impact of the Web on the 1998 campaign as it unfolded.[199] And in 1999, the leading trade publication, *Campaigns & Elections*, inaugurated a monthly column by Michael Cornfield called "The Online Campaigner."

At a more micro level, the technical skills, Web production philosophy, and personality of the individual or individuals who create and maintain a campaign's Web presence can also be expected to have a significant impact on a campaign's Web practice. Some of the more noteworthy innovations in Web practices in recent years have been attributed to a technically creative and politically savvy Webmaster who was given free rein, such as Phil Madsen in Jesse Ventura's 1998 gubernatorial campaign, Max Fose in John McCain's 2000 presidential primary campaign, and Joe Trippi in Howard Dean's 2004 presidential primary campaign.

Our analysis of the impact of experiences, attitudes, and values of individual Web producers draws on the Web-based survey of producers we conducted just after the 2002 election. Given the difficulty of surveying this particular population, we were pleased to receive nearly one hundred valid responses from individuals who identified themselves as responsible for producing a campaign Web site during the 2002 election. Although the size of our respondent pool makes it difficult to conduct statistical analyses, especially among subgroups of respondents, we can nevertheless see directions and trends in this data that enable us to suggest some potential relationships.

Our survey method allowed us to distinguish among three groups of respondents, based on the features we had observed on the sites they produced. About 70 percent of our respondents produced sites that offered an opportunity for the site visitor to become involved in the campaign by signing up to volunteer, agreeing to receive email, or contributing funds. About 15 percent of our respondents produced sites that provided both opportunities for involvement as well as a feature that facilitated mobilizing, such as sending links or encouraging letters to the editor. The remaining 15 percent of our respondents produced sites that had neither involving nor mobilizing features. In the discussion that follows, we refer to these three groups as producers of involving sites, of mobilizing sites, and of non-involving sites.

Our data suggest that there are important differences between these three groups of Web producers in experiences and attitudes. Webmasters of mobilizing sites tended to be more experienced in producing political Web sites and less concerned about perceived dangers and negative effects of the Web. As illustrated in table 7.3, producers of mobilizing sites, on average, reported having worked in more previous election cycles than did producers of either involving or non-involving sites. In addition, this group of producers reported having produced more campaign Web sites in either current or previous elections than did the other producers surveyed. At the same time, the producers of mobilizing sites reported less overall experience on the Internet. It may be that the earliest adopters of the Internet are not those working with campaigns engaged in the broadest array of Web campaigning practices.

Attitudinally, we found that Web producers of mobilizing sites expressed a lower level of concern when asked about some perceived Internet or Web dangers, either to themselves as users or to the polity as a whole, than did producers of non-involving sites. Web producers of mobilizing sites were less concerned that others might inappropriately track the Web sites they

Table 7.3
Differences in Background of Site Producers and Campaign Commitment to Web Campaigning among Producers of Campaign Web Sites, 2002

Types of Web Sites Produced by Survey Respondent in 2002		Background of Site Producers			Campaign Commitment to Web		
		Number of Previous Election Cycles During which Producer Created Web Sites	Total Number of Campaign Web Sites Created by Producer, All Election Cycles	Number of Years Producer Has Used the Internet	Percent of Campaign Budget Committed to Web by Campaign	Hours per Week Spent by Campaign on Site	Number of Staff Members Committed to Web Site by Campaign
No Involving or Mobilizing Features	Mean	0.46	1.77	9.15	27.69	7.31	2.00
	N	13	13	13	13	13	9
	Std. Deviation	0.66	0.83	3.05	36.55	4.39	0.00
Involving Features, No Mobilizing Features	Mean	0.50	1.95	8.03	14.03	8.44	2.52
	N	64	64	60	62	64	23
	Std. Deviation	0.78	1.25	3.06	20.52	7.39	1.06
Involving and Mobilizing Features	Mean	1.14	2.71	7.21	13.57	13.57	2.44
	N	14	14	14	14	14	9
	Std. Deviation	1.46	1.64	2.64	22.40	9.49	0.77
All Survey Respondents	Mean	0.59	2.04	8.07	15.96	9.07	2.39
	N	91	91	87	89	91	41
	Std. Deviation	0.92	1.29	3.01	23.92	7.60	0.88

visit, read their email, or obtain their credit card number. More broadly, the producers of mobilizing sites were less concerned than were producers of non-involving sites about the giving of political information by unqualified people, the posting of false or inaccurate news reports online, and the use of the Web to spread false political rumors. Of course, the organizational context within which a campaign Webmaster works also plays a significant role in shaping the extent to which a campaign engages in Web campaigning.

Campaigns in an Organizational Context

Individuals producing Web sites for campaigns work within highly structured campaign organizations. Thus, campaigns' Web practices should be understood as also manifesting organizational patterns of technology adoption. Pablo Boczkowski's (2004) study of the processes of technology adoption in news organizations found that they are not only triggered by technological developments but also shaped by production factors such as organizational structures, work practices, and representations of users. The ways in which campaigns adopt and deploy Web technologies are undoubtedly influenced by these kinds of organizational and production factors. However, a thorough investigation of such factors would require internal analyses of campaign organizations, such as those provided by Howard's (2006) study of what he labels "hypermedia" campaign organizations, that are generally beyond the scope of this book. We can make some preliminary comments on the degree to which the structure of these organizations and the competing aspects of their electoral arenas influence the Web campaigning practices in which they engage.

The necessary strategic, rhetorical, structural, and aesthetic choices in Web production are made within the context of the campaign as a sociotechnical organization. In our 2002 survey of Web producers, described in detail previously, we found that the extent to which particular campaigns engage in Web campaigning was affected by the general commitment of each campaign to Web production. We assessed the reported commitment of the campaign to the Web with three measures: the number of staff members assigned to develop and maintain the Web site, the number of hours per week spent on updating and maintaining the Web site, and the percentage of campaign budget devoted to the Web site. As the number of hours per week and the number of staff members committed to Web production increase, the extent of Web campaigning increases, as illustrated in table 7.3. Producers of involving and mobilizing sites reported nearly twice the number of weekly hours and about 25 percent more staff members committed to Web production as did producers of sites without involving features.

Paradoxically, however, we found that producers of non-involving sites reported about twice the proportion of their campaign's budget was committed to the Web than producers of involving sites or of involving and mobilizing sites. While our finding on budget commitment runs counter to expectations, we do find limited evidence that increased commitment by the campaign, in terms of hours and staffing assignments, is associated with expanded Web campaigning. One explanation for the finding with regard to the campaign budget commitment could be that campaigns with relatively low budgets may have invested more heavily in the Internet but still been too short of funds to develop a wide array of Web features.

Campaigns' Web practices also appear to be related to the target audiences identified for the Web site and the goals that organizations have for their Web site. As shown in table 7.4, producers of non-involving sites reported that their organizations were more likely to target undecided voters, their opponent's supporters, curious nonvoters, and journalists; producers of involving and mobilizing sites indicated their target audiences to be supporters. Producers of non-involving sites indicated that their goals were more likely to be informing visitors, getting out the vote, increasing issue awareness, and persuading undecided voters. By contrast, producers of mobilizing sites claimed that their goals were signing up volunteers and publicizing events (see table 7.5). From these data, we conclude that at least some of the explanation for the variance in Web campaigning we observed is related to specific factors associated with individual campaigns and their political strategies. However, other factors present in the political system or the electoral context may also play a role.

As we discussed in chapter 1, some analysts have suggested that as the Internet emerges as an important component of many social, economic, and political sectors, its impact would be less revolutionary than first predicted (and hoped for) by those who were optimistic or utopian. Some scholars were skeptical due to uneven access to the Internet as a result of

Table 7.4

Differences in Audiences Targeted among Producers of Campaign Web Sites, 2002

Types of Web Sites Produced by Survey Respondent in 2002		Importance of Target Audience to Web Site Producers				
		Un-decided Voters	Sup-porters	Oppo-nents' Sup-porters	Curious Non-voters	Journal-ists
No Involving or Mobilizing Features	Mean	4.62	3.69	3.46	3.62	4.15
	N	13	13	13	13	13
	Std. Deviation	0.77	1.44	1.45	1.61	1.28
Involving Features, No Mobilizing Features	Mean	4.22	4.06	2.70	3.25	3.67
	N	64	64	64	63	64
	Std. Deviation	0.81	0.89	1.24	1.29	1.05
Involving and Mobilizing Features	Mean	4.29	4.21	2.43	3.21	3.43
	N	14	14	14	14	14
	Std. Deviation	0.73	0.70	1.16	1.25	1.50
All Survey Respondents	Mean	4.29	4.03	2.77	3.30	3.70
	N	91	91	91	90	91
	Std. Deviation	0.79	0.96	1.28	1.33	1.17

Note: Survey responses to questions asking priority different groups had as "target audiences," where 1 indicated very low and 7 indicated very high.

the so-called digital divide (e.g. Davis and Owen 1998; Norris 2001). Others focused on the likelihood that traditional forms of power would shape the new political environment of the Internet. This argument, most clearly articulated by the title of Margolis and Resnick's (2000) book *Politics as Usual*, contended that politics and political practice on the Internet would closely resemble politics offline and that traditional factors affecting the distribution of political resources would shape the way that political actors use the Web. Therefore, the Internet would have minimal impact on politics. As Margolis and Resnick (2000) observe, in the offline world, characteristics of constituencies and the distribution of campaign resources largely predict the adoption of familiar campaign approaches such as the reliance on television advertising, the preparation of bilingual campaign materials, and the

Table 7.5
Differences in Goals among Producers of Campaign Web Sites, 2002

Types of Web Sites Produced by Survey Respondent in 2002		Recruit Volunteers	Inform Site Visitors	Increase Voter Turnout	Increase Issue Awareness	Cost-Efficient Campaigning	Publicize Offline Events	Persuade Undecided Voters	Distribute Campaign Materials	Manage Campaign Schedule	Solicit Financial Contributions	Coordinate Volunteer Activities
No Involving or Mobilizing Features	Mean	2.15	8.69	6.08	8.85	8.69	5.00	8.46	3.67	2.62	1.62	2.00
	N	13	13	13	13	13	13	13	12	13	13	13
	Std. Dev.	2.23	0.85	2.99	0.38	0.75	3.08	0.88	3.08	2.75	1.04	2.04
Involving Features, No Mobilizing Features	Mean	4.95	8.06	4.67	7.43	6.69	5.45	6.37	5.03	3.24	4.58	2.90
	N	64	62	63	61	64	64	62	63	63	62	63
	Std. Dev.	2.65	2.06	2.83	2.29	2.76	2.92	2.50	2.85	2.80	2.60	2.45
Involving and Mobilizing Features	Mean	6.07	7.23	4.71	6.64	5.64	6.14	5.58	5.93	4.00	6.14	4.50
	N	14	13	14	14	14	14	12	14	14	14	14
	Std. Dev.	2.34	2.92	2.84	2.56	2.76	2.28	2.54	2.62	2.88	2.54	2.68
All Survey Respondents	Mean	4.73	8.03	4.88	7.51	6.81	5.49	6.57	4.99	3.27	4.39	3.02
	N	91	88	90	88	91	91	87	89	90	89	90
	Std. Dev.	2.76	2.10	2.87	2.24	2.69	2.84	2.47	2.88	2.80	2.73	2.51

Note: Means based on survey responses to questions assigning values on scale of 1–7, where 1 indicated the goal was not at all important, and 7 indicated the goal was very important.

development of field operations. The normalization hypothesis, to which some recent studies lend support (e.g. Bimber and Davis 2003), suggests that politics in the online world should, over time, come to resemble politics in the offline world. Political system factors such as incumbency, political party, level of race competitiveness, and office sought are generally useful in explaining the adoption of distinct types of campaign practices in the offline world. To the extent this hypothesis provides an explanation of the Web practices of campaign organizations, these factors ought to be useful in explaining the adoption of distinct types of practices and strategies on candidate Web sites. It could also be expected that higher levels of Internet penetration among constituencies would be associated with more extensive Web campaigning to the extent campaigns view their own electorates as audiences for their Web campaigning efforts. To determine the degree to which constituency effects and political-structural factors were associated with Web campaigning practices, we examined the relationship between nine measures of these factors and the occurrence of specific features on campaign Web sites launched to support candidates for Senate, House, and governor in 2002.

Three factors are associated with the constituency in which the campaign is being waged: the level of Internet penetration (by state) in homes, the median family income, and the percentage of the population with college degrees. A clear and consistent relationship has been observed between median family income, educational attainment, and Internet use in the household. Higher household incomes and higher levels of educational attainment have been found to be associated with both computer use and Internet use starting from the mid-1990s and continuing through at least 2002 (National Telecommunications and Information Administration 2002). To the extent that political campaigns gauge their Web campaigning strategy on the basis of their target electorate's use of the Internet, both family income and level of education serve as reasonable proxies of these factors. In addition, the state-level measure of the percentage of homes with Internet access provides a direct measure of this factor; however, given the large number of House campaigns examined, it is a somewhat imprecise measure.

We also examine the impact of six political system factors: the incumbency status of the candidate, the office sought, the major-party affiliation, the party affiliation of the candidate, the competitiveness of the race, and the campaign's receipts. Analysts frequently distinguish campaigns by these political-structural factors and expect different behavior depending on the status of the campaign. For example, incumbents and major-party candidates are generally less likely to seek debates and appearances with their opponents, and they have a lower need to use campaign resources to increase name recognition (Herrnson 2003; Fenno 1996; Bradshaw 1995). Studies of race intensity have shown that intense races, in which candidates are well-known and outcomes are uncertain, produce more—and more widely publicized—public position taking among candidates than low-key races between poorly matched candidates where the victory of the stronger candidate is a foregone conclusion (Simon 2002; Westlye 1991; Kahn and Kenney 1999).

Table 7.6 presents a descriptive summary of the constituency and political system variables we employed in our attempt to explain the distribution of cases on the indices of these practices. Data for three measures were derived from the 2000 U.S. Census. The proportion of Internet penetration ranged from 41 percent to 90 percent statewide. The median family income and the percentage of the population with a college degree, measured at the district level for House candidates and the state level for Senate and

Table 7.6
Descriptive Statistics of Political System Variables

	Cases	Minimum Value	Maximum Value	Mean	Std. Deviation
Incumbency	1163	0	1.00	0.25	0.43
Major-party Status	1168	0	1.00	0.75	0.43
Race Intensity	1159	1.00	4.00	1.85	1.12
House Candidate	1774	0	1.00	0.82	0.38
Senate Candidate	1774	0	1.00	0.07	0.25
Per Capita Campaign Expenditures	881	0	16.56	1.29	1.63
Percent Online, State	1159	40.70	90.00	64.55	11.77
Percent College-Educated, District	1129	6.30	56.90	24.74	8.09
Mean Family Income, District, $	1130	20,924.00	91,571.00	51,475.00	11,193.48
Democratic Candidate	1774	0	1.00	0.23	0.42
Republican Candidate	1774	0	1.00	0.26	0.44
Valid N (Listwise)	844				

gubernatorial candidates, ranged from $20,974 to $91,571. Six of the independent variables were measured dichotomously: incumbency status, major-party affiliation, Democratic party identification, Republican party identification, House candidacy, and Senate candidacy (with the value of one indicating that an individual case had this characteristic).

The competitiveness of the race was derived from ratings presented in the *Cook Political Report* and reported in the *National Journal*. *Cook Political Report* assigns each race a rating assessing the most likely outcome of the campaign: strong Republican, likely Republican, leaning Republican, toss-up, leaning Democrat, likely Democrat, and strong Democrat. Candidates in "strong" and "likely" races were assigned to the "low" competitiveness level; candidates in "leaning" races were assigned to "medium" competitiveness level; and candidates in "toss-up" races were assigned to the "high" competitiveness level. Campaign receipt data, provided by campaigns to the Federal Election Commission, are processed and made publicly available by several public interest groups.[200] The per capita receipts measure indicates the number of dollars received by candidates divided by the population of the district or state. They ranged from zero to $16.56. We did not employ data on the outcomes of the races that were represented in our sample of candidates, since outcomes, obviously, cannot be salient factors in the campaigns' decisions regarding Web practices during a campaign season.

We used traditional ordinary lest squares (OLS) methods to test the explanatory power of the political system and the constituency variables with respect to the campaigns' Web practices. Specifically, we regressed the number of features associated with each practice on our constituency and political system variables with respect to campaigns' Web practices. Table 7.7 presents four regression models explaining the extent to which campaigns engaged in the practices of informing, involving, connecting, and mobilizing during the 2002 electoral year. The political system variables explained only about a fifth of the variance in the practice of informing and even less of the variance in the practices of involving, connecting, or mobilizing. With respect to informing, three factors made statistically significant contributions to explaining its variance. Campaigns in more competitive races and with higher per capita campaign expenditures were more likely, other things being equal, to engage in the practice of informing; candidates running for House seats were less likely to do so. There were

Table 7.7

Impact of Political System Variables on Level of Web Campaigning Practices by Campaign Organizations, 2002

Independent Variable	Web Campaigning Practice Explained by Model			
	Informing	Involving	Connecting	Mobilizing
House Candidate	−0.24*	−0.08	−0.01	−0.04
Senate Candidate	0.08	0.05	0.01	0.19*
Major-party Candidate	0.14	0.09	−0.12	−0.06
Democratic Candidate	−0.10	0.12	−0.02	0.27
Republican Candidate	−0.06	0.11	−0.06	0.24
Incumbent	−0.08	−0.07	−0.13*	0.06
Race Competitiveness	0.17*	0.18*	0.04	0.15*
Per Capita Campaign Expenditures	0.21*	0.17*	0.12*	0.04
Percent Online, State	0.07	0.11*	0.16*	0.01
Percent College-Educated, District	0.01	−0.01	0.10	−0.02
Mean Family Income, District	0.05	−0.06	0.02	−0.04
Constant	2.62	3.34	0.97	0.04
R-Squared	0.22	0.13	0.11	0.09
N	387	411	352	411

Note: Standardized beta coefficients are displayed. * Indicates significant at .05 or higher.

no significant relationships between informing and the major-party status, the incumbent status, the party identification, the percentage of state population online, the mean family income, or the percentage of district residents with a college degree.

In contrast, the model explained only 13 percent of the variance in the practice of involving. As with informing, campaigns in more competitive races and with higher per capita campaign expenditures were more likely, other things being equal, to engage in the practice of involving. In addition, campaigns from states with higher proportions of their populations online were more likely to engage in the practice of involving. There were no significant relationships between involving and the office sought, the major-party status, the incumbent status, the party identification, the mean family income, or the percentage of district residents with a college degree.

With respect to the practice of connecting, our model predicts 11 percent of the variance observed. As in the involving model, the per capita campaign expenditures and the percentage of the state population online were statistically significant factors. Campaigns for incumbent candidates were less likely to engage in the practice of informing, other things being equal. The other political system factors, referenced previously, did not make statistically significant contributions to the model.

Finally, our fourth model, providing an explanation of the variance in the practice of mobilizing, explains only nine percent of the variance. Campaigns in more competitive races, and those involving Senate candidates, were more likely to engage in this practice, other things being equal. The other political system factors did not make statistically significant contributions to the model. In summary, our regression models suggest that political system factors do little to explain the extent to which campaigns engage in the four types of Web campaigning practices under study. Among the nine factors examined, the competitiveness of the race and the campaign expenditures per capita are the most useful factors to explain Web campaigning.

The Web in the Context of Genre

In the preceding sections of this chapter, we have explored the ways in which two types of factors might shape the Web campaigning practices of campaign organizations: those associated with individual Web producers or the professional Web production community, and those associated with the electoral context in which campaigns compete. In this section, we focus on the extent to which Web campaigning practices are influenced by the Web itself and the behavior of other campaign organizations on the Web.

One way in which the Web may influence the Web campaigning practices of campaign organizations is through the pressures of conforming to a genre of Web sites. Such a process of conforming is itself a structuring practice—one that shapes and molds the activities of campaign Web site producers. A genre is "a distinctive type of communicative action, characterized by a socially recognized communicative purpose and common aspects of form," (Orlikowski and Yates 1994, p. 543). A genre in any medium entails a set of genre "markers" that serve as interpretive heuristics for users and benchmarks for producers. Burnett and Marshall (2003) explain that genres develop as a constantly cycling interplay between audience expectation and producer satisfaction of audience expectation. "Genre is neither completely an audience conceptualization nor an industry conceptualization but a constantly developing though relatively stable constellation or pattern that links the audience to the industry" (Burnett and Marshall 2003, p. 90).

Some research on communication practices on the Web has focused on the emergence of distinct and identifiable genres of Web sites (Crowston and Williams 2000; Herring et al. 2005), most commonly in reference to personal home pages or blogs. Dillon and Gushrowski's (2000) survey of user perceptions of personal home pages sought to determine the correlation between personal Web site features, or "elements," and user preferences and expectations of these features when surfing. Their findings support the notion of recognizable and stable sets of site features that hold the elements of genre as seen in other media. Genres exert pressure on would-be producers to conform by employing the pertinent genre markers, and at the same time provide tracks from which to improvise and diverge. Over time, improvisation and divergence can lead to the expansion and evolution of the genre. If, indeed, campaign Web sites as a group had developed to the point where they were a recognizable genre, suggesting the possibility that other political actors, including journalists, activists, and voters had come to recognize certain elements as part of the "common aspects of form," we could explain the presence of some aspects of Web campaigning as conforming to the genre.

As early as 1998, journalistic analysis had detected the aspects of a typical campaign Web site: "Typically, there is a photograph of the candidate, a biography, a list of positions, some news clippings and the usual kind of exaggeration and misrepresentation of their opponents' positions often seen in TV ads" (Booth 1998). The emergence and standardization of the campaign site genre is evidenced by a range of studies demonstrating the increasing prevalence of particular kinds of features and content types on campaign Web sites produced for U.S. House, Senate, and gubernatorial elections between 1996–2002 (Democracy Online Project 1998; Benoit and Benoit 2000; D'Alessio 1997, 2000; Davis 1999; Dulio, Goff, and Thurber 1999; Margolis, Resnick, and Tu 1997; Puopolo 2001; Harpham 1999).

Our analysis of campaign Web sites produced by House, Senate, and gubernatorial candidates in the 2000, 2002, and 2004 campaigns, as well as our review of scholarly and journalistic assessments of the Web in the 1996 and 1998 campaigns, has led us to conclude that a genre of campaign Web sites had emerged by the 1998 election cycle. We also conclude that this genre has steadily evolved in subsequent election cycles, and that the pressures to conform to the genre are shaping the extent to which organizations engage in various Web campaigning practices. Our approach to determining the set of features that can be considered genre markers is to examine a substantial number of sites and identify those features that are found on at least 80 percent of campaign sites examined within a single electoral cycle. While the 80 percent figure is arbitrary, we believe it represents a significant threshold that distinguishes the associated features from those found on fewer sites.

We further classify features as "near genre" if found on at least 60 percent but fewer than 80 percent of the sites examined within a single electoral cycle. We are especially interested in examining the extent to which the presence of near-genre features creates pressure in subsequent campaigns for organizations to adopt similar features, because evidence of this pressure would indicate the emergence of near genre features as genre markers on Web sites deployed in subsequent campaigns.

Table 7.1 presents a compilation of findings from several analyses examining campaign Web sites launched during the election cycles from 1998, 2000, 2002, and 2004. The campaign Web site genre in 1998 and 2000, as practiced and enacted by candidates for House, Senate, or gubernatorial positions, included only features associated with the practice of informing. In 1998, a biographical statement about the candidate was included on 90 percent of campaign Web sites, and statements outlining the candidate's issues positions were found on 88 percent of campaign Web sites. Our data for 2000 indicate that these features were found on 89 percent and 75 percent of Web sites, respectively.[201]

Biographical and issue position statements were the only two features of more than one dozen examined in each of the two electoral cycles to be found on more than 80 percent of the sites in either election. Three features associated with the practice of involving were found on more than 60 percent of the sites in 1998 and 2000, thus indicating near-genre status. The most significant growth was seen in the number of campaign Web sites accepting online contributions, which grew from 19 percent in 1998 to 60 percent in 2000. Similarly, in 1998, more than 70 percent of the sites provided information about donating to the campaign (a comparable figure is not available for 2000). Nearly 70 percent of the sites examined in 2000 included functionality to allow individuals to sign up as campaign volunteers, growing from 55 percent two years earlier. No features associated with the practice of either connecting or mobilizing were found on more than 60 percent of the sites; in fact, fewer than 10 percent of the campaign Web sites included any of the features associated with the practice of mobilizing. Our data do not indicate any shift in the identification of markers for the genre of campaign Web sites from the 1998 to the 2000 campaign. Although the proportion of candidates with Web sites grew from 35 percent, 52 percent, and 75 percent respectively among House, Senate, and gubernatorial candidates in 1998 to 75 percent, 55 percent and 82 percent in 2000 (Howard 2006), there is no evidence that the presence of significant numbers of campaign sites with specific features in the earlier campaign stimulated developments in the genre of campaign Web sites in the later campaign.

By the 2002 and 2004 campaign cycles, the genre of Web sites produced for House, Senate, and gubernatorial campaigns included features associated with the practice of involving as well as the practice of informing. Slightly more than 80 percent of the campaign Web sites examined included information enabling contact with the campaign, specifically an email address, postal address or a telephone number. Unfortunately, there is no data available indicating the proportion of campaign Web sites with these features in 1998 or 2000. We can, however, infer that features associated with the practice of involving would not have hit the threshold for genre markers in 1998 or 2000. Additionally, the proportion of sites providing information about making donations to the campaign increased beyond the 80 percent level, starting with the 2002 election. This provides further evidence that the practice of involving had become part of the genre of campaign Web sites starting in 2002.

Other involving features, such as providing the opportunity to sign up as a campaign volunteer or to receive email from the campaign, were found on between 60 percent and 80 percent of the sites examined, lending further credence to the proposition that the practice of involving had become part of the genre by 2002. One feature associated with the Web campaigning practice of connecting—providing links to external sites—achieved near-genre status in 2002, featured on 76 percent of sites reviewed, a substantial increase from the 1998 measure of 51 percent. However, none of the other features examined that were associated with connecting were even close to near-genre status. With respect to the practice of mobilizing, no more than 10 percent of sites contained such features in either 2002 or 2004.

The overall view of the prevalence of Web campaigning practices on candidate Web sites between 1998 and 2004 lends support to the notion that the genre has expanded beyond the practice of informing to include the practice of involving. We further conclude that these trends indicate an expansion of the genre in the near future to include the practice of connecting, but based on evidence from 1998 to 2004, the practice of mobilizing will remain outside the genre at least through the next electoral cycle.

Another perspective on the influence of the dynamics of the Web environment on Web campaigning practices is based on the notion that campaign organizations react to the behavior of other campaign organizations. They do this by striving for either symmetry (by keeping up with their competitors) or a one-upmanship form of asymmetry (by matching yet staying distinctively ahead of their competitors). Campaign organizations compete in several arenas. Most obviously, of course, campaigns compete in the electoral arena against their opponents. In addition, campaigns compete against other campaigns for scarce resources. In this way, for example, Democratic candidates for U.S. Senate are competing with each other for contributions from individuals and political action committees, as well as for attention from the national media.

Statements from the site producers of two competing campaigns in a 2000 congressional race illustrate this dynamic of symmetry and one-upmanship. The campaign manager for an Independent congressional candidate in 2000 explained:

We want to be able to match what other campaigns are doing, so we consistently monitor their Web sites to see what they have up on the Web ... It's almost a competition with other campaigns. You want to make sure you're matching what they have up on the Web ... and in some cases, maybe we could take the lead on some of those things in putting some of this stuff up.

Although interviewed separately, the Webmaster for the Democratic candidate in the same congressional race in 2000 gave a nearly identical explanation:

Interviewer: Have you ever visited any of [your] opponents' Web sites?

Webmaster: Oh yes, all the time.

Interviewer: Really. And what are you looking for when you go to their sites?

Webmaster: I want to go see how nice it looks, how fast it loads. That was an important consideration for me. I wanted to make sure that the Web site didn't take forever to load over a modem.

Interviewer: You wanted to make sure the [your candidate's] site didn't take so long, so you were comparing, timing the other Web sites.

Webmaster: Yeah. Because I have high-speed access here, I get fed up pretty fast if I'm on a slow modem now. For all I know, people who've never had anything but a 56K modem, that doesn't bother them; that's how they think it should be. But I just didn't want to turn anybody else off by having the Web site be slow. But I look at the other candidates and see how they design their sites. I went and looked at them all before we got this one set up, and while I was working on it to see what kinds of things they had done. I look to see what kind of content they have, whether there are some ideas they have, or features they have that we should be having. I think we all have just about the same. Well, [one opponent], because she's the endorsed candidate, she has a lot of endorsements. She was a member of the [state] House of Representatives, and I think she's been endorsed by that, and she put some of those up. So she has a lot of endorsements. [My candidate] doesn't have so many endorsements, and neither do the other candidates. Most all of them have position papers, biographies, and a brief statement from the candidate. We started putting pictures on ours, just for fun, and to make it look more human and more interesting. [Other campaigns] have lists of events.

Interviewer: Do you have any idea whether people from other campaigns are coming to visit [your candidate's] site?

Webmaster: I don't know.

These two site producers, representing competing campaigns, illustrate the way that symmetry and one-upmanship play out on the Web—and shape campaigns' Web practices.

Our survey of Web producers sheds further light on how the symmetry dynamic works. When campaign site producers were asked how often they visit opponents' sites, only 6 percent of respondents claimed to have never done so. Thirty-six percent reported visiting their opponent's site weekly, 11 percent visited daily, and a handful acknowledged having checked their opponent's site several times a day during the campaign season. The fact that 28 percent of Web producers responded on their Web sites to changes in the content, features, or links on an opponent's site evidences those campaigns' perceived need to be responsive to an opponent's Web strategy.

In summary, the Web context contributes to the shaping of Web campaigning practices to the extent that campaign organizations react to the behavior of other campaign organizations with whom they are competing for votes or resources.

The Structuring Effects of Practice

Just as the pressures of conforming to genre shape practices, the extent to which individual campaigns engage in some practices structures their engagement in others. We formulated these relationships in chapters 3–6 based on qualitative analyses of campaign Web sites and through survey and interview data. We now use site feature data to formalize and test the model we have proposed, postulating the relationships among the four practices as depicted in figure 7.1. To review, we view the practice of informing as a foundational practice to the other three Web campaigning practices. The practices of involving and connecting build on the practice of informing, in separate and distinct ways. In other words, we would not be surprised to see campaigns engage in connecting but not involving, or vice versa. Furthermore, the practice of mobilizing builds on both the practices of involving and connecting.

To test the degree to which our feature analysis data provides additional empirical support for this model, and to determine if it provides a better explanation for the variance observed in the four practices than do the political system variables previously discussed, we present three additional regression models; see table 7.8. Specifically, we add those practices predicted by the theoretical model to the list of independent variables tested in the previous models. This allows us to assess the extent to which the explana-

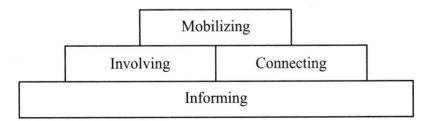

Figure 7.1
Proposed Relationships Between Four Web Campaigning Practices

Table 7.8
Impact of Level of Other Web Campaigning Practices and Political System Variables on Level of Web Campaigning Practices by Campaign Organizations, 2002

Independent Variable	Web Campaigning Practice Explained by Model		
	Involving	Connecting	Mobilizing
Level of Informing Practice	0.32*	0.17*	0.17*
Level of Involving Practice		0.10	0.10
Level of Connecting Practice	0.09		0.19*
House Candidate	−0.02	0.05	0.01
Senate Candidate	0.00	0.01	0.21*
Major-party Candidate	0.06	−0.19	−0.08
Democratic Candidate	0.18	0.04	0.33
Republican Candidate	0.15	−0.03	0.30
Incumbent	−0.09	−0.10	0.08
Race Competitiveness	0.10	−0.02	0.08
Per Capita Campaign Expenditures	0.07	0.08	−0.08
Percent Online, State	0.07	0.14*	−0.08
Percent College-Educated, District	−0.08	0.09	0.00
Mean Family Income, District	−0.01	0.03	−0.09
Constant	2.32	−0.41	−0.36
R-Squared	0.22	0.14	0.21
N	334	334	334

Note: Standardized beta coefficients are displayed. * Indicates significant at .05 or higher.

tory power provided by the level of Web campaigning practices is distinct from that provided by the political system variables.

In all three cases, the level of Web campaigning practices explains more variance than any of the political system variables alone; in fact, it generally supplants those variables in the models. With respect to involving, the amount of variance explained by informing increases to 22 percent from 13 percent. Other things being equal, campaigns with Web sites providing more online structures associated with the practice of informing were more likely to engage in involving. As predicted by the model, the level of connecting does not add to the explanation of the level of involving. Furthermore, none of the three political system factors that were statistically significant—race competitiveness, per capita expenditures, and percentage of state population online—remain so when the level of informing is considered.

Similar, though less dramatic, results were obtained in the model explaining the level of connecting. The level of informing again has a significant and positive effect. As predicted, the level of involving practice does not. Among the political system factors, only the percentage of state population online continues to make a significant contribution; neither incumbency nor per capita campaign expenditures do so.

Finally, adding the level of other Web campaigning practices to our model explaining mobilizing more than doubles the amount of variance explained. Both the level of informing and the level of connecting are positively and significantly associated with the level of mobilizing. Although the level of involving is not statistically significant at the 0.05 level, its coefficient is in the predicated direction, and the significance level observed (0.07) suggests the presence of a relationship. Among the political system variables, only the office sought is still significant.

These regression models support our theory of the interrelationships between the four Web campaigning practices. Our data indicate that informing is foundational to the other practices; campaigns engaging in this practice are more likely to engage in the other three practices. The lack of a relationship between the level of involving and the level of connecting indicates, as predicted, that these are distinct practices that are not dependent on each other. The fact that the level of connecting contributes to explaining the variance in the level of mobilizing supports our theory that mobilizing is a distinct and specialized form of the practice of connecting. The lack of a statistically significant relationship, as it is typically viewed, between the level of involving and the level of mobilizing is more likely to reflect flaws associated with our measures than in our theoretical model. Based on face validity as well as extensive interview and survey data, we maintain that mobilizing builds on involving as much as it builds on connecting.

Shaping Web Practices

In this chapter, we have focused on the factors associated with the tendency of organizations to engage in specific Web campaigning practices and modeled the interrelationships between practices. We conclude this chapter with an integrative discussion of each of the four Web campaigning practices in relationship to sets of factors associated with the following four arenas: Web campaigning practice, Web producers and the professional community in which they operate, the electoral context in which campaign organizations compete, and the Web itself (such as genre and symmetry effects).

The high incidence of informing suggests the presence of both genre and professional norms as significant causal factors. As noted, basic informing features have been found on nearly all campaign Web sites since 1998. Indeed, it is difficult to conceive of a campaign Web site without features such as a candidate biography or issue positions. The ubiquity of these features is itself evidence of the strong pressures to conform to the genre characteristics. Part of this pressure comes from the presence of so many campaign Web sites that include these features. An additional pressure comes from the professional norms of Web producers, which state clearly the importance of basic information to the campaign Web site in the best practices literature.

By contrast, we do not find the characteristics of Web dynamics, operating through the conforming pressures of genre, to be an explanatory factor in the practice of involving. We might expect to see the pressure from other Web sites increase, but we believe that this is more likely to be a result of professional norms and best practices than of genre pressures. Nor do we see evidence in the current data that would suggest that the campaign context provides an explanation for involving as a practice. The relatively low explanatory power provided by political system variables in the explanation of the variance in involving as a practice supports this view. However, this view could change, perhaps as early as the 2006 cycle, based on the experience of the 2004 presidential campaign. To the extent that specific types of candidates view the experience of 2004 as suggestive that their organizations ought to use their Web sites to galvanize supporters— and to the extent that these candidates share a common strategic characteristic such as incumbency status or party type—the electoral context might begin to play a more significant role in shaping the extent to which the Web campaigning practice of involving is engaged.

Our assessments of the final two Web campaigning practices, connecting and mobilizing, share a common theme. We suggest that the best explanation for the relatively low level of either practice, especially when compared to informing and involving, stems from the context in which campaigns as organizations operate. As discussed throughout the book, Web campaigning highlights an inherent tension within a campaign organization between the desire for centralized control and the decentralizing dynamic of Web-based communication. This is particularly evident in the practices of connecting and mobilizing, both of which require a campaign to allow site visitors or users, at a certain level, to have control of key messages or resources. We see little evidence that the best practices literature, which has championed both connecting and mobilizing practices since the run-up to the 2000 campaign, has managed to overcome this strong pressure from the campaign organization. However, as other campaigns—especially the Dean 2004 presidential primary campaign—demonstrate the utility and potential of both connecting and mobilizing in a live electoral context, Web effects associated with symmetry and producer effects associated with award structures and best practices may combine to overcome the organizational drag on these practices.

In addition to campaign context, Web context, and political system factors, we find that the structuring effects of practice are critical to explaining Web campaigning practices. The interrelationships among the levels of engagement in these four practices reveal these structuring effects. The model we have presented (supported empirically by our qualitative analyses of sites, statistical analysis of site feature data, surveys and interviews) demonstrates that informing is a foundational practice to the other three practices and that both involving and connecting are foundational to mobilizing. We anticipate that this model will hold true for the foreseeable future, and that campaign context, Web context, and political systems factors will continue to shape Web campaigning as well. In the concluding chapter we take a look ahead.

8 Web Campaigning: Implications and Trajectory

The Future Observed

On October 15, 2012, three days before the start of the second Presidential debate, the Chief Information Officer for the Republican nominee's campaign was briefed by her Digital Communication Group (DCG). The briefing focused on three core projects the group had launched, with mixed results, in conjunction with the first debate two weeks earlier, and on the modifications that had been made to resolve the most troublesome aspects of the project.

The DCG reported that "Debate Chat" has been thoroughly retooled, in the hope of avoiding further embarrassment to the campaign, that of being associated with a technical meltdown. The programming firm is confident that its adjustments to the code, as well as its tripling of the number of servers, will handle the projected crush of 2.5 million simultaneous participants. (Two weeks ago, the campaign projected one million simultaneous participants, and was mortified when twice that many attempted to log on to the service, overwhelming the system and rendering it inoperable for most of the evening.) The software is designed to funnel users into small groups of ten participants to interact in real-time text chats during the debate; a proposal for video chat was rejected because use-monitoring software was not cost-effective.

Participants are placed into groups based on a complex algorithm accounting for their affiliations, political positions, personal traits, educational and occupational status, and computer experience. A menu of preprogrammed comments and questions is available to the participants to select from based on these demographic data, to reduce keyboard input that participants may find laborious to type (and thereby would slow down the discussion). The goal of the chats is to provide a positive and stimulating experience for participants without exposing them to the unpredictable climate of public chat rooms. All participants have previously registered with the campaign, and most have participated in several events prior to this week's debate. The campaign employs real-time monitoring software scanning the text to identify trouble spots in the chats; 2,500 trained chat moderators are routed to difficult chats to resolve conflicts and remove unruly participants.

The next projects discussed were based on the campaign's controversial and pioneering use of "ClickStick" technology. The ClickStick was invented in 2009 and is now a wildly successful, nearly ubiquitous hand-held wireless device that, among other things, allows individual users to "click" on embedded links (called QClicks) in large-screen video programming and display associated content on personal screens. The DCG's two ClickStick projects—one based on interactive, real-time ratings of the candidates, the other focused on providing additional information to interested debate viewers—were the first political uses of the three-year old technology, and caused considerable consternation among both privacy advocates and deliberative democracy enthusiasts.

The "How's She Doing?" project borrows from the "dial group" concept used in traditional focus group settings. Debate viewers can continuously record their reaction to any of the candidate's statements using a rating wheel on their ClickSticks. ClickStick data from users who participated during the first debate was analyzed immediately and an auto-generated "personalized" message was sent to four million individuals who had identified themselves as potential supporters but who had negative reactions during the debate. The messages addressed the aspects of the debate performance that generated the negative response and invited the recipients to respond. Email responses were received from 150,000 of the recipients of the auto-generated messages. Prior to the debate, the campaign had recruited nearly 10,000 supporters to be members of the "Debate Response Squad," and had developed an algorithm to match the email responders to these volunteers, based on affinity groups, political views, and other factors. The volunteers who crafted follow-up letters were given templates and key information (such as group membership, religion, and geographic region) on each individual to whom they would write. However, the volunteers were able to complete only 100,000 follow-up letters. For the final debate, the campaign has recruited an additional 10,000 volunteers, which the project team expects to able to keep pace with the demand.

The DCG's "Tell Me More" project used the ClickStick and the campaign's own broadcast of the debate to provide interested viewers with a vast amount of additional information during the actual debate. Interested viewers (no reg-istration required) simply tuned into the debate on the national party's channel and used the QClick links embedded into the broadcast as pointers to addi-tional materials. During the course of a ninety-minute debate, nearly seventy-five links are displayed on the party broadcast (by contrast, the Debate Commission feed provided only seven links and the Unified News feed only thirty-two links). There were some missed opportunities, however, as the DCG staff had not been well integrated with the debate preparations team. In an at-tempt to rectify this shortcoming, members of the DCG were invited to ob-serve the full set of preparations for this final debate, and thus to develop a more comprehensive integration plan. The DCG is hoping for an explicit men-tion of their work during the debate and have scripted a line for inclusion into one of the question answers: "But don't just take my word for it. If you're watching on the Republican Channel, you can just QClick on the factcheck.org link on your screen right now and get the facts for yourself." While the DCG is hopeful the message gets delivered correctly by the candidate, they are confi-dent that their QClick link will enable debate viewers to get the information the campaign desires them to have.

The DCG is also preparing to integrate ClickStick responses into a video ar-chive of the debate for posting on the campaign Web site, so that individuals who missed the debate, or want to see how others responded to the debate, can experience the debate later. By examining the ClickStick and Debate Chat responses, the DCG can create a wide array of specific voter personas and then highlight the candidate's points they believe will be most persuasive and rele-vant to different kinds of voters. Through integration of the campaign's data resources—the feedback from the debate viewers through the Debate Chat and ClickSticks—with the campaign's message, the DCG will create a persua-sive record of the debate for undecided voters to access at their convenience.

Summing Up Web Campaigning

In the ten short years between 1994 and 2004, Web campaigning moved from the exotic and exploratory fringes of the electoral arena to its very core. It has moved more quickly and more fully than many would have imagined. In some ways, Web campaigning has become so synonymous with electoral campaigning, its edges so blurred and indistinct, that it is dif-ficult to isolate its impact or even clearly define what, precisely, it consists of. Perhaps this is why some have dismissed the role of the Web in politics as anything but revolutionary.

We disagree. We believe that despite the near-ubiquity of the Web and the consequent blending of the offline with the online, a practice-based approach enables analysts to discern the unique and specific effects of the Web on electoral campaigning and campaign organizations. Based on our analysis, we conclude that the advent of Web campaigning has had profound and significant effects on the electoral arena. In this book, we have attempted to show how and why this has occurred, with a particular emphasis on how organizations have enacted Web campaigning practices.

Clearly, the electoral arena can no longer be considered apart from the electoral Web sphere. The practices of Web campaigning reflect meso-level organizational structures and the macro-level political system. At the same time, these practices spawn a myriad of online structures through which organizational structures and processes, and the political system itself, are being reshaped. As campaigns adopt techniques of Web production in relation to other actors, the electoral Web sphere becomes coproduced, hyperlinked and interwoven with the offline realm. As a result the electoral arena gains an additional dimension, grows more complex, and provides expanded opportunities for political action.

Our primary aim in writing this book has been to provide a historical accounting of campaigns' use of the Web during this ten year period, tracking changes as they emerged in order to uncover the germ cells of profound shifts in campaigning that will become more fully evident over the next decade. In chapters 3–6, we laid out how electoral campaigns employed Web technologies to enact and extend campaign activities during this period. We focused on how the use of the Web manifested challenges and tensions in the campaigning process, resolving some tensions but aggravating others. We analyzed how the techniques of coproduction, linking, and convergence were employed differentially within all four practices. In addition, we identified the techniques of documentation and position taking in correspondence with informing, then went on to consider how transaction relates to involving, association to connecting, and empowerment to mobilizing. In our examination of Web campaigning practices, we found that they were employed with increasing breadth, depth, and technical sophistication across the last three elections. In chapter 7, we analyzed four types of factors that help explain why Web campaigning practices have diffused in particular ways to date. We found that the social-professional context of campaign site producers, political system factors, the context of the Web itself, and the structural nature of practice all shape the extent to which particular campaigns engage in informing, involving, connecting, and mobilizing.

In this final chapter we summarize our findings concerning the relationship between the Web and electoral campaigning, and then address the question of what Web campaigning might look like in the future or under different organizational, political, and technological circumstances. But first we reflect on how the framework of Web sphere analysis, and the practices and techniques we have employed in this study of Web campaigning, may be useful in studies of other Web phenomena and discuss the limitations of our approach.

Reflections on Web Sphere Analysis

Our notion of a Web sphere as a macro-level unit of analysis enables analysts to think theoretically about the Web manifestations of any kind of social, political, and cultural phenomena, and about the types of actors who may be producing Web objects in relation to those phenomena. It can be useful in bounding a study, as well as in conceptually guiding a systematic way of identifying the constitutive sites that are relevant for analysis The Web sphere concept provides researchers with a context for interpreting the Web activity of any set of actors in relation to others, and thus strengthens analyses of Web phenomena. In this study, we chose to focus primarily on campaigns as key actors within electoral Web spheres. Foregrounding a different actor type in a study of electoral Web spheres would undoubtedly yield different insights.

The multimethod framework applied in this study could be useful in studies of other complex, multiactor phenomena that have Web dimensions. Studies using this approach focus on Web observation and incorporate other methods that elicit the perspectives of producers and users of sites within a Web sphere. Web observation methods include a wide range of techniques such as ethnographic approaches and feature and content analysis. Surveys, interviews, and focus groups are among the methods that can be used to interrogate producers and users. Through these methods, Web production practices and the sociopolitical relations these practices mediate among producers, among users, and between producers and users, can be understood more fully.

The concept of Web practices, or acts of making on the Web, corresponds closely with ideas about media production practices that have been investigated broadly in relation to offline media. Any set of Web producers engage in Web practices of some kind, and the Web objects they produce reflect the practices in which they engage. A practice-based approach to studies of Web phenomena grounds such studies in the actual rather than the assumed uses of Web technologies. In illuminating the ways in which Web technologies are employed, the approach makes possible analyses of the underemployment or absence of specific practices that may carry cultural, social, or political significance.

The particular Web practices we have examined—informing, involving, connecting, and mobilizing—are not solely employed by electoral campaigns. This set of practices is used by many kinds of actors involved in persuasive activities. For example, issue advocates employ these practices in political activities that are not necessarily electoral in focus; savvy marketers employ them in promoting goods or services; and government entities employ them to engineer social changes such as healthier lifestyles. Each one of the practices is used individually by an even larger array of actors. A news organization inviting and enabling feedback or commentary from readers on articles on its site engages in involving, whether its motive is stimulating civic engagement or building a customer base. A phone company site enabling customers to recruit friends and relatives as customers is attempting to mobilize via the Web. A health care institution providing online structures for patients suffering from a particular disease to interact with each other is engaging in connecting, in the hope that facilitating the exchange of support between patients will enhance the health of all. The four practices upon which we have focused in regard to Web campaigning could be useful lenses through which to analyze many other kinds of Web activity.

Similarly, the techniques we have analyzed in correspondence with Web campaigning practices are employed in other Web activities and thus may be useful for studies of other kinds of Web phenomena. As we have demonstrated, there are many production techniques that are employed across practices. Coproduction, linking, and convergence are readily observable on and between many kinds of sites. Comparative analyses of the variants of these techniques across domains of activity or different Web spheres could be enlightening. For example, patterns of relations between types of actors such as political parties and civic organizations could be analyzed through a comparison of the coproduction technique, both in the context of an electoral Web sphere and in the aftermath of a natural disaster such as Hurricane Katrina in 2005.

Although our practice-based approach to the study of Web campaigning has proved fruitful in many ways, there are limitations and drawbacks to this approach in general and to the particular way we have implemented it in this study. In general, a focus on practices as evidenced primarily in their manifestations in Web objects makes it difficult to analyze offline campaign strategies, organizational dynamics, and the roots and impacts of individual leadership or cultures of innovation within campaigns, much less examine the ways site visitors make sense of online structures. The survey, interview, and focus group data we collected from campaign site producers and visitors were helpful in this regard. However, there are some questions that would only be answerable through in-depth participant observation research within campaign organizations over time.

More specifically, as we stated in chapter 1, the particular practices on which we have focused in this book do not cover the full spectrum of Web practices in which campaigns engage. For instance, the rhetorical dimensions of persuasion, while implicit in each of the four practices we analyzed, were not directly addressed by any of them. Similarly, the production techniques we have examined, though diverse, were by no means exhaustive of those employed by campaigns. Although we chose not to analyze visual or aesthetic production techniques, analysts with different areas of expertise than we have might focus on those techniques or others that are also salient to understanding Web campaigning.

Finally, every data set is shaped by the theoretical and methodological lenses through which the data are collected, as well as by the constraints of available time and financial resources and technical limitations. Although we amassed a substantial data corpus, there are other kinds of data that are also relevant to understanding campaigns as sociotechnical networks but were beyond our scope. We focused on the use of the Web by campaigns, but campaigns' use of email also deserves in-depth analysis. We concentrated on the production practices underlying what campaigns have done on the publicly accessible Web. However, analysts looking under the hood of some campaigns' Web productions at the code and databases would undoubtedly find other ways that linking, coproduction, convergence, and other techniques were employed. For example, online structures for involving on the public Web are often undergirded by databases built, maintained, and shared among campaigns within a party and across elections (Howard 2006). Other kinds of questions about digital, networked technologies, and campaigning remain to be explored, and these will require other kinds of data than those collected for this study.

Web Impacts

In spite of the limitations previously outlined, we believe that our analysis points towards a wide range of significant impacts of Web campaigning on electoral and political processes. Most broadly, the emergence of the Web and the expansion of Web campaigning have fundamentally altered the ways in which campaigns are organized and the ways in which campaign organizations perceive themselves and their roles. Similarly, the tendency of campaigns to engage in Web campaigning has coincided with significant shifts in the ways that citizens and other political actors perceive themselves, and their roles, in the political process. It has also changed the ways that citizens are perceived by campaigns. We contend that politics on the Web has proven to be anything but "politics as usual," as Margolis and Resnick (2000) suggested in their seminal work carrying that title, based on the 1996 and 1998 elections. Despite the irony of their subtitle, "The Cyberspace 'Revolution,'" we suggest that revolution—connoting a dramatic and far-reaching change in the organization or conceptualization of a phenomenon—might be just the word to describe the implications of the practices we have documented and analyzed in this book.

Campaign organizations have clearly been upended by the introduction of Web and other information technology, and information technology specialists, into their milieu. Howard (2006) identified four types of political power wielded by campaign Web site producers and other IT staff: (1) the power to define and extend an organization; (2) the power to filter, destroy, or protect information for the campaign organization; (3) the power to synchronize and network individuals who share a concern about a specific issue; and (4) the power to cause organizational deadlock, including, at times, the power of veto if minor project goals come into conflict with policy that has been openly declared on the Web site. As Howard explains,

The code they [campaign IT staff] write, the material schema that take shape as they make hardware and software decisions, give their political organization an important performative power. Especially when it comes to Web site design, code reveals and conceals features of the organization to the outside world, enabling candidates or political parties to show different aspects of their ideologies to different people (p. 168–169).

To the extent that the presence of the Web and other information and communication technologies in the campaign organization contributes to the shift of power from one set of individuals to another, we can say that the Web has changed the power structure and organizational culture within campaigns. In just the few years since the turn of the twenty-first century, the archetypal campaign Webmaster has morphed from the candidate's nephew who is tangential to the campaign, to a key strategic player in the upper hierarchy of the campaign management team.

Perhaps the most foundational change to campaigning, evoked by the widespread adoption of the Internet in American life, has been that most candidates have come to recognize the Web as a realm in which they must have a presence to be credible. In 2000, even some citizens who did not own computers themselves commented in a focus group that candidates for federal office who did not have Web sites were "out of touch." One said, only half jokingly, "I'd wonder if [a candidate without a Web site] had indoor/outdoor plumbing." Campaign site producers were aware of this dynamic; one noted "The Web site brought [our] campaign a huge dose of credibility." As Max Fose, McCain's Webmaster in 2000, predicted, "[The campaign Web site] is definitely here to stay, not only as a fundraising tool, but also as an organizational tool and as an informational tool." Another campaign Webmaster noted the importance of an early Web presence, saying if he could redo the campaign he "would have launched [the site] earlier in the campaign—possibly even pre-campaign." Several expressed regret over not having created online structures for involving, such as features for online contributions and volunteer sign-up. A couple wished they had better facilitated offline distribution by "making parts of the site 'printer friendly.'" Other features campaign producers wished they had used included better navigation, links to opponents' sites, more issues information, a calendar of upcoming events, and "a specific email option asking people if they were voting for me, another asking if not, why?"

One window into the impact of the Web on campaigning is through campaign site producers' regrets, or, put another way, their reflections on what they wish they had done differently. Many site producers in 2002 indicated that they saw potential in Web technologies that remained untapped by the campaigns on which they worked. This was summed up by one producer's comment that "not enough attention was paid to what the site could do for the campaign." Several wished they had promoted the campaign site more extensively, both online and in offline media. Such Webmasters' statements as "It was incredibly underutilized. The campaign was oblivious to the potential and never gave it enough consideration," and, "This year, we showed the campaign what the Internet is capable of. Hopefully, the Web will be more prominent in the 2004 election season," indicate the ferment within campaigns over how best to employ Web technologies.

Reflecting on broader issues about Web production within the context of general campaign activity, several producers wished they had updated the site more frequently, and one commented that, given another chance, "[I would have] kept campaign workers abreast of [Web site] developments." In a more extended reflection, a campaign Webmaster explained lessons he learned the hard way:

I would have actually had a budget for more than just the cost of the Web hosting. I would have looked for more ways to engage people. It's a simple (if not easy) matter of increasing our "market share," and of offering the "story" of my candidate and the "story" of our opponent in a far more compelling manner. I would have done more task analysis of what visitors would want to accomplish on the site, and improved the ease with which they could do those tasks. A bit of usability testing would have been a boon, as well.

The regrets noted by respondents to our survey indicate the ways in which Web campaigning will evolve in future elections.

Along with regrets, campaign site producers identified many benefits that the Web had provided them. A first-time candidate (and first-time site producer) indicated, "the Web site allowed us to look professional." "The Web is giving 'poor' campaigns a chance," one Webmaster said. Another noted, "Our campaign was a low-budget, all-volunteer, grassroots campaign. Having very little money for other advertising, we relied heavily on the Internet to spread the word across the state." Beyond campaign sites, the Internet provides ample material for opposition research. As one campaign Webmaster explained: "[The Web is an] EXCELLENT resource. We researched the Internet and came up with eight hundred pages of information on my opponent, which was then used to influence voters. For instance ... he says he is anti-ACLU, yet accepted donations from the ACLU." Others mentioned the extended reach that the Web provided their campaigns (both among their constituency and beyond), the speed of information dissemination, and the cost efficiency it afforded.

Webmasters, especially from several third-party campaigns, commented that the Web had some leveling influence on the political playing field. In this vein of response, one characterized the Web as an "easier method of distributing info. Slight leveler of the field for third-party candidates who can't afford traditional advertising [sic]." Another provided a more expansive assessment: "[The Web is a] real boon to minor-party and independent candidates who typically can't afford TV ads. We can publish tons of info about our candidates and issues at a very low cost. People can view our info when/where they want and then make truly informed decisions. If used appropriately and fully, the Internet could revolutionize the election process!" Other comments on ways the Web affected campaigning, and thus the political system as a whole, included the following:

The Internet allowed me to effectively get my message out to the media for little cost. The Internet makes it easier to compete against corrupt establishment candidates, and [the Web provides] much needed opening to honest dialogue. A breakthrough in the absolute control money has on our political dialogue.

Third-party candidates are indeed much more visible in the electoral Web sphere than in broadcast media. Like major-party candidates, most third-party candidates adopt the basic genre of campaign sites, providing biographical and issue stance information that is relatively comparable to that offered by major-party candidates.

As an information environment, the Web has affected the functioning and organization of campaigns and the process of campaigning. It does this by extending the duration of the campaign, regularizing the flow of information over time and across audiences, and altering the traditional timetable of various kinds of campaign communication. Several campaign Webmasters reported feeling pressure to have had a campaign site posted as soon as the candidacy was official, and they regretted not having generated more detailed issue information before the site was launched. Although in 2000 most campaign sites went dark immediately after the election, by 2004 many candidates kept their sites online weeks and even months after the election, a phenomenon we discuss more thoroughly later. The need to maintain the campaign's Web presence influenced other communication strategies, as one site producer explained: "[Having a campaign site] affected the timing of many decisions and releases of information, because we often didn't want to 'go public' with something until we were ready to launch it on the Web simultaneously." The more strategically a campaign views its site, the more it attempts to coordinate Web production with other aspects of campaign communication.

In addition to impacting the way campaign organizations communicate with outside individuals and groups, internal communication processes have been affected as well. Unsurprisingly, the impact of the Web on intra-campaign organizing has been mixed. Some small campaigns have not attempted to use the Internet for internal communication because face-to-face interaction has sufficed. However, many larger campaigns have experimented with employing it as an organizational tool. One Webmaster expressed disappointment with the ways Internet technologies were employed organizationally in his campaign: "We attempted a 'distributed office' model of campaign organization relying heavily on telecommuting. It didn't work very well. Face-to-face contact must not be underestimated, and failing that, voice-to-voice. It is not possible to persuade people via e-mail. Next time, we'll have a storefront office." Another reflected on a painful lesson learned in this regard:

[Internet technologies] can help plan and involve people, but only if everyone using them has the same goal. Lack of communication within campaigns on online campaigns can cause less than desirable results, which tends to dishearten people who know what can be done with online campaigns if used properly.

Unsurprisingly, these comments demonstrate that the process of technology adoption in intra-campaign communication is rife with challenges.

However, many other campaign site producers cited significant benefits to the use of Internet technologies for intra-campaign organizing. "Technology was an important factor in keeping volunteers informed of campaign activities," reported one Webmaster. "The campaign was entirely run by busy volunteers, so 90 percent of communication was by email," commented another. The Webmaster of a campaign that developed a database of contacts explained, "the centralized database made it possible for multiple staffers to manage contact information. [It] allowed greater decentralization of tasks, and better utilization of volunteers." Campaigns that successfully migrate internal communication to the Web reap the benefits of greater efficiency.

Just as the organizations that manage and produce political campaigns have changed as the Web has grown in significance, the number of those who use the Web for political information, and their expectations and perceptions, have evolved as well, particularly during electoral cycles (Institute for Politics, Democracy, and the Internet 2004). Web use creates different, and in some ways, higher expectations on the part of users than do other media. As campaigns become aware of this dynamic, they feel compelled to increase the resources they invest in Web production far beyond the posting of a basic HTML page.

Campaigns strive to respond to at least three kinds of user expectations. First, users expect substantive content on a campaign site, not sound bites. As a Webmaster explained, "Unlike mail which can be thrown away, people come to a Web page expecting something, so it was important not to have fluff, but real information content." Second, visitors that take action on campaign sites expect some kind of appropriate response. If they sign up for email from the campaign, they expect confirmation of the subscription; if they make an online donation, they expect an immediate receipt. The mechanisms necessary for managing even these basic types of transactions require greater programming skills than does the provision of information in HTML. Third, Web users' expectations regarding transparency and the flow of information also affect campaigns' investment in Web production. Although it is common knowledge that campaigns produce different messages for different audiences in offline media, such as advertisements for particular television markets, Web users expect to see a unified, coherent message on a campaign site. Taken together, these expectations can be summed up in a site producer's observation that "[the Web] is engendering an increased expectation for a responsive political process."

A responsive Web campaign strategy also builds what we termed in chapter 4 a transactional relationship between campaigns and site visitors. Transactional relationships, which are at the core of the practice of involving, are predicated on the credibility and trustworthiness of a candidate (and thus a campaign) and a willingness on the part of supportive site visitors to become involved, remain involved and, in the ideal scenario from a campaign's perspective, retain a relationship with the candidate, whether that candidate wins or loses. The carefulness by which staff members of a Republican congressional campaign in 2000 sought to preserve site visitors' trust in their candidate exemplifies a growing number of campaigns' efforts to foster strong transactional relationships:

We've been very proactive not to sell, trade, or distribute our email lists to any outside parties, even though they may be affiliated with our campaign, like Republican groups. We made sure not to distribute that stuff because we don't want people to get our email addresses. We don't want people to feel like they can't trust [our candidate].

However, this kind of careful attention to the boundaries of the transactional relationship between campaigns and site visitors was unusual in the earliest incarnations of campaign Web sites, many of which did not even include privacy policies, as we demonstrated in chapter 4.

The Electronic Privacy Information Clearinghouse reports that "online users have strong reservations about the use and abuse of the personal information." They go on to note, however, that, to date, many Web users have naively assumed that the mere presence of any privacy policy on a Web site ensured that the site producer would not share a user's personal information with others (Hoofnagle 2005). As more Web users grow increasingly concerned about the spread of their personal information, the absence of a campaign site privacy policy, or the presence of a policy that offers weak or ambiguous protection to users, may become a significant detriment to campaign's efforts to involve and mobilize site visitors.

In view of these expectations, the resources required to actively maintain a campaign's Web presence have increased significantly, especially for those campaigns with extensive online structures or multiple sites. Monitoring and managing what is happening elsewhere on the Web regarding the campaign requires further effort. Rogers (2002) borrows the naval term "managing the bubble" to describe how various actors on the Web engage in Web surveillance and rapid response in order to have strategic engagement in that realm. Voters' assumption that serious candidates will have a Web presence has increased some campaigns' opportunities and workload, and, at the same time, created anxiety. Fears revolve primarily around the need to produce accurate and appropriate content for the site, the possibility of alienating prospective voters, and the requirement of contending with hackers.

Most campaigns are aware that they must find ways to promote their site in order to draw traffic. One Webmaster observed that "people must be enticed to visit a Web page and once there they must find a reason to stay." As John Birrenbach, Web consultant and site producer for several campaigns, explained, "Putting up a Web site is much like putting up a store. Unless you put a sign out front, and turn on the open sign, do some advertising, and tell people where you are, nobody comes" (Birrenbach 2000). Many campaigns used print brochures and radio and television ads to promote their sites; one characterized the site as "the central communication hub for the campaign" and pointed to it in every message the campaign put out in offline media. Still, campaigns wished they had attracted more visitors to their sites. One Webmaster reflected: "[Our campaign's use of the Internet was] not as effective as hoped. We tried very hard to drive voters to our Web site, but only with limited success. It can be an effective tool, but you must still be able to reach voters with traditional methods. A Web site is an excellent addition to effective campaigning, but not a substitute for other proven methods."

As the Web has become more of an integral part of campaigning in the United States, campaign Web sites have coalesced around a distinct genre with identifiable and regular patterns. This tendency introduces new dynamics into the broader campaign information environment. As we demonstrated in chapter 7, the campaign site genre includes the provision of basic biographical information along with issue positions. Thus, previously variable and dynamic aspects of campaigns are regularized substantively and temporally through the process of being rendered online. For voters with access to the Internet, this means that the familiar information flow of campaigns, characterized by a dynamic stream of paid political advertising and stories about the campaign appearing in news media, is now supplemented by an easily accessible stock of basic candidate information. One campaign site producer welcomed this change, saying, "I hope that [the Web] is opening up campaigning to all sorts of issues that the conventional news does not wish to cover, such as the war on drugs, mandatory minimums, fully informed juries, third-party candidates, alternate forms of taxation, different methods of solving the Social Security mess. The major parties try to limit the debate to what they want to focus on, but hopefully the Internet will make them take a stand on all issues." The emergence of the campaign site genre creates an environment in which it is more noticeable if a candidate, such as an incumbent, does not provide such issue content.

This regularized form of basic campaign information presentation on the Web has also altered the traditional pattern by which campaign messages evolve over the course of an election season. In 2000, as noted previously, Lynn Reed articulated conventional wisdom about the timing of various kinds of campaign communication. She viewed the campaign site as fitting into that progression:

The [campaign site] has a communications role and that communications role changes throughout the life of the campaign. In the early life of the campaign, when the general public really isn't paying attention, it's about communicating with activists and communicating with the press. So our first communications task was to prove that this was a legitimate campaign. Is it possible to pose a legitimate challenge to the sitting vice president? So the Web site had to play that role (and we can come back and get into the specifics of all of this). In the latter part of the campaign, when it's actually the time when people are voting, hopefully, if you have done your work right, it is a place for undecided voters to go, who are trying to learn more information about the candidates and make up their minds. (Reed 2000)

However, as the campaign activity on the Web extends in both directions—beginning earlier and lasting longer—this pattern of phasic communication is changing. Whereas the traditional development of campaign messages tends to move from simple recognition and introductory messages (like the familiar biographical advertisements that appear early in a campaign) toward strategic issue-related appeals later on, the genre of Web campaigning is forcing candidates to make some aspects of all of these types of communication available at all times during the campaign. Thus, the agenda-setting effects created by strategic timing of paid advertising and other communications are diluted by Web campaigning. Webmasters' comments illustrate this: "[The Web] allows voters to obtain unfiltered, unedited information. It provides an extension of the campaign that heretofore wasn't available. It gives easy access to much more information than has traditionally been available," and "More information is available to the public [on the Web] and [it] allows many more voices to be heard." Such comments reflect the perspectives of many campaign site producers regarding the changing information environment.

We will highlight one final impact of the Web on campaigning. Web technologies allow candidates to develop digital resources that can be migrated across elections, allowing what we call a "continuous campaign" to emerge. This is visible, at its most basic level, in the maintenance of a Web presence from election to election. The plan one Webmaster sketched for an ongoing Web presence illustrates this Web-enabled shift in campaigning: "For the next two years (my candidate did not win), I would like to post comparisons between the incumbent's voting record, and how my candidate would have voted on the same issues. I think it will be a powerful voice for the next campaign."

Continuous campaign Web sites vary with respect to the Web practices they employ and the attempts they make to be tied closely to their original purposes. Some former candidates use their campaign sites post-election to continue advancing issue positions. The Web site produced for John Kerry's 2004 presidential campaign (www.johnkerry.com) began life promoting his 2002 Senate campaign,[202] and it continued at least a year after the presidential election, acting as a vehicle to advance Kerry's agenda and, perhaps, to point toward a future presidential or Senatorial campaign. In its October 2005 incarnation, the Web site offered few of the involving or connecting features—and none of the mobilizing features—that were prominent during the campaign.[203]

In October 2005, the organization, Friends of John Kerry, Inc., made extensive use of email as a mobilization tool, but offered little else on their Web site. In contrast, one of Kerry's rivals for the 2004 Democratic nomination, Dennis Kucinich, engaged in the practices of involving and mobilizing through his Web site through October 2005, using the same www.kucinich.us URL as was used during the 2004 campaign.[204] Interestingly, the Re-elect Congressman Kucinich Committee framed the Web site as a vehicle to both promote Kucinich's national agenda and serve his re-election campaign. In fact, browsers directed to the URL www.kucinichforcongress.us resolved to the same page as did browsers directed to www.kucinich.us.[205]

Other ex-candidates from 2004 continued to use their campaign domains to maintain a Web presence in anticipation of a future campaign. For example, both Lois Herr (D-PA-16)[206] and John Russell (D-FL-5),[207] who lost bids for seats in the U.S. House in 2004 and announced their intention to run again for the same seats more than a year prior to the 2006 elections, not only maintained the same URL but also the same underlying site design and site content. The fact that many candidates do not embed an election year, state name, or office sought in their campaign domain names indicates a strategic understanding of the importance of a continuous URL. Conversely, campaign URLs that are year-, state-, or office-specific mark candidates who lacked a long-term strategic view of the Web, such as

Joe Lieberman (www.joe2004.com), Barack Obama (www.obamaforillinois
.com), or Jay Dickey (www.jaydickeyforcongress.com).

The phenomenon of continuous campaigning involves a deeper set of
practices than just maintaining a Web presence after election day, however. We suggest that the Web has enabled the expansion of the permanent
campaign beyond the sense of constantly seeking public support for both
policy and electoral initiatives (Blumenthal 1980; Medvic and Dulio 2004)
to encompass the creation and maintenance of a dedicated infrastructure to
accomplish these and other goals. The infrastructure enables the organization to engage in the same practices that its electoral incarnation had established, and to build on the databases cataloging transactional relationships
previously established with voters, supporters, contributors, journalists, and
other political actors. The Web-enabled campaign is continuous with respect to a blurring of boundaries, easing distinctions between the offline
and the online, and between producers and users. We turn our attention
next to the future of continuous campaigning and other aspects of Web
campaigning.

Looking Ahead

Back in the spring of 2000, an Arizona state senate candidate asked Max
Fose, McCain's presidential campaign Web producer, whether his campaign needed a Web site. Even after running the McCain campaign's Web
presence, Fose admitted to having never thought about whether a state
senate candidate should have a Web site. He replied:

The obvious answer is yes. I said, "Yes, and here's why … if you get a hundred
people on your email list and you send them something, maybe not daily because
you don't have enough to say, but maybe send them something weekly. Then when
you ask them to do something, they're going to be there because they're going to be
a part of your campaign" (Fose 2000).

Between the general elections of 2000 and 2004, this dynamic became obvious to most if not all campaigns. Having assessed the impacts to date of
the Web on campaigning, we now look ahead.

Based on the developments we have observed in 2000 through 2004, and
on current trends in technology innovation and use, we anticipate significant changes in Web campaigning over the next few elections. We expect
that the act of producing a basic campaign Web site will be nearly ubiqui-

tous among candidates for elected office, raising the baseline of political information available to online citizens. Most practices are fairly enduring, and will evolve gradually over time. However, we expect that Web production techniques, which emerge with and evolve alongside new technologies, will change rapidly and dramatically, and thus, will reshape each of the practices of Web campaigning.

In the coming election cycles, the techniques used by campaigns to engage in the practice of informing can be expected to change modestly. We expect the technique of documentation to play an increasingly significant role, and the techniques of convergence and coproduction, as associated with informing, to become more mature and developed. In addition, we expect new techniques to emerge in relation to technologies that enable information provision through a wide variety of interfaces other than Web browsers, for instance, via highly mobile and wireless devices other than computers. Correspondingly, Internet access via wireless portable devices is a very different kind of user experience. For these reasons, the 2004 U.S. election may well be remembered as the endgame of the first generation of Web campaigning.

Online structures supporting documentation will be increasingly cross-referenced to support assertions, positions, and data presented by campaign organizations. The information provided will be deeper, broader, and more ambitiously indexed, allowing campaign site visitors to obtain biographical and issue information customized to the level of detail desired. The key informational objects produced by campaigns will continue their spread from the Web to the streets and neighborhoods of the candidate's constituency via portable devices carried by canvassers and volunteers, and will be distributed on demand in both paper and digital form.

As a response to the challenge of producing greater quantities of information that is fresh and interesting (created partially by increased demand for new and relevant content from site visitors), campaigns will increasingly coproduce information with other actors that share their agenda through syndication and other means. Campaigns will begin informing earlier in the electoral season, and continue long after the election, contributing to the phenomenon of continuous campaigning. Contributing to this development will be the increasing tendency to record or archive the content of Web sites by journalists, political opponents, advocacy groups, and even ordinary citizens, which will establish a sense of permanency for campaign Web materials. Some campaigns will respond by providing comprehensive access to biographies and issue position statements for longer periods of time, perhaps even providing permanent and sustained archives of key documents, as they seek to control their own history.

In view of a campaign's increasing need to manage the collection and dissemination of informational resources, we expect to see significant sections of campaign information environments accessible only to registered users. This will increase the proportion of campaign Web presence that is private—accessible only to supporters or members. Different levels of access to the campaign's Web presence will be based on a visitor's contributions and volunteer activities. This will also enable campaigns to engage in greater segmentation of the audience and more refined targeting of their messages and informational resources. As Howard (2006) argues, "The new forms of campaign organization, and the new technologies, are deliberately designed to alter the structure of political communication in the United States by privileging narrowcasting tools and strategies over mass communication tools and strategies" (p. 171).

More significant and perhaps more dramatic development can be expected in the ways and extent to which campaigns engage in the practices of involving and connecting. With respect to involving, we anticipate greater convergence between the online and offline worlds and a much more extensive use of transaction-based online structures. Campaigns will increasingly use calendaring features and reservation systems to attract audiences and crowds to significant events. Location-aware technology, such as GPS-enabled cell phones, will be used by campaign organizations to assemble small groups of highly committed supporters on short notice at events sponsored by other actors, such as state fairs, sporting events, political rallies, and the like. Campaigns will increasingly manage citizen involvement and view the relationship through a transactional lens. Campaigns will develop rewards and incentives for individuals to provide credentials, through a user ID and password, to access more and more of their Web sites and information environments. For example, features that track visitor interactions will emerge, similar to online structures on e-commerce sites, suggesting additional activities based on profiles of similar involved citizens. In sum, the campaign's Web site will increasingly be seen as the primary mechanism through which individuals interested in being involved with the campaign will negotiate and manage their involvement with the campaign organization.

With respect to connecting, we expect increased linking to other political actors and the extensive development of structures to facilitate quasi-independent interactions among political supporters. Fewer campaign Web sites will be constructed on the cul-de-sac model that assumed providing links to other actors was the way to lose the attention of site visitors. Instead, the campaigns will cede more control over the messages to which visitors may be exposed when they follow links to sites produced by other actors. Position papers and supporting documents produced by other political actors, including advocacy groups, parties and journalists, will be routinely linked, if only to provide credibility in a culture that rhetorically demands and technically insists on citations and footnotes. More broadly, campaigns will increasingly position themselves as traffic circles, carefully steering visitors to the sites of carefully selected actors, and increasingly seeking to control messages through techniques like framing and syndication. Campaigns will also dramatically expand their use of social network software like Meetup.com's to organize and interconnect citizens by geography, identity, and affinity into volunteer-to-volunteer networks (Ayres 2004).

Of all the practices we have described, we anticipate mobilizing will develop furthest in the coming election cycles. The emphasis on mobilizing activities, especially relative to informing and involving, will increase dramatically, as campaign organizations develop online structures using the techniques of convergence, coproduction, and empowerment. In some aspects, campaigns will deepen the commitment of involved citizens and more effectively turn them into advocates. Campaigns are becoming increasingly aware that they need to not only post a Web site, but also manage their Web presence as it is mediated across the electoral Web sphere on sites that they do not and cannot control. This will result in more coproduction of online structures. Following the approach employed by the Kerry site producers and a few others in 2004, site visitors will be encouraged to go to other sites with the purpose of promoting the candidate. It will be increasingly strategic for campaigns to foster multivoiced dialogue about candidates, on their own sites as well as on others' sites. The dispatching of campaign site visitors to other Web sites to promote the candidate stimulates coproduction of the campaign's Web presence and of the electoral Web sphere.

Refining the use of social networking software to move beyond providing connections between like-minded supporters will allow campaigns to facilitate interaction between advocates and undecided voters. Undecided voters will be identified and characterized through polling and database mining; this data will then be integrated with similar data about campaign advocates, who will be given specific mobilization tasks. Social network software will facilitate both online and offline interactions. Campaigns will also expand their capabilities to support coproduction of materials by providing templates, graphics, audio, video, and text to individuals interested in creating Web sites, pages, documents, and multimedia presentations for both online and offline distribution. The growth of what we have termed e-paraphernalia from a relatively modest effort into a significant and robust set of tools will equip advocates with a set of underlying resources, the implementation of which will take greater advantage of the heretofore untapped hardware and software capacity available in the homes and offices of supporters. Campaigns will use these techniques to enhance not only the work of individual supporters, but to integrate their message and materials with those of civic and advocacy groups that support their candidacy. The ease of movement of digital resources will increase cross-campaign fertilization among candidates from the same party seeking both the same office from different constituencies and different offices from overlapping constituencies. This activity may presage a new and expanded role for political parties as information brokers.

We anticipate that these developments in and across all four Web practices will reshape the campaign organization by redistributing power within the organization. Decentralization of some kinds of labor will be facilitated by increased centralization in digital infrastructure. The increasingly viral nature of politics as it is practiced on the Web also indicates decentralization and a redistribution of power, both within the electoral arena and the campaign organization. The potential for relative seamlessness within a distributed campaign organization, exemplified by Dean's 2004 campaign, reflects viral politics and indicates extensive coproduction between organizations. Finally, we anticipate that campaigns will face increased accountability from the public as their Web objects and emails are more permanently inscribed through ubiquitous archiving and indexing techniques.

The Value of Practice

Over the last ten years, campaign organizations have adapted traditional practices and developed new techniques integrating the Internet—especially the Web—into their ways of being and methods of doing. We have sought to capture and analyze the shifts in their practices, including the factors that are responsible for these shifts, as they are evidenced in the Web artifacts created by campaign organizations. We suggest that an understanding of these processes can be found in a close, systematic examination of the relationships between these artifacts and the sociotechnical networks within which they were produced. As Web campaigning practices evolve over time, the reciprocal relationship between these practices and the structures of the campaign organization and the electoral arena becomes more evident. While the influence of existing structures on Web campaigning practices is clear, as seen in the political system factors examined in chapter 7, the influence of evolving Web practices on organizational and political structures must also be taken into account.

In chapter 1, we defined Web campaigning as those activities with political objectives that are manifested in, inscribed on, and enabled through the Web. Our definition was intended to focus our analysis on how and why campaign organizations created specific online structures as they sought to enact and extend campaign activities. We found that concerns about control underlie many of the Web production decisions campaigns make, and that the evolving norms of campaign Web production shaped the choices made by individual campaign site producers. We also found that political system factors tended to be of less value in explaining Web campaigning practices than the structuring effects of practice on practice. These findings highlight the importance of focusing on Web campaigning as a set of practices. As a campaign Web site producer told us in 2002, "It ultimately matters less what the tools are and more how effectively and creatively the tools are used. Can we excite our visitors? Can we engage their hearts? Can we shake them out of their apathy enough to stand up and be counted?" Web campaigning restructures the practice of politics and, in so doing, reshapes our democratic practice.

Appendix

METHODS

Overview

As noted in Chapter 2, Web sphere analysis is a multimethod approach involving contemporaneous and retrospective interrogation of Web objects and interactions with Web producers and Web users. The analysis presented in this book is based on data collected using this approach. This Appendix describes the specific data collection and analysis activities by which we generated the findings for this book. Separate sections of the Appendix present methodological details of our demarcation of electoral Web spheres, campaign site analyses, user focus groups, user survey, site producer interviews, and site producer survey.

Electoral Web Sphere Demarcation

Our analysis of campaign Web sites in the 2000, 2002, and 2004 elections required the demarcation of an electoral Web sphere for each election to identify Web sites that were to be included. We used the campaign sites identified as constituents of the Web sphere as a universe from which samples of sites to be analyzed could be selected. Identifying the producers of this sample of campaign sites then served as the basis for recruiting respondents to our producer interviews and survey. In addition, the sample of sites served as stimulus materials to share with users during our focus groups. To illustrate the process we followed to demarcate the 2000, 2002, and 2004 electoral Web spheres in the United States, we provide below a description of the specific processes we followed to demarcate the 2002 general federal election Web sphere. Although our processes were not as formally implemented in 2000, and were slightly different in 2004, the 2002 process is also a useful illustration because an extensive archive of the multiple impressions of the full collection of sites identified is publicly available as the "Election 2002 Web Archive" at the U.S. Library of Congress.[208] It should be noted that our processes for demarcating the 2002 electoral Web sphere were shaped by our collaboration with the Library of Congress in building the archive, and thus became, in part, a task of operationalizing the collection policy statement developed in conjunction with the Library (Schneider 2004).

Systematic identification of sites within the 2002 election Web sphere took place between July 1, 2002 and election day 2002, and was guided by a definition of the Web sphere with the topical focus of elections for U.S. House, Senate, and gubernatorial seats. To facilitate consistent identification of sites across the research team, we developed a sleuthing guide for all research team members to use. The guide provided search strategies and definitions of six Web producer types: candidate, civic or advocacy group, citizen, government, political party, and press. Sites produced by candidates were identified using a Web-based search strategy for candidates in the races under analysis: 436 House races (including the Delegate race in the District of Columbia), thirty-seven gubernatorial elections, and thirty-four campaigns for the U.S. Senate. Using a variety of Web-accessible databases, including those from local secretary of state offices as well as commercial and nonprofit databases produced by the *National Journal*, the *Washington Post*, and politics1.com, individual candidates in each race were identified, and, for those with Web sites, URLs were identified and reviewed. A candidate Web site was identified on the basis of two characteristics: (1) being clearly focused on advancing a particular candidate for a specific office, and (2) not identified as being produced by any organization other than one controlled by the candidate. In this way, Web sites produced by political parties or advocacy groups, for example, even though advancing specific candidates for office, were not included as candidate Web sites. This process proved to be cumbersome and somewhat unwieldy, as new candidate sites were launched throughout the campaign period, candidates changed URLs during the campaign, new candidates emerged during the campaign, various sources identified different sites as associated with individual candidates, some candidates maintained multiple URLs and some candidates sought multiple offices simultaneously. By November 2002, a total of 1,550 URLs had been identified as candidate Web sites.

Identification of sites produced by citizens with content related to the 2002 election was handled very differently. We focused on identifying citizen blog sites, which were then rapidly emerging as the dominant form of citizen site for election-related content. Our identification process involved submitting queries to the Google search engine with a candidate name, state, office sought, and the word *blog*, for example "FL Governor Bush blog" or "GA Senate Cleland blog." A total of 1,552 queries were submitted; up to one hundred returned URLs were collected for each of the queries, yielding 84,587 total links distributed across 3,381 unique URLs. These URLs were then filtered to include only those with the text blog, resulting in a list of 1,449 URLs. We then ranked this list of URLs based on the number of Google queries returned, and selected the one hundred sites that, collectively, accounted for the most queries. Our analysis suggests that the returned links were concentrated in relatively few blog sites. Ranked by the number of links, the first twenty-five sites included 26 percent of the links. Including the top one hundred of the identified blog sites encompassed 49 percent of the links identified by Google to our 1,552 queries.

Other sites in the Web sphere included those produced by press organizations, civic and advocacy groups, and government entities. The set of press sites included in the Web sphere was defined as the Web sites produced by the one hundred largest newspapers (ranked by circulation) in the United States., as well as the largest newspaper (by circulation) in each state capital. In addition, the Web sites produced by produced by national broadcast and cable television networks were included. A total of 163 press sites were included in the Web sphere. Civic and advocacy groups were identified from a variety of sources, including the Washington Information Directory, organizations identified as financial contributors registered by the Federal Election commission, and directories of national- and state-level nonprofit organizations with election or voting emphasis. A total of 663 organizations were identified. Government sites included in the electoral Web sphere included those produced by the U.S. House, U.S. Senate, the Federal Election Commission, state and territorial central government sites, and the sites produced by election boards or secretaries of state for each state and territory. A total of eighty-nine government sites were identified.

Campaign Web Site Analyses

We used the universe of campaign Web sites identified as constituent elements of the 2000, 2002, and 2004 electoral Web spheres to generate samples of sites for feature analysis. During the 2000 campaign, we helped coordinate a research team at the University of Pennsylvania's Annenberg Public Policy Center. The team developed, through a grounded theory process, a set of coding rules for interrogating campaign Web sites to identify the presence of salient features. We examined more than seven hundred election-related sites between July 2000 and November 2000, and an additional one hundred sites following the election. Our process was informed by the set of best practices described by the Democracy Online Project (1999) as we incorporated suggested features into our coding protocols. Our process yielded a set of campaign Web site features; trained undergraduate and graduate student coders spent between five and ten minutes on candidate Web sites identifying the presence or noting the absence of each of these features.

Based on this work, in 2002 we developed comprehensive templates of campaign Web site features and a structured sampling process to examine campaign Web sites produced by candidates seeking election that year. Operational definitions of the features we evaluated on campaign sites are provided in table A.1. A group of undergraduate and graduate students were trained as coders through a rigorous process designed to ensure intercoder reliability. All coders participated in training workshops and coded a shared set of 10 campaign Web sites, selected for the variety of features provided. The level of agreement between coders on each measure, based on our coder training exercises, is also reported in table A.1.

During the months of August, September, and October, we analyzed a distinct sample of 325 to 425 candidate sites each week, stratified to include a representative sample of candidates from major parties and third parties in races of varying levels of race competitiveness. Our measure of race competitiveness was based on ratings provided by the *Cook's Political Report*, as published by the *National Journal*. Samples were selected to ensure that all candidate sites were evaluated at least once during each month's evaluation cycle. Our population of Web sites was defined as the "party candidacies" in each race, where *party candidacies* refer to all of the candidates from one of the two major parties, or from third parties. This technique allowed us to maintain a flexible sample throughout the primary season, since specific candidates could be removed from the sample without altering the representation of a particular party candidacy. We stratified our sampling to overrepresent those Web sites associated with the most competitive races. Each week, our trained coders analyzed sampled candidate Web sites using the templates developed for this project. Each template included measures of the presence or absence of specific features and/or types of information on campaign sites. Each of the sites in the weekly sample was evaluated with one standard coding template and one of four rotating coding templates. We evaluated a total of 1,045 Web sites between August 1 and October 31, 2002. Coders were instructed to examine the first and second levels of pages linked from the front page for evidence of the item, then to follow links to access the item itself.

For 2004, we report a set of data obtained from a random sample of 119 campaign Web sites, selected from among the universe of campaign Web sites identified by Project Vote Smart[209] examined as part of a larger study of features on Web sites within 2004 general federal election. In the 2004 study, the presence or absence of a subset of the features measured in 2002 was coded by trained site evaluators, using similar procedures employed for the 2002 study. Coders were instructed to examine the first and second levels of pages linked from the front page for evidence of the item, then to follow links to access the item itself. Systematic coding of the sample of identified sites for features and types of information took place during a period of two weeks ending three days prior to the election.

In each election year, coders used the WebArchivist Resource Coder, which enabled distributed, Web-based coding and coordination of resources to be coded. The WebArchivist Resource Coder was introduced in training sessions, and employed in intercoder reliability coding and coding of sites for generating project data.

Data from 1998 was drawn from several studies conducted by other scholars (Democracy Online Project 1999; Kamarck 1999; Harpham 1999). These earlier studies did not use strictly comparable measures, and in some cases clear operational definitions of features examined were not available. In addition, the studies were conducted with various methodological considerations and levels of precision—some, for example, reported inter-rater reliability scores, while others did not. In addition, these studies necessarily identified a subset of all possible features available on campaign Web sites.

Table A.1
Operational Definitions and Percent Agreement Scores for Web Features Analyzed on U.S. Campaign Web Sites, 2002–2004

Practice	Feature	Operational Definition	2002		2004	
			N	% Agreement	N	% Agreement
Informing	Biography	The personal/political history of the candidate	1,045	91%	119	100%
	Issue Positions	Discusses the candidate's assessment of what issues are relevant for the race and/or the candidate's goals pertaining to those issues	1,045	85%	119	80%
	Campaign News	Section containing news on the campaign progress	589	85%		
	Position Substantiation	Presence of rationale in the description of candidate's position on first two issues	815	82%		
	Speech Texts	Text of candidate speeches	589	90%	119	90%
	Campaign Ads	Online reproduction ads distributed also on TV, radio, press, or other offline media	589	90%		
Connecting	Link to Any Other Site	Links to Web pages other than those clearly sponsored or produced by the campaign organization	826	87%		
	Party Affiliation	A succinct, visible reference to the candidate's party, such as a logo, label or slogan.	1,044	82%		
	Endorsements	Section dedicated to listing the names and positions of those who have endorsed the candidate	589	89%	119	70%
	Link to Government Site	A link to any site produced by a U.S., state or local government entity.	822	87%		

Link to Party Site	A link to any business, organization, or service affiliated with a local community	822	92%		
Voter Registration	Feature that allows visitors to start the process of voter registration	1,044	85%	119	100%
Link to Civic/Advocacy Group Site	A direct link to any civic, advocacy, interest, or ideological group: Civic groups include national and state level non-profit organizations with a civic, voting, or election emphasis. Advocacy and interest groups include national and state level cause-oriented groups that may have a legislative/policy agenda. Ideological groups include those that represent themselves as 'conservative,' 'liberal,' 'progressive,' etc.	817	87%		
Link to Press Site	A link to any newspaper, news program, or magazine (e.g., any organization that produces news content and delivers it online); does not include portal sites that just deliver news (e.g., msn.com, yahoo.com).	825	87%		
Position Alignments	Presence of statement aligning issue position to a named individual or group on first two issue positions.	815	86%		
Position Comparison to Opponent	Presence of statement distinguishing issue position from opponent on first two issue positions.	815	94%		
Link to Local Site	A link to any business, organization, or service affiliated with a local community.	830	85%		
Position Comparison to Other	Presence of statement distinguishing issue position from position of other named individual or group on first two issue positions.	815	86%		

Table A.1
(continued)

Practice	Feature	Operational Definition	2002		2004	
			N	% Agreement	N	% Agreement
	Link to Portal Site	A link to any general interest (e.g. yahoo.com, msn.com) or special interest portal.	830	89%		
	Comparison Section	Presence of section distinct from issues section in which candidate directly compares him/herself to opponent.	818	86%	119	80%
	Link to Citizen Site	A link to any Web site produced by a citizen working as an individual; that is, not as an employee of an organization.	828	93%		
	Link to Opponent Site	A link explicitly identified as an opponent's site.	831	99%		
Involving	Donation Information	Instructions or system for making offline or online contributions.	1,044	85%	119	100%
	Contact Information other than email	Telephone number or address of the campaign.	589	87%	119	100%
	Email Address	Email address of the campaign.	1,045	87%	119	100%
	Volunteer Sign-up	Feature that provides visitors with the information and/or tools they need register as a volunteer for the campaign.	1,044	84%	119	90%
	Email List Sign-up	Feature that allows visitors to subscribe to the campaign listserv.	1,044	91%	119	80%
	Photos of Campaign Events	Photographs of campaign events available online.	589	85%		

	Campaign Calendar	Allows visitors to locate upcoming events on the candidate's schedule.	1,044	84%	119	80%
	Visitor Comments	Feature that allows visitors both to contribute their own comments and view those sent in by others.	865	98%	119	90%
	Online Polls	Feature that allows visitors to respond to a closed-ended question by selecting from among options presented on the Web page.	865	99%		
	Online Events	Live event Webcast over the site, or an archive of such an event.	865	97%		
Mobilizing	Offline Distribution of Materials	Materials available for printing and offline distribution.	589	95%	119	80%
	Send Links	Feature that allows visitors to send a link about the campaign site, via email, to a friend.	865	95%	119	80%
	Electronic Paraphernalia	Electronic, downloadable campaign items such as campaign buttons, bumper stickers, etc.	865	93%	119	100%
	Send Letters to Editors	Feature on the site to help visitors draft or send letters to send to local newspapers.	939	96%	119	90%

Nevertheless, we believe that as a general indicator of trends in campaign Web site features over the six year period in question, this data compilation provides the richest and most robust reading that is available. Furthermore, given the lack of adequate archives for analysis of campaign Web sites from 1998, it is unlikely that future research will yield better estimates of the practices exhibited in the earliest years of Web campaigning.[210]

Focus Groups

All of the citizen focus group findings we report in this study were generated from a series of thirteen focus groups with U.S. citizens in New Hampshire in January, 2000, two weeks prior to the presidential primary elections. This series of focus groups was conducted in collaboration with three research assistants; we worked in two teams in order to conduct all of the focus groups within a four-day span. We recruited participants for the focus groups a few weeks in advance by tapping social networks of one of the researchers. Thirteen people of various ages residing in towns across central and southern New Hampshire agreed to host a focus group in their home. Employing a snowball sampling method, we asked each host to invite four to six additional people (for a total of seventy-eight participants) to spend two hours viewing and discussing election-oriented Web sites and the role of the Internet in the political process. While viewing campaign sites, citizens were asked to talk about what they saw, what they liked and disliked, and what they thought was missing or what they expected to see on the campaign sites.

Using a laptop computer, access to an Internet service provider, an LCD projector, and a portable screen, each group was shown at least two presidential campaign sites, one from each major party. Participants in the focus groups were directed to the home page of a campaign site, and then asked to comment and reflect on what they saw. They were then encouraged to navigate the Web site collectively, discussing the site as they explored it. An assistant moderator took detailed notes on each group discussion, and the focus groups were videotaped. The audio tracks of the videotapes were fully transcribed, indexed, and coded thematically in correspondence with the specific Web pages under discussion. Aided by qualitative data analysis software, we made comparisons between every instance of focus group talk that pertained to the concepts we investigated, noting how prevalent the expressed perceptions were both within each focus group and across groups, as well as the discursive aspects of the interaction.

By conducting focus groups in homes, we were able to participate in, as well as observe, the real-world experiences of citizens exploring election-oriented Web sites in preparation for the 2000 presidential primary. Although we employed a standardized agenda of discussion-starting questions in each group, we sought to cultivate an informal atmosphere in order to facilitate dialogue between participants in the groups regarding the Web sites, rather than simply between the moderator and individual participants. Fieldnotes taken by members of the research team after each focus group added insights to the dynamics of the discussion.

We wanted the focus groups to be composed of people covering a wide spectrum of ages and having varying levels of experience with the technology and with politics. Because we were seeking to elicit a range of citizens' impressions of campaign Web sites and their perceptions of the sites' interactive potential, we were interested to learn what people with little experience online think as well as those who are regular users. People unfamiliar with the technology may be more observant of the features of the medium than those who use it routinely, or they may bring a different set of observations than routine users. Similarly, those who do not look at political sites may bring perspectives to the discussion overlooked by regular political Web users but illuminating to researchers.

At the time of this focus group study, age tended to correspond with Internet use, with younger people being more likely to use the Internet than older people in 2000 (Pew Internet and American Life, 2001). In order for the focus group participants to reflect the full range of Internet experience levels characteristic of the U.S. population at the time of this study, our priority in recruiting participants was to have a well-distributed range of ages. The ages of the focus group participants ranged from eighteen to eighty-one across the groups, with an average of forty-three (SD = 18), and the groups were composed of slightly more women than men (57 percent female, 43 percent men).

Our participants were similar to the general U.S. population in overall Web use. Twenty-two percent of our participants never or rarely went on-line. Similar to findings by the Pew Center for the People and the Press

(1998), a majority of our participants (58 percent) rarely or never went online to get news and information on current events, public issues, or politics. Similarly, 82 percent reported never going online to communicate with other people through forums such as newsgroups, discussion lists, or chat groups. In the discussions we had with our participants, very few reported having visited a campaign Web site. Most suggested in the conversations that they did not realize that the candidates had Web sites. The fact that some of our participants had little or no experience with the Internet, and many had never visited political Web sites, helped stimulate robust discussion within the focus groups, which is the goal of this method of data generation (Kitzinger and Barbour 1999).

Our participants were wealthier and better educated than the New Hampshire population. All participants were Caucasian (the general population of New Hampshire is 95 percent Caucasian). Fifty-three percent of our participants reported earning $50,000 or more a year, while the median household income in New Hampshire is $42,000. Seventy-two percent of the participants reported having a bachelor's degree or a professional degree, while only 14 percent of New Hampshire's population had a college degree, according to the U.S. Census 2000. Eight percent of the participants reported having no more than a high school education. The group was also more Republican than the general New Hampshire population. Over three-fourths reported being active in religious, labor, social, or political organizations in their communities. In a follow-up survey after their primary elections, the vast majority (86 percent) reported having voted in the primary—a rate higher than national or state averages. It is possible that participation in these focus groups increased motivation to vote in the primary. For more findings from this focus group series, see Stromer-Galley and Foot (2002).

Web User Survey

Our Web user survey data was generated from a panel of Internet users created by the Wharton School at the University of Pennsylvania in the autumn of 2000. Panel respondents were asked to describe questions concerning their use of the Internet for political purposes, their reasons for getting news and information about politics from the Web, and their interest in a subset of the features for which we were measuring prevalence in our contemporaneous campaign Web site analysis. Panel respondents were recruited through banner ads with attempts made to recruit from sites that would generate a demographically representative sample. The survey was administered twice during the 2000 election season, and the same respondents were asked to answer the survey both times. Response rates were higher the second time (73%, N = 850) than the first time (56%, N = 651). As a result, statistics provided in the analysis are generated from the second survey. The first survey ran from October 7 through October 14, 2000. The second survey ran from October 28 through November 5, 2000.

Although all efforts were made, there were still disproportionate representations of specific groups. On the whole, our survey sample had more women, more white participants, was more highly educated, and younger than the general population (p < .0005) than the U.S. Census and the General Social Survey indicates. Perhaps the most significant difference was in gender. While women composed approximately 51.2 percent of the U.S. population, they made up 69.4 percent of the participants in our survey. With regard to race, whites were overrepresented, and blacks underrepresented; 92.4 percent of participants were white, compared to 82.4 percent in the population at large, and only 2.5 percent were black, compared to 12.8 percent in the general population. Our survey participants when compared to the results of the General Social Survey were less likely to have stopped their education at or before high school (15.0 percent versus 45.8 percent for the population at large) and more like to have some college or a Bachelor's degree (69.6 percent versus 40.9 percent). Finally, our survey respondents were younger than the population as compared to the results from the General Social Survey. Their mean age, 37.2, was approximately seven years below the mean age of 44.3 recorded in the General Social Survey in 1994. Because of these marked differences between our sample and the population, generalization to the population may not be possible. The Pew Center for the People and the Press's surveys of Internet users in 2000 suggests that the Internet population was beginning to look like the population in the United States. When controlling for socioeconomic factors, there was no longer a gender gap. The Internet population, however, remained slightly younger, whiter, and better educated than the general population.

Producer Interviews

To better understand the process of producing a campaign Web presence, we conducted eleven in-depth interviews with a total of thirteen campaign site producers during the autumn of 2000 with the help of three research assistants. Most interviews were held in person; some were conducted over the telephone. All interviews were audio-recorded with the permission of the interviewees, and all recordings were fully transcribed.

After the 2000 presidential primary season ended, we interviewed site producers from the defeated Republican and Democratic campaigns. Due to time constraints and strategic concerns on the part of the presidential campaigns during the general election season, it was not possible to interview anyone from the Bush or Gore campaigns during the autumn of 2000. To identify other prospective campaigns for interviews, we first selected several congressional districts in different regions of the country in which there were competitive races, and in which at least two candidates had campaign sites with an email address for the campaign. If there were competitive Senate races in the same states with campaign sites, we contacted those campaigns as well.

Our initial contact with each campaign was via email, using whatever address the campaign site provided. We explained our research interests and requested an interview with whomever was responsible for the campaign Web site. The campaigns that responded decided internally who should talk with us. Most of the interviewees were Webmasters; some were campaign managers responsible for Web strategy. In two instances, at the initiative of the campaigns, we interviewed the campaign manager and the Webmaster together. Those interviewed represented a wide range of experience in producing campaign Web sites, from low-budget third-party House campaigns to presidential primary contenders.

The interviews were semistructured. All of the interviewers employed a common interview agenda with a prioritized list of questions, but were encouraged to probe interesting responses more deeply. Question topics included the organizational position and prior experience of the interviewee, the role of the campaign's Web presence in the campaign's overall strategy, specific aspects of the campaign's Web presence including its linking strategy and its online structures for involving and mobilizing. Each interview concluded with questions about the interviewee's goals, concerns, fears, and doubts about Web campaigning, and about whether and how the Internet impacts the electoral process.

Producer Survey

Based in part on findings from our interviews during the 2000 elections, we collaborated with two other researchers in the autumn of 2002 to develop a Web survey for campaign site producers. The survey contained 100 questions; most were structured as multiple-choice or select-any-format and a few were open-ended. Question topics included demographics, previous political and Web production experience, the use of Web technology in internal campaign communication, organizational aspects of Web production within the campaign, goals and anticipated users of the campaign's main site, and attitudes toward technology and politics.

After categorizing each campaign site based on our observational data, as either noninvolving (that is, not having any features associated with the practices of involving or mobililizing), involving only, or involving and mobilizing, we collected the email addresses of the campaigns in each category from their sites. We created three identical installations of the survey, each accessible via a different URL. The invitation emailed to each campaign contained one of the three survey URLs, corresponding with the category of that campaign's site. We could thereby correlate the survey responses with the Web production patterns we had observed while protecting the identity of the campaign responders. We had decided to wait until a few days after the election in November 2002 to issue the survey invitation, in the hope that campaigns would be more likely to respond after the campaign had ended. Three days after the election we emailed the initial survey invitations to the email addresses associated with 1001 campaign sites: ninety-nine sites categorized as non-involving, 740 categorized as involving only, and 162 sites categorized as involving and mobilizing. A week later we sent a reminder invitation. A significant number of invitations did not reach the intended recipients, due to errors in the email addresses posted on campaign sites and to the fact that some campaign organizations cancelled their campaign email accounts within two days after the election. The response was proportional across the three categories. A total of ninety-three recipients, approximately 10 percent from each category, completed the survey.

Notes

A Note on Sources

In this book, we reference archived copies of Web pages wherever possible. When referencing an archived page, we identify the archive holding a copy of the page, the original URL, and the date the page was archived. We reference pages from two publicly accessible archives:

• The 2002 Election Web Archive, U.S. Library of Congress. This collection of materials from the 2002 U.S. elections includes daily captures of House, Senate and Gubernatorial candidate Web sites from July through November of 2002. The collection can be accessed via the Web at http://lcweb2.loc.gov/cocoon/minerva/html/elec2002/elec2002-about.html (accessed 02/27/2006). Pages from this collection include (LC2002) in the reference.

• The Wayback Machine, Internet Archive (IA). This general collection of more than 50 billion Web pages includes materials from elections since 1996. The collection can be accessed via the Web at http://web.archive.org (accessed 02/27/2006). Pages from this collection include (IA) in the reference.

Some pages referenced are from our personal collection of pages gathered between 2000 and 2006. Pages from this collection include (PC) in the reference.

1. http://www.pbs.org/newshour/vote2004/debates/vpdebate/part3.html, archived 10/09/2004 (IA).

2. http://www.factcheck.org/article272.html, archived 10/14/2004 (IA).

3. http://www.georgesoros.com, archived 10/12/2004 (IA).

4. http://blog.lextext.com/blog/_archives/2004/10/6/155847.html, archived 02/26/2005 (PC).

5. http://www.debates.org/pages/trans2004b.html, archived 02/26/2005 (PC).

6. http://www.whitehouse.gov/news/releases/2004/10/20041006.html, archived 02/26/2005 (PC).

7. http://www.bufordforcongress.com/, archived 11/03/2004 (PC).

8. http://www.stanley2002.org/Rickscauses.htm, archived 11/01/2002 (LC2002).

9. http://www.stanley2002.org/midocs.htm, archived 11/01/2002 (LC2002).

10. http://www.stanley2002.org/national.htm, archived 11/01/2002 (LC2002).

11. http://www.stricklandforcolorado.com/pageinpage/ontheissues.cfm, archived 11/02/2002 (LC2002).
http://www.allardforsenate.com/aboutAllard.html#, archived 11/01/2002 (LC2002).

12. http://www.stanley2002.org/lpnews12_19_01.htm, archived 10/04/2002 (LC2002).

13. http://www.stanley2002.org/endorsements.htm, archived 11/01/2002 (LC2002).
http://www.stanley2002.org/letters.htm, archived 11/01/2002 (LC2002).

14. http://www.stanley2002.org/, archived 11/01/2002 (LC2002).
http://www.purepolitics.com/rickstanleysenco.htm, archived 01/11/2003 (IA).

15. http://www.saxby.org/media/speech/default.asp, archived 11/01/2002 (LC2002).
http://www.johnkerry.com/site/PageServer, archived 09/22/2002 (LC2002).

16. http://jaydickey2002.com/, archived 11/01/2002 (LC2002).
http://www.tomharkin.com/features/tv-ads.cfm., archived 11/01/2002 (LC2002).

17. http://www.dougose.com/press.htm, archived 11/01/2002 (LC2002).
http://www.colemanforsenate.com/index.asp?Type=B_PR&SEC={D11D264B-868F-45EA-99BD-DA0ED0B62CE9}, archived 10/07/2002 (LC2002).

18. http://www.dawnbly.com/, archived 11/01/2002 (LC2002).

19. http://www.scottmcinnis.com/, archived 11/01/2002 (LC2002).
http://www.captainorin.com/biography.htm, archived 11/01/2002 (LC2002).

20. http://www.wilhoit410gov.com/bio.html, archived 11/01/2002 (LC2002).

21. http://www.flattaxamendment.org/longprof.html, archived 10/01/2002 (LC2002).
http://www.stan2002.com/plan.html, archived 11/01/2002 (LC2002).
http://www.feeley2002.com/issues.asp, archived 11/01/2002 (LC2002).

22. A copy of this page is archived in "Election '96: The Online Campaign Web Archive," a collection of the Internet Archive. http://ftp.archive.org/96_Elections/forbes2/forbes96.htm, accessed 06/01/2005.

23. http://www.statonforcongress.org/default2.htm, archived 08/30/2002 (LC2002).
http://herndon2.sdrdc.com/cgi-bin/dcdev/forms/C00369926/33217/sa/ALL, archived 08/30/2002 (LC2002).
http://www.peopleforplatts.com/, archived 11/01/2002 (LC2002).

http://herndon1.sdrdc.com/cgi-bin/fecimg/?H0PA19053., archived 11/01/2002
(LC2002).

24. http://www.colemanforsenate.com/index.asp?Type=B_BASIC&SEC={8CFD7A12
-E5D3-4DFD-8464-063BBABAA941}, archived 10/04/2002 (LC2002).

25. http://www.bebout4governor.com/other_images/r&e.pdf, archived 10/31/2002
(IA).

26. http://www.bebout4governor.com/other_images/FinanceReport4.pdf, archived
10/31/2002 (IA).

27. http://www.tancredo.org/, archived 07/01/2002 (LC2002).
http://www.tancredo.org/supporters/supporters.htm, archived 07/01/2002 (LC2002).
http://www.tancredo.org/, archived 11/05/2002 (LC2002).

28. http://www.chandlerforcongress.com/, archived 11/01/2002 (LC2002).

29. http://www.voteforgood.com/, archived 11/01/2002 (LC2002).

30. http://www.feeley2002.com/issues.asp, archived 11/01/2002 (LC2002).

31. http://www.beauprezforcongress.com/textonly/issues.htm, archived 11/01/2002
(LC2002).

32. http://www.voteforgood.com/, archived 11/01/2002 (LC2002).

33. http://www.feeley2002.com/index.asp; 11/01/2002 (LC2002).
http://www.beauprezfacts.com/, archived 11/01/2002 (LC2002).

34. http://www.elizabethdole.org/multimedia.asp, archived 10/30/2002 (LC2002).

35. http://www.gopatgo2000.org/radio_ads.asp, archived 11/12/2000 (IA).

36. http://www.gwu.edu/%7Eaction/2004/parties/iafairbooths.html, 02/01/2006
(PC).
http://www.gwu.edu/%7Eaction/2004/parties/mnbooths0904.html, archived 02/01/
2006 (PC).

37. http://www.andyhorning.org/, archived 11/01/2002 (LC2002).
http://members.aol.com/higginslp/index.html?mtbrand=AOL_US, archived 11/01/
2002 (LC2002).

38. http://www.schiff4congress.com/, archived 11/01/2002 (LC2002).
http://www.house.gov/schiff/, archived 11/01/2002 (LC2002).
http://www.peopleforplatts.com/, archived 11/01/2002 (LC2002).
http://www.house.gov/platts/, archived 10/14/2002 (IA).

39. http://www.johngraham4congress.com/background.html, archived 11/01/2002
(LC2002).
http://web.gsm.uci.edu/~jgraham/, archived 11/01/2002 (LC2002).

40. http://www.feeley2002.com/index.asp, archived 11/01/2002 (LC2002). http://www.beauprezfacts.com/, archived 11/01/2002 (LC2002).

41. http://www.stan2002.com/voterinfo.html, archived 10/31/2002 (LC2002). http://www.tomharkin.com/voting-info/index.cfm., archived 11/01/2002 (LC2002).

42. http://www.sneary.com/press_.html, archived 08/18/2000 (IA). http://www.allardforsenate.com/, archived 11/01/2002 (LC2002).

43. http://www.schiff4congress.com, archived 11/01/2002 (LC2002). http://www.schiff4congress.com/news/as_latimes_102902.htm, archived 11/01/2002 (LC2002).

44. http://www.secstate.wa.gov/elections/voterguides/?u=2004Primary, archived 06/20/2005 (PC).

45. http://www.miriamforcongress.com/, 11/01/2002 (LC2002).

46. For example, the 2002 campaigns of Ralph Hall (D-TX-4) and Sandy Thomas (Lib-GA-Senate) requested that access to their sites be restricted in the Library of Congress 2002 Election Web Archive. See http://lcweb4.loc.gov/elect2002/catalog/1857.html, accessed 06/01/2005 and http://lcweb4.loc.gov/elect2002/catalog/1934.html, accessed 06/01/2005.

47. http://www.edpastor.com/, archived 11/02/2002 (LC2002).

48. http://www.johngraham4congress.com/youcanhelp.html, archived 09/01/2002 (LC2002).

49. http://www.joe2004.com/site/PageServer?pagename=getin_mojoe, archived 01/19/04 (PC).

50. http://www.joe2004.com/site/PageServer?pagename=state_AZ, archived 01/19/04 (PC).

51. http://www.joe2004.com, archived 1/19/04 (PC).

52. http://www.joe2004.com/site/PageServer?pagename=targeted_dogsforjoe, archived 01/19/04 (PC).

53. http://www.joe2004.com/site/PhotoAlbumUser?view=UserAlbum&AlbumID=5925, archived 02/11/2004 (IA).

54. http://community-2.webtv.net/@HH!F9!75!85F6E32C97A2/zone_0/GEORGENLYNE/, archived 09/01/2002 (LC2002).

55. http://www.votemarkgreen.com/, archived 09/01/2002 (LC2002).

56. http://www.theron.net/umphress/contact.htm, archived 09/01/2002 (LC2002).

57. http://www.brianbaird.com/send/index.html, archived 11/01/2002 (LC2002).

58. http://www.johngraham4congress.com/youcanhelp.htm, archived 11/01/2002 (LC2002).

59. http://www.mccotterforcongress.com/McCotter-The%20Band.pdf, archived 11/03/2004 (PC).

60. http://home.attbi.com/~jgs3d/, archived 09/01/2002 (LC2002).

61. http://www.jimnussle.com/nussle/wrapper.jsp?PID=4086-681, archived 02/20/2006 (PC).

62. http://www.dickgephardt2004.com/plugin/template/gephardt/Volunteer/*, archived 01/19/2004 (PC).

63. http://www.mccotter2002.com/volunteer.asp, archived 09/01/2002 (LC2002).

64. http://www.mccotterforcongress.com/volunteen.asp 06/30/2005 (PC).

65. http://www.marybono.com/Privacy.cfm, archived 11/01/2002 (LC2002).

66. http://www.tomharkin.com/privacy/index.cfm, archived 11/01/2002 (LC2002).

67. http://www.larrycraig.com/priv.cfm, archived 09/30/2002 (LC2002).

68. http://www.georgewbush.com/, archived 10/06/1999 (IA).
http://www.georgewbush.com/Volunteer/volunteer.html, archived 10/11/1999 (IA).
http://www.georgewbush.com/Volunteer/volunteer.html, archived 05/08/1999 (IA).

69. http://www.georgewbush.com/disclaimer/privacy.html, archived 11/28/1999 (IA).

70. http://www.georgewbush.com/Privacy.asp, archived 10/01/2000 (IA).

71. http://www.georgewbush.com/Privacy.htm, archived 06/06/2003 (IA).

72. http://www.georgewbush.com/PrivacyPolicy.aspx, archived 10/08/2003 (IA).

73. http://www.georgewbush.com/PrivacyPolicy.aspx, archived 06/22/2004 (IA).

74. http://carolforpresident.com/content.php?page=schedule, archived 01/19/2004 (PC).
http://carolforpresident.com/content.php?page=kit, archived 01/19/2004 (PC).

75. http://www.meetup.com/about/, archived 03/12/2005 (IA).

76. http://press.meetup.com/watch/archives/000696.html, archived 03/29/2005 (IA).

77. http://clark04.com/meetup/, archived 02/02/2004 (IA).
http://wesleyclark.meetup.com/, archived 04/12/2004 (IA).

78. http://www.tancredo.org/helping_tom.htm, archived 12/14/2000 (IA).
http://www.mapquest.com/cgi-bin/ia_find?link=btwn/twn-map_results&event=find_

search&SNVData=njij9-qw7;vdduvj&7cl56,cjtsc(u,f7c3m(0,c2j%7cx0672u.3rs;_
wd672u.q8k8)c2j&7cx0472u.q8k8)cw8%7c.h472u6,3iqcme5%7c;rom6(.gv2js
-$kdq(.xif1m88;,hxggm-eqej;xmwjs8$bcjsol@klqr(0,rxhqje;libbdf$5s34l9
-&country=United+States&address=609+w+littleton+blvd,+Suite+200&city=
Littleton&State=CO&Zip=80121&Find+Map=Get+Map, archived 12/14/2000 (IA).

79. http://mccain2000.com, archived 10/07/1999 (IA).
http://www.mccaininteractive.com/, archived 11/28/1999 (IA).

80. See http://politicalweb.info/2004/2004.html, archived 06/28/2005 (PC).

81. http://www.leadingwithintegrity.com/involved/index.htm, archived 12/04/2003
(IA).

82. http://www.tancredo.org/, archived 10/09/2000 (IA).
http://www.tancredo.org/helping_tom.htm, archived 08/16/2000 (IA).
http://www.tancredo.org, archived 11/01/2002 (LC2002).
http://www.tancredo.org/volunteer/volunteer.htm, archived 11/01/2002 (LC2002).

83. http://www.tancredo.org/index.html, archived 03/06/2005 (IA).
http://www.tancredo.org/info/volunteer.html, archived 03/06/2005 (IA).

84. http://www.udall2002.com/, archived 09/17/2002 (IA).

85. http://www.votesoph.com/, archived 11/01/2002 (LC2002).

86. http://deanforamerica.com, archived 01/27/2004 (PC).

87. http://www.deanforamerica.com/, archived 02/08/2004 (IA).

88. http://www.richardromeroforcongress.com/, archived 09/26/2004 (IA).

89. http://www.charleslaws.org/, archived 10/31/2002 (IA).

90. http://www.bonnieb2000.org/weblog/blogger.html, archived 01/25/2001 (IA).

91. http://blog.deanforamerica.com/archives/000396.html, archived 10/11/2003
(IA).

92. http://www.dickgephardt2004.com/plugin/template/gephardt/Volunteer/*,
archived 01/19/2004 (PC).

93. http://www.boehlert.com/content.cfm?id=27, archived 02/01/06 (PC).

94. http://www.johnkerry.com/, archived 07/01/2005 (PC).

95. http://bonnieb2000.com/releases/0830.html, archived 02/17/2001 (IA).

96. http://bonnieb2000.com/weblog/blogger.html, archived 01/26/2001 (IA).

97. http://bonnieb2000.com/soundoff.html, archived 02/02/2001 (IA).

98. http://www.bonnieb2000.org/links.html, archived 01/25/2001 (IA).

99. http://www.bonnieb2000.org/cyber.html, archived 01/25/2001 (IA).

100. http://www.raytricomo.org/endorsements.php, archived 11/01/2002 (LC2002).

101. http://www.er2004.com/jdonjd1.html, archived 10/09/2004 (IA).

102. http://www.liberaldebbie.com/, archived 08/16/2000 (IA).

103. http://firetaft.com/, archived 09/22/2002 (IA).
http://www.taftquack.com/, archived 08/30/2002 (IA).
http://www.timhaganforgovernor.com/, archived 08/30/2002 (LC2002).

104. http://www.timhaganforgovernor.com/, archived 08/30/2002 (LC2002).

105. http://www.taftquack.com/, archived 09/22/2002 (IA).

106. http://www.taftquack.com/press_releases.htm, archived 10/01/2002 (IA).
http://www.timhaganforgovernor.com/gi/volform.html, archived 10/02/2002 (IA).
http://www.timhaganforgovernor.com/gi/contribute.html, archived 10/02/2002 (IA).

107. http://www.taftquack.com/billboard.jpg, archived 10/12/2002 (IA).
http://www.taftquack.com/commercials.htm, archived 10/14/2002 (IA).

108. http://www.georgewbush.com/KerryMediaCenter/, archived 06/22/2004 (IA).

109. http://www.gopatgo2000.org/schedule/, archived 10/28/2000 (IA).

110. http://www.georgewbush.com/Calendar.asp, archived 08/15/2000 (IA).

111. http://www.georgewbush.com/Calendar.asp, archived 10/04/2000 (IA).

112. http://www.georgewbush.com/Calendar.asp, archived 10/21/2000 (IA).

113. http://www.georgewbush.com/, archived 12/18/2003 (IA).

114. http://www.georgewbush.com/calendar/, archived 01/10/2004 (IA).

115. http://georgewbush.com/calendar/, archived 02/13/2004 (IA).

116. http://georgewbush.com/calendar/CalendarDetail.aspx?ID=331, archived 02/27/2004 (IA).
http://georgewbush.com/calendar/CalendarDetail.aspx?ID=335, archived 02/27/2004 (IA).
http://georgewbush.com/calendar/CalendarDetail.aspx?ID=340, archived 02/27/2004 (IA).

117. http://www.georgewbush.com/calendar/SendEvent.aspx, archived 02/06/2004 (IA).

118. http://www.pam4congress.net/, archived 08/16/2000 (IA).

119. http://clear2000.com/c2/, archived 08/23/2000 (IA).
http://login.delphi.com/dirlogin/index.asp?webtag=CLEAR2000&lgnDST=http%3A
%2F%2Fwww%2Edelphi%2Ecom%2Fclear2000%2Fstart%2F, accessed 07/06/2000.

120. http://www.tim2002.com/, archived 11/01/2002 (LC2002).

121. http://www.tim2002.com/timcontents/endorsements/, archived 06/22/2003
(IA).

122. http://www.chandlerforcongress.com/davesarticles.html, archived 11/01/2002
(LC2002).
http://www.jeffconews.com/n2294ta.html, archived 11/01/2002 (LC2002).
http://rockymountainnews.com/drmn/election/article/
0,1299,DRMN_36_1474861,00.html, archived 11/01/2002 (LC2002).

123. http://www.annaeshooforcongress.com/, archived 10/17/2002 (LC2002).
http://www.annaeshooforcongress.com/hot_off_the_press.html, archived 10/17/
2002 (LC2002).
http://query.nytimes.com/search/abstract?res=
F70E12F73A540C738DDDAC0894DA404482, archived 10/17/2002 (LC2002).
http://www.paweekly.com/paw/morgue/2002/2002_02_20.digest20.html, archived
10/17/2002 (LC2002).

124. http://www.georgewbush.com/wstuff/NewsFeed.aspx#Terms, archived 11/03/
2004 (PC).
http://www.bufordforcongress.com/issues/index.html, archived 11/03/2004 (PC).

125. http://www.garrettforgovernor.org/music.html, archived 10/21/2002 (LC2002).
http://www.e-sites.net/roberthoyt/, archived 10/21/2002 (IA).

126. http://www.jimrogan.org/, archived 10/16/2000 (IA).
http://w.moreover.com/, archived 08/15/2000 (IA).

127. http://www.drdan2004.com/site/PageServer?pagename=links_home, archived
10/11/2004 (IA).

128. http://www.johngraham4congress.com/aboutopponents.html, archived 09/01/
2002 (LC2002).

129. http://www.murraysabrin.com/, archived 10/19/2000 (IA).
http://www.murraysabrin.com/corzine.html, archived 06/19/2001 (IA).

130. http://www.er2004.com/jdonjd2.html, archived 09/19/2005 (IA).

131. http://jdhayworth.com/press.html, archived 12/06/2003 (IA).

132. http://www.flynnforcongress.com/political_searchers.html, archived 08/19/
2000 (IA).

133. http://blogforamerica.com, archived 01/26/2004 (IA).

134. The fish photo at http://www.slade2000.com/contents/tourdiary/pic_wbuster2
.jpg, archived 08/17/2000 (IA), was linked to from http://www.cantwell2000.com/
content/buster.html, archived 08/17/2000 (IA).

135. http://www.slade2000.com/contents/rumors/oldmill2.shtml, archived 08/22/
2000 (IA).

136. http://www.cantwell2000.com/content/buster.html, archived 08/17/2000 (IA),
which linked to http://www.w3.org/People/Berners-Lee/FAQ.html, archived 08/17/
2000 (IA) as the source of the quote by Berners-Lee.

137. http://www.fordean.org/ForDean, archived 10/15/2005 (IA).

138. http://www.johnkerry.com/onlinehq/, archived 06/15/2004 (IA).

139. http://www.johnkerry.com/onlinehq/mediacorps, archived 06/15/2004 (IA).

140. http://www.johnkerry.com/signup/mediacorps.php, archived 06/06/2004 (IA).

141. http://www.johnkerry.com/onlinehq/bbn.html, archived 06/10/2004 (IA).

142. http://www.johnkerry.com/onlinehq/, archived 06/15/2004 (IA).

143. http://kerry2004.meetup.com/, archived 06/15/2004 (IA).
http://www.johnkerry.com/download/buttons/toolkit.pdf, archived 06/09/2004 (IA).

144. http://18minutegap.com, 08/03/2003, archived as http://18minutegap
.blogspot.com/2003_08_03_18minutegap_archive.html, 02/21/06 (PC).

145. http://www.johnkerry.com/onlinehq/, archived 06/15/2004 (IA).

146. http://www.johnkerry.com/signup/online_pledge.html, archived 06/09/2004
(IA).

147. http://www.votevan.org/page7.html, archived 10/12/2004 (IA).

148. http://www.votevan.org/page3.html, archived 02/21/2006 (PC).

149. http://www.kahnforcongress.com/media.htm, archived 11/01/2002 (LC2002).

150. http://www.gogeorgego.com/index.asp?Type=B_BASIC&SEC={81B97C16-EC37
-4DF0-A027-50CC11F23B62}, archived 10/03/2002 (LC2002).

151. http://www.jimryanforgovernor.com/Downloads.asp?FormMode=Download&
Type=Wallpapers, archived 10/12/2002 (LC2002).
http://www.wallyherger.com/wall.htm, archived 10/01/2002 (IA).

152. http://www.georgewbush.com/WStuff/downloads.aspx, archived 07/15/2004
(IA).

153. http://www.georgewbush.com/Postcards.asp, archived 12/17/2000 (IA).
http://www.jimryanforgovernor.com/EPostcard.asp, archived 10/12/2002 (LC2002).
http://www.betseybayless.com/Team/Tell.cfm, archived 09/07/2002 (LC2002).

154. http://www.votenader.com/downloads/download.html, archived 11/07/2000 (IA).
http://www.votenader.com/publicmedia.html, archived 11/07/2000 (IA).

155. http://www.carolforpresident.com/content.php?page=kit, archived 12/11/2003 (IA).

156. http://www.gopatgo2000.org/, archived 11/07/2000 (IA).
http://www.gopatgo2000.org/library/default.asp?id=131, archived 11/19/2000 (IA).

157. http://www.kahnforcongress.com/media.htm, archived 11/01/2002 (LC2002).

158. http://www.jimnussle.com/nussle/wrapper.jsp?PID=4085-683, archived 11/03/2004 (PC).

159. http://www.abraham2000.net/Volunteer.asp, archived 10/18/2000 (IA).
http://www.abraham2000.net/NewspapersForm.asp, archived 08/18/2000 (IA).
http://netelection.org/notes/notedisplay.php3?ID=1, archived 01/12/2001 (IA).

160. http://www.pattymurray.com/privacy.php?PHPSESSID=a2e924d0bbfaaa5435866ddfc7324082, archived 08/18/2005 (IA).

161. http://www.pattymurray.com/lte.php, archived 11/03/04 (PC).
http://www.pattymurray.com/lte_winner.php, archived 11/03/04 (PC).

162. http://www.johnkerry.com/onlinehq/mediacorps/, archived 06/15/2004 (IA).

163. http://www.mccaininteractive.com/feedback/feedback.cfm?r=10, archived 03/03/2000 (IA).

164. http://volunteer.johnkerry.com/event/plan/?type=18, archived 10/13/2005 (IA).

165. http://www.votenader.com/materials/houseparty/index.html, archived 11/07/2000 (IA).
http://www.votenader.com/materials/houseparty/HousepartyKit.html, archived 11/07/2000 (IA).

166. http://www.laurawells.org/pages/volunteer6.php?project_id=6, archived 10/13/2002 (IA).

167. http://www.getthefedout.com/volunteer/vol-houseparty.htm, archived 10/31/04 (IA).
http://www.charleswsanders.org/html/wwwboard/bulletin.html, archived 10/24/04 (IA).
http://www.electgregharris.com/DesktopDefault.aspx?tabindex=3&tabid=54, archived 06/19/2004 (IA).

168. http://www.getthefedout.com/volunteer/vol-houseparty.htm, archived 07/10/2004 (IA).

169. http://volunteer.johnkerry.com/event/plan/?type=18, archived 10/13/2005 (IA).

170. http://www.johnedwards2004.com/travel-nh-asp, archived 01/19/2004 (PC).

171. http://newhampshire.deanforamerica.com/primaryweek, archived 01/19/2004 (PC).
http://newhampshire.deanforamerica.com/ridestonh, archived 01/19/2004 (PC).

172. http://www.georgewbush.com/, archived 10/30/2004 (IA).

173. http://www.electgregharris.com/DesktopDefault.aspx?tabindex=3&tabid=12, archived 06/19/2004 (IA).

174. http://www.mccotterforcongress.com/about.asp, archived 11/03/2004 (PC).

175. http://www.mccotterforcongress.com/volunteer.asp, archived 11/03/2004 (PC).

176. http://www.carolforpresident.com/kit/cmb_signin_sheet.pdf, archived 08/19/2003 (IA).

177. http://www.inez2004.com/portal/index.php?module=article&view=67, archived 10/31/2004 (PC).

178. http://www.inez2004.com/portal/index.php?module=article&view=67, archived 10/31/2005 (PC).
http://www.inez2004.com/portal/index.php?module=pagemaster&PAGE_user_op=view_page&PAGE_id=20&OLTARGET=involved_2, archived 10/11/2004 (IA).

179. http://www.joeturnham.com/tellafriend.asp, archived 11/01/2002 (LC2002).

180. http://deanforamerica.com, archived 01/27/2004 (PC).

181. http://www.deanforamerica.com/, archived 02/08/2004 (IA).
http://www.fordean.org/ForDean, archived 08/22/2005 (IA).

182. http://www.electharris.org/links.html, archived 10/31/2002 (LC2002).

183. http://www.kaygranger.com/, archived 05/24/2004 (IA).
http://stomp4victory.org/, archived 06/08/2004 (IA).

184. http://volunteer.johnkerry.com/contribute, archived 11/02/2004 (IA).

185. http://www.marybono.com/team/TeamList.cfm?c=20, archived 11/01/2002 (LC2002).

186. http://www.laurawells.org/pages/volunteer6.php?project_id=6, archived 10/12/2004 (IA).

187. http://www.marybono.com/team/TeamList.cfm?c=20, archived 11/01/2002 (LC2002).

188. http://dir.webring.com/rw, archived 06/15/2004 (IA).

189. http://q.webring.com/hub?ring=unofficialjohnfk, archived 10/13/2004 (IA).

190. http://h.webring.com/hub?ring=electralphnaderi, archived 10/13/2004 (IA).
http://s.webring.com/hub?ring=bushcheney04, archived 10/13/2004 (IA).

191. http://www.jimnussle.com/nussle/wrapper.jsp?PID=4085-680, archived 11/03/2004 (PC).

192. http://www.georgewbush.com/GetActive, archived 10/31/2004 (PC).

193. http://www.georgewbush.com/Secure/BushTeamLeaderSignUp.aspx, archived 07/11/2004 (IA).

194. http://www.garymcleod.org/, archived 09/24/2004 (IA).
http://www.garymcleod.org/cgi-bin/affiliates/signup.cgi, archived 10/09/2004 (IA).

195. http://volunteer.johnkerry.com/, archived 11/01/2004 (IA).

196. http://volunteer.johnkerry.com/contribute, archived 11/02/2004 (IA).

197. http://volunteer.johnkerry.com/event/plan/?type=hp&1=1, archived 10/09/2004 (IA).

198. See, for example, Web pages produced by New Media Communications (http://www.technomania.com/awards.asp), NetCampaign (http://netcampaign.com/projects/), Liberty Concepts (http://www.libertyconcepts.com/golden_dot.htm), and NetPolitics Group (http://www.netpoliticsgroup.com/awards.html). Archived 02/26/2006 (PC).

199. The first issue of Campaign Web Review is archived in the "Interesting People Mailing List Archive." http://www.interesting-people.org/archives/interesting-people/199807/msg00061.html, archived 02/26/2006 (PC).

200. We appreciate the invaluable service provided by both the Center for Responsive Politics (http://opensecrets.org) and the Institute on Money in State Politics (http://followthemoney.org) in making available the data they collect on campaign finance.

201. 75 percent, of course, falls below the genre threshold of 80 percent. Given the trend line, we attribute the lower measure in 2000 to measurement error.

202. http://www.johnkerry.com, archived 09/24/2001 (IA).

203. http://www.johnkerry.com, archived 10/12/2005 (PC).

204. http://www.kucinich.us, 10/17/2005 (PC).

205. http://www.kucinichforcongress.us, archived 10/12/2005 (PC).

206. http://www.loisherr.us/, archived 10/12/2005 (PC).

207. http://johnrussellforcongress.com, archived 09/26/2004 (IA).
http://www.johnrussellforcongress.com/, archived 10/12/2005 (PC).

208. http://www.loc.gov/minerva/collect/elec2002/index.html, accessed 02/27/
2006.

209. http://www.vote-smart.org, accessed 09/20/2004.

210. Campaign Web sites produced by presidential candidates and some
congressional candidates in the 2000 U.S. election were preserved by the Library
of Congress and the Internet Archive; archival impressions are Web accessible
(http://web.archive.org/collections/e2k.html, accessed 05/21/06). Additional
congressional and gubernatorial sites from 2000 were included in the Annenberg
2000 Election Web Archive, accessible onsite at the Annenberg School of
Communication Library, University of Pennsylvania. Archival impressions of
campaign Web sites produced by House, Senate, and gubernatorial candidates in the
2002 U.S. elections are available in the Election 2002 Web Archive, Library of
Congress (http://www.loc.gov/minerva/collect/elec2002/index.html, accessed
05/21/06). Campaign Web sites produced during the 2004 election were preserved
by the Library of Congress. Public access to the archive was "coming soon" as of
05/21/06 (http://www.loc.gov/minerva, archived 05/21/06 (PC)).

References

Abbate, Janet. 1999. *Inventing the Internet*. Cambridge, MA: MIT Press.

Abramson, Jeffrey B., F. Christopher Arterton, and Gary R. Orren. 1988. *The Electronic Commonwealth: The Impact of New Media Technologies on Democratic Politics*. New York: Basic Books, Inc.

Adamic, Lada A., and Eytan Adar. 2001. "You Are What You Link." Paper read at The 10th International World Wide Web Conference, May 1–5. [Accessed June 20 2005]. Available from http://www10.org/program/society/yawyl/YouAreWhatYouLink.htm.

Adatto, Kiku. 1990. *Sound Bite Democracy: Network Evening News Presidential Campaign Coverage, 1968 and 1988*. Joan Shorenstein Center on the Press, Politics and Public Policy, June 1990 [Accessed June 23 2005]. Available from http://www.ksg.harvard .edu/presspol/Research_Publications/Papers/Research_Papers/R2.PDF.

American Association of Political Consultants. 1999. *Pollie Awards 1999*. American Association of Political Consultants, [Accessed September 7 2005]. Available from http://www.theaapc.org/content/pollieawards/pastwinners/pastwinners1999.asp.

———. 2005. *Pollie Awards 2005*. American Association of Political Consultants, 2005 [Accessed September 7 2005]. Available from http://www.theaapc.org/content/ pollieawards/pastwinners/pastwinners2005.asp.

Arena, Robert K. 1996. *Dole/Kemp '96*. Presage Internet Campaigns [Accessed October 2 2005]. Available from http://www.presageinc.com/contents/experience/dolekemp .shtml.

Arms, William, Roger Adkins, Cassy Ammen, and Allene Hayes. 2001. "Collecting and Preserving the Web: The MINERVA Prototype." *RLG DigiNews*, April 15, 2001. [Accessed March 20 2005]. Available from http://www.rlg.org/preserv/diginews/ diginews5-2.html.

Atkinson, Rowland, and John Flint. 2001. "Accessing Hidden and Hard-to-Reach Populations: Snowball Research Strategies." *Social Research Update* Summer 2001

(33). [Accessed July 10 2005]. Available from http://www.soc.surrey.ac.uk/sru/SRU33.html.

Ayres, Bruno. 2004. "Volunteer Work, Information and Digital Networks." Paper read at International Association for Volunteer Effort World Volunteer Conference, at Barcelona, Spain. [Accessed September 20 2005]. Available from http://www.barcelona2004.com/eng/banco_del_conocimiento/documentos/ficha.cfm?idDoc=2363.

Barber, Benjamin R. 1984. *Strong Democracy: Participatory Politics for a New Age.* Berkeley: University of California Press.

Barnes, John A. 1954. "Class and Committees in a Norwegian Island Parish." *Human Relations* 7:39–58.

Beaucar Vlahos, Kelley. 2003. *Political "Meet-ups" Double as Singles Events.* Fox News, December 9, [Accessed June 30 2005]. Available from http://www.foxnews.com/story/0,2933,105206,00.html.

Beaulieu, Anne. 2005. "Sociable Hyperlinks: An Ethnographic Approach to Connectivity." In *Virtual Methods: Issues in Social Research on the Internet,* edited by C. Hine. Oxford: Berg.

Benoit, William L., and Pamela J. Benoit. 2000. "The Virtual Campaign: Presidential Primary Websites in Campaign 2000." *American Communication Journal* 3 (3). [Accessed September 12 2005]. Available from http://acjournal.org/holdings/vol3/Iss3/curtain.html#4.

Benoit, William L., John P. McHale, Glenn Hansen, P. M. Pier, and John P. McGuire. 2003. *Campaign 2000: A Functional Analysis of Presidential Campaign Discourse.* Lanham: Rowman & Littlefield.

Berelson, Bernard. 1952. *Content Analysis in Communication Research.* Glencoe, IL: Free Press.

Berg, S. 1988. "Snowball Sampling." In *Encyclopaedia of Statistical Sciences,* edited by S. Kotz and N. L. Johnson. New York: John Wiley.

Berners-Lee, Tim. 2000. *Weaving the Web: The Original Design and Ultimate Destiny of the World Wide Web.* New York: HarperCollins.

Besag, David Haydn. 2001. "An Evaluation of the Web Sites of 'Third' Political Parties in the United States of America." MA, Department of Information and Library Management, University of Northumbria at Newcastle, Newcastle.

Bimber, Bruce, and Richard Davis. 2003. *Campaigning Online: The Internet in U.S. Elections.* New York: Oxford University Press.

Birrenbach, John. 2000. Interview by Kirsten Foot. St. Paul, MN, August 31.

Blumenthal, Sidney. 1980. *The Permanent Campaign: Inside the World of Elite Political Operatives*. Boston: Beacon Press.

Boczkowski, Pablo. 2004. "The Processes of Adopting Multimedia and Interactivity in Three Online Newsrooms." *Journal of Communication* 54 (2):197–213.

Booth, William. 1998. *More Politicians Use Web as Campaign Tool*. Washington Post, October 17, [Accessed September 14 2005]. Available from http://www.washingtonpost.com/wp-srv/politics/campaigns/keyraces98/stories/netizens101798.htm.

Bradshaw, Joel. 1995. "Who Will Vote for You and Why: Designing Strategy and Theme." In *Campaigns and Elections American Style*, edited by J. A. Thurber and C. J. Nelson.

Bucqueroux, Bonnie. 2000. Interview by Tresa Undem. Philadelphia, PA, October 22.

Burbules, Nicholas C., and Thomas A. Callister. 2000. *Watch IT: The Risks and Promises of Information Technologies for Education*. Boulder, CO: Westview Press.

Burnett, Robert, and P. David Marshall. 2003. *Web Theory: An Introduction*. New York: Routledge.

Casey, Chris. 1996. *The Hill on the Net: Congress Enters the Information Age*. Boston: AP Professional.

Castells, Manuel. 1996. *The Rise of the Network Society*. Vol. 1, *The Information Age: Economy, Society and Culture*. Cambridge, MA: Blackwell.

Cohen, Joshua, and Joel Rogers. 1995. *Associations and Democracy*. New York: Verso.

Connelly, Joel. 2000. *Gorton Campaign Accuses Cantwell of Web "Hacking."* Seattle Post-Intelligencer, June 14, [Accessed September 29 2005]. Available from http://seattlepi.nwsource.com/local/cant14.shtml.

Crowston, Kevin, and Marie Williams. 2000. "Reproduced and Emergent Genres of Communication on the World Wide Web." *The Information Society* 16 (3):201–215.

Crumlish, Christian. 2004. *The Power of Many: How the Web is Transforming Politics, Business, and Everyday Life*. Alameda: Sybex.

D'Alessio, David. 1997. "Use of the World Wide Web in the 1996 U.S. Election." *Electoral Studies* 16 (4):489–500.

———. 2000. "Adoption of the World Wide Web by American Political Candidates, 1996–1998." *Journal of Broadcasting and Electronic Media* 44 (4):556–568.

Davis, Richard. 1999. *The Web of Politics: The Internet's Impact on the American Political System*. New York: Oxford University Press.

Davis, Richard, and Diana Owen. 1998. *New Media and American Politics*. New York: Oxford University Press.

December, John. 1996. "Units of Analysis for Internet Communication." *Journal of Computer Mediated Communication* 1 (4). Available from http://www.ascusc.org/jcmc/vol1/issue4/december.html.

Democracy Online Project. 1999. "Online Campaigning: A Primer." Washington, DC: Graduate School of Political Management, George Washington University.

———. 1998. *Characteristics of 1998 Campaign Web Sites*. Democracy Online Project, [Accessed October 3 2005]. Available from http://www.ipdi.org/UploadedFiles/Characteristics%20of%201998%20Campaign%20Web%20Sites.pdf.

Dillon, Andrew, and Barbara A. Gushrowski. 2000. "Genres and the Web: Is the Personal Home Page the First Uniquely Digital Genre?" *Journal of the American Society for Information Science* 51 (2):202–205.

Downing, John. 1989. "Computers for Political Change: Peacenet and Public Data Access." *Journal of Communication* 39 (3):154–162.

Downs, Anthony. 1957. *An Economic Theory of Democracy*. New York, NY: Harper and Row.

Dulio, David A., Donald L. Goff, and James A. Thurber. 1999. "Untangled Web: Internet Use During the 1998 Election." *PS: Political Science and Politics* 32 (1):53–58.

Earl, Jennifer, and Alan Schussman. 2002. "The New Site of Activism: On-line Organizations, Movement Entrepreneurs, and the Changing Location of Social Movement Decision-making." In *Consensus Decision-making, Northern Ireland and Indigenous Movements*: Elsevier.

Endres, Danielle, and Barbara Warnick. 2004. "Text-based Interactivity in Candidate Campaign Web Sites: A Case Study from the 2002 Elections." *Western Journal of Communication* 68 (3):322–342.

Engeström, Yrjö. 1990. *Learning, Working and Imagining: Twelve Studies in Activity Theory*. Helsinki: Orienta-Konsultit.

———. 2005. *Developmental Work Research—Expanding Activity Theory in Practice*. Berlin: Lehmanns Media.

Evans, Sara M., and Harry Chatten Boyte. 1986. *Free Spaces: The Sources of Democratic Change in America*. 1st ed. New York: Harper & Row.

Eveland, William P., Jr., and Sharon Dunwoody. 2001. "User Control and Structural Isomorphism or Disorientation and Cognitive Load?" *Communication Research* 28:48–78.

Faler, Brian. 2004. "Kerry's E-mail List Continues to be a Valuable Resource." *The Washington Post*, December 25, A2. [Accessed May 23 2005]. Available from http://www.washingtonpost.com/wp-dyn/articles/A24796-2004Dec24.html?nav=rss_politics.

Fenno, Richard F. 1996. *Senators on the Campaign Trail*. Norman, OK: University of Oklahoma Press.

Foner, Eric. 2004. *Tom Paine and Revolutionary America*. Updated ed. New York: Oxford University Press.

Foot, Kirsten A., and Steven M. Schneider. 2004. "Online Structure for Civic Engagement in the Post-9/11 Web Sphere." *Electronic Journal of Communication* 14 (3–4). [Accessed October 13 2005]. Available from http://www.cios.org/www/ejc/v143toc.htm.

Fose, Max. 2000. Interview by Jennifer Stromer-Galley. Washington, DC, April 21.

Fuller, Wayne Edison. 1972. *The American Mail: Enlarger of the Common Life, The Chicago History of American Civilization*. Chicago: University of Chicago Press.

Gamson, William A., and Andre Modigliani. 1989. "Media Discourse and Public Opinion on Nuclear Power: A Constructionist Approach." *American Journal of Sociology* 95 (1):1–37.

Gibson, Rachel Kay, Andrea Rommele, and Stephen Ward, eds. 2004. *Electronic Democracy: Mobilisation, Organisation, and Participation via New ICTs*. London; New York: Routledge.

Giddens, Anthony. 1984. *The Constitution of Society: Outline of the Theory of Structure*. Berkeley: University of California Press.

Graber, Doris, and James Smith. 2005. "Political Communication Faces the 21st Century." *Journal of Communication* 55 (3):479–507.

Graduate School of Political Management. 1998. *The Golden Dot Awards*. George Washington University, December 7, [Accessed September 7 2005]. Available from http://web.archive.org/web/19990506025812/www.gspm.org/politicsonline/goldendot.html.

Harpham, Edward J. 1999. "Going On-line: The 1998 Congressional Campaign." Atlanta: American Political Science Association.

Harris, John F. 2004. "In Ohio, Building a Political Echo." *The Washington Post*, May 12, 1.

Hemingway, Sam. 2003. "How Did Dean Surge to the Front?" *The Burlington Free Press*, November 2.

Herring, Susan, Lois Ann Scheidt, Sabrina Bonus, and Elijah Wright. 2005. "Weblogs as a Bridging Genre." *Information, Technology & People* 18 (2):141–172.

Herrnson, Paul S. 2003. *Congressional Elections: Campaigning at Home and in Washington*. 4th ed. Washington, DC: Congressional Quarterly Press.

Hine, Christine. 2000. *Virtual Ethnography*. Thousand Oaks, CA: Sage.

Hoofnagle, Chris Jay. 2005. *Privacy Self Regulation: A Decade of Disappointment.* Electronic Privacy Information Center, March 4, [Accessed October 10 2005]. Available from http://www.epic.org/reports/decadedisappoint.html#_edn15.

Howard, Philip N. 2005. "Deep Democracy, Thin Citizenship: Digital Media and the Production of Political Culture." *Annals of the American Academy of Political & Social Science* 597.

———. 2005. *New Media Campaigns and the Managed Citizen.* New York: Cambridge University Press.

Howard, Philip N., and Steve Jones, eds. 2003. *Society Online: The Internet in Context.* Thousand Oaks: Sage.

Hunter, Christopher D. 2002. "Political Privacy and Online Politics: How E-campaigning Threatens Voter Privacy." *First Monday* 7 (2). [Accessed October 5 2005]. Available from http://www.firstmonday.org/issues/issue7_2/hunter/.

Hyman, Herbert Hiram. 1955. *Survey Design and Analysis: Principles, Cases, and Procedures.* Glencoe, IL: Free Press.

Institute for Politics, Democracy, & the Internet. 2004. "Political Influentials Online in the 2004 Presidential Campaign." Washington DC: The George Washington University.

Institute for Politics, Democracy, and the Internet. 2002. "Online Campaigning 2002: The Primer." Washington DC: The George Washington University.

———. 2005. *Golden Dot Awards.* George Washington University 2004 [Accessed September 7 2005]. Available from http://www.ipdi.org/politicsonline/goldendotrequirements.htm.

———. 2004. "Putting Online Influentials to Work for Your Campaign." Washington, DC: The George Washington University.

International FidoNet Association. 1989. *FidoNet News.* International FidoNet Association [Accessed September 21 2005]. Available from http://www.fidotel.com/public/fidonews/archive/1989/fido609.htm.

Iozzi, David P., and Lance Bennett. 2004. *Crossing the Campaign Divide: Dean Changes the Election Game.* Center for Communication and Civic Engagement, University of Washington 2004 [Accessed July 7 2005]. Available from http://depts.washington.edu/ccce/assets/documents/iozzi_bennet_crossing.pdf.

Johnston, Hank, and Bert Klandermans. 1995. *Social Movements and Culture, Social Movements, Protest, and Contention; v. 4.* Minneapolis: University of Minnesota Press.

Jones, Stanley Llewellyn. 1964. *The Presidential Election of 1896.* Madison: University of Wisconsin Press.

Kahle, Brewster. 1997. "Preserving the Internet." *Scientific American* 276 (3):82–83.

Kahn, Kim Fridkin, and Patrick J. Kenney. 1999. *The Spectacle of U.S. Senate Elections.* Princeton: Princeton University Press.

Kamarck, Elaine Ciulla. 1999. "Campaigning on the Internet in the Elections of 1998." In *Democracy.com?: Governance in a Networked World*, edited by E. C. Kamarck and J. S. Nye. Hollis, NH: Hollis Publishing.

Keep, Christopher, Tim McLaughlin, and Robin Parker. 1993. "The Electronic Labyrinth." Available from http://www.iath.virginia.edu/elab/elab.html.

Keller, Ed, and Jon Berry. 2003. *The Influentials.* New York: The Free Press.

Kitzinger, Jenny, and Rosaline S. Barbour. 1999. "Introduction: The Challenge and Promise of Focus Groups." In *Developing Focus Group Research: Politics Theory and Practice*, edited by R. S. Barbour and J. Kitzinger: Sage.

Klandermans, Bert, Hanspeter Kriesi, and Sidney Tarrow, eds. 1998. *International Social Movement Research. From Structure to Action: Comparing Social Movement across Cultures.* London: JAI Press.

Klotz, Robert. 1997. "Positive Spin: Senate Campaigning on the Web." *PS: Political Science & Politics* (30):482–486.

———. 2005. "Internet Campaigning and Participation." Paper read at American Political Science Association, September 3, 2005, at Washington, DC.

Kotamraju, Nalini P. 2004. "Art versus Code: The Gendered Evolution of Web Design Skills." In *Society Online: The Internet in Context*, edited by P. N. Howard and S. Jones. Thousand Oaks: Sage.

Kuutti, Kari. 1996. "Activity Theory as a Potential Framework for Human–Computer Interaction Research." In *Context and Consciousness*, edited by B. Nardi. Cambridge, MA: MIT Press.

Lamb, Roberta, Steve Sawyer, and Rob Kling. 2000. "A Social Informatics Perspective on Socio-Technical Networks." Paper read at Americas Conference on Information Systems, at Long Beach, CA. [Accessed April 20 2005]. Available from http://lamb.cba.hawaii.edu/pubs/stnwtppr.htm.

LaPointe, Mark Eugene. 1999. "Cyber Campaigning for the United States Senate: A Content Analysis of Campaign Web Sites in the 1998 Senate Elections." MA, University of Nevada, Reno.

Lasswell, Harold. 1948. "The Structure and Function of Communication in Society." In *The Communication of Ideas*, edited by L. Bryson. New York: Harper and Row.

Lazarsfeld, Paul F., Bernard Berelson, and Hazel Gaudet. 1944. *The People's Choice.* New York: Duell, Sloan and Pearce.

Leont'ev, Alexei Nikolaevich. 1978. *Activity, Consciousness, and Personality*. Englewood Cliffs: Prentice-Hall.

Lewin, James. 2003. "Is Your Site Sticky?" *Computer World*, March 18. Accessed April 26 2005]. Available from http://www.computerworld.com.au/index.php?id=3822760 &eid=-44.

Lusoli, Wainer, Stephen Ward, and Rachel Gibson. 2002. "Political Organizations and Online Mobilisation: Different Media—Same Outcomes?" *New Review of Information & Networking* 8:89–108.

MacKenzie, Donald, and Judy Wajcman, eds. 1985. *The Social Shaping of Technology: How the Refrigerator Got Its Hum*. Philadelphia: Open University Press.

Madsen, Phil. 1998. *Notes Regarding Jesse Ventura's Internet Use in His 1998 Campaign for Minnesota Governor*. Jesse Ventura for Governor Volunteer Committee, December 7, [Accessed September 7 2005]. Available from http://web.archive.org/web/19990424134224/http://www.jesseventura.org/internet/netnotes.htm.

Manovich, Lev. 2001. *The Language of New Media*. Cambridge, MA: MIT Press.

Margolis, Michael, David Resnick, and Chin-Chang Tu. 1997. "Campaigning on the Internet: Parties and Candidates on the World Wide Web in the 1996 Primary Season." *The Harvard International Journal of Press/Politics* 2 (1):59–78.

Margolis, Michael, and David Resnick. 2000. *Politics as Usual: The Cyberspace "Revolution."* Thousand Oaks, CA: Sage.

McAdam, Doug. 1988. "Micromobilization Contexts and Recruitment to Activism." In *From Structure to Action: Comparing Social Movement Research across Cultures*, edited by B. Klandermans, H. Kriesi and S. Tarrow. Greenwich, CT: JAI Press.

McAdam, Doug, John D. McCarthy, and Mayer N. Zald. 1996. *Comparative Perspectives on Social Movements: Political Opportunities, Mobilizing Structures, and Cultural Framings, Cambridge Studies in Comparative Politics*. New York: Cambridge University Press.

———. 1996. "Introduction: Opportunities, Mobilizing Structures, and Framing Processes—Toward a Synthetic, Comparative Perspective on Social Movements. In *Comparative Perspectives on Social Movements*, edited by D. McAdam, J. D. McCarthy and M. N. Zald. New York: Cambridge University Press.

McLeod, Jack M., Gerald M. Kosicki, and Douglas M. McLeod. 1994. "The Expanding Boundaries of Political Communication Effects." In *Media Effects: Advances in Theory and Research*, edited by J. Bryant and D. Zillman. Hillsdale, NJ: Lawrence Erlbaum.

McQuail, Denis, and Sven Windahl. 1981. *Communication Models for the Study of Mass Communications*. London: Longman.

Meadow, Robert G. 1986. "The Electronic Machine: New Technologies in Political Campaigns." *Election Politics* 3 (3):26–31.

Medvic, Stephen K., and David A. Dulio. 2004. "The Permanent Campaign in the White House: Evidence from the Clinton Administration." *White House Studies* 4 (3):301–317.

Miettinen, Reijo. 1998. "Object Construction and Networks in Research Work: The Case of Research on Cellulose Degrading Enzymes." *Social Studies of Science* 38:423–463.

Mitchell, Michele. 1998. *A New Kind of Party Animal: How the Young are Tearing Up the American Political Landscape*. New York: Simon & Schuster.

Mitra, Anandra. 1999. "Characteristics of the WWW Text: Tracing Discursive Strategies." *Journal of Computer-Mediated Communication* 5 (1). [Accessed October 15 2005]. Available at http://jcmc.indiana.edu/vol5/issue1/mitra.html.

Moldashcl, Manfred, and Wolfgang G. Weber. 1998. "The Three Waves of Industrial Group Work: Historical Reflections on Current Research in Group Work." *Human Relations* 51 (3):347–388.

Mueller, Carol McClurg. 1992. "Building Social Movement Theory." In *Frontiers in Social Movement Theory*, edited by A. D. Morris and C. M. Mueller. New Haven, Conn.: Yale University Press.

National Telecommunications and Information Administration. 2002. *A Nation Online: How Americans Are Expanding Their Use of the Internet*. National Telecommunications and Information Administration, February, [Accessed September 5 2005]. Available from http://www.ntia.doc.gov/ntiahome/dn/nationonline_020502.htm.

Nelson, Theodor H. 1978. *Dream Machines: New Freedoms through Computer Screens—A Minority Report, Issued with "Computer Lib."* South Bend, IN: The Distributors.

Neuman, W. Russell. 1991. *The Future of the Mass Audience*. New York: Cambridge University Press.

Nicolini, Davide, Silvia Gherardi, and Dvora Yanow. 2003. "Introduction: Toward a Practice-based View of Learning and Knowing in Organizations." In *Knowing in Organizations: A Practice-based Approach*, edited by D. Nicolini, S. Gherardi and D. Yanow. Armonk, NY: M.E. Sharpe.

———, eds. 2003. *Knowing in Organizations: A Practice-based Approach*. New York: M.E. Sharpe.

Nicolini, Davide, and Richard Holti. 2001. "Practice-based Theorising and the Understanding of Participative Change in Organizations." Paper read at 4th International Conference on Organizational Learning & Knowledge Management, June 1–4, at London, Ontario.

Norris, Pippa. 2001. *Digital Divide: Civic Engagement, Information Poverty, and the Internet Worldwide*. New York: Cambridge University Press.

Oldenburg, Ray. 1989. *The Great Good Place: Cafes, Coffee Shops, Community Centers, Beauty Parlors, General Stores, Bars, Hangouts, and How They Get You Through the Day*. 1st ed. New York: Paragon House.

———. 2001. *Celebrating the Third Place: Inspiring Stories About the "Great Good Places" at the Heart of Our Communities*. New York: Marlowe & Co.

Orlikowski, Wanda J. 1992. "The Duality of Technology: Rethinking the Concept of Technology in Organizations." *Organization Science* 3 (3):398–427.

Orlikowski, Wanda J., and JoAnne Yates. 1994. "Genre Repertoire: The Structuring of Communicative Practices in Organizations." *Administrative Sciences Quarterly* 35:541–574.

Overfelt, Maggie. 2003. *Taking America Offline* (September). Fortune Small Business 2003 [Accessed June 28 2005]. Available from http://www.fortune.com/fortune/smallbusiness/technology/articles/0,15114,490011,00.html.

Page, Benjamin. 1978. *Choices and Echoes in Presidential Elections*. Chicago, IL: University of Chicago Press.

Park, Han Woo. 2003. "Hyperlink Network Analysis: A New Method for the Study of Social Structure on the Web." *Connections* 25 (1):49–61.

Pasley, Jeffrey L. 2001. *"The Tyranny of Printers": Newspaper Politics in the Early American Republic, Jeffersonian America*. Charlottesville: University Press of Virginia.

Peng, Foo Yeuh, Naphtali Irene Tham, and Hao Xiaoming. 1999. "Trends in Online Newspapers: A Look at the U.S. Web." *Newspaper Research Journal* 20 (2):52–64.

Pew Internet and American Life Project. 2005. *Usage over Time* [Spreadsheet], January, [Accessed June 25 2005]. Available from http://www.pewinternet.org/trends/UsageOverTime.xls.

Pew Research Center for People and the Press. 1995. *Americans Going Online . . . Explosive Growth, Uncertain Destinations*. Pew Research Center for People and the Press, October 16, [Accessed September 26 2005]. Available from http://people-press.org/reports/display.php3?ReportID=136.

Pickering, Andrew. 1995. *The Mangle of Practice: Time, Agency, and Science*. Chicago: University of Chicago Press.

Pinch, Trevor, and Wiebe E. Bijker. 1987. "The Social Construction of Facts and Artifacts: Or How the Sociology of Science and the Sociology of Technology Might Benefit Each Other. In *The Social Construction of Technological Systems: New Directions in the Sociology and History of Technology*, edited by W. E. Bijker, T. P. Hughes and T. Pinch. Cambridge, MA: MIT Press.

Politics Online. 2000. *Political Milestones on the Internet.* Politics Online 2000, [Accessed September 15 2005]. Available from http://web.archive.org/web/20040610120120/http://www.politicsonline.com/pol2000/politicalfirsts.asp.

Puopolo, Sonia. 2001. "The Web and U.S. Senatorial Campaigns 2000." *American Behavioral Scientist* 44 (12):2030–2047.

Putnam, Robert D. 2000. *Bowling Alone: The Collapse and Revival of American Community.* New York: Simon & Schuster.

Rainie, Lee, Michael Cornfield, and John Horrigan. 2005. "The Internet and Campaign 2004." Washington, DC: Pew Internet and American Life Project.

Raney, Rebecca Fairley. 1998. "Former Wrestler's Campaign Got a Boost from the Internet." *New York Times,* November 6.

Reed, Lynn. 2000. Interview by Jennifer Stromer-Galley. Washington, DC, April 20.

Rein, Lisa. 2004. *Interview with Brewster Kahle.* O'Reilly Open P2P 2004 [Accessed May 19 2005]. Available from http://www.openp2p.com/pub/a/p2p/2004/01/22/kahle.html.

Rheingold, Howard. 1993. *The Virtual Community: Homesteading on the Electronic Frontier.* Reading, MA.

Rogers, Everett M. 1986. *Communication Technology: The New Media in Society.* New York: Free Press.

———. 1995. *Diffusion of Innovations.* 4th ed. New York: Free Press.

Rogers, Richard. 2002. "Operating Issue Networks on the Web." *Science as Culture* 11 (2):191–214.

Rogers, Richard, and Noortje Marres. 2000. "Landscaping Climate Change: A Mapping Technique for Understanding Science & Technology Debates on the World Wide Web." *Public Understanding of Science* 9 (2):141–163.

Saco, Diane. 2002. *Cybering Democracy: Public Space and the Internet.* Thousand Oaks: Sage.

Sadow, Jeffrey D., and Karen James. 1999. "Virtual Billboards? Candidate Web Sites and Campaigning in 1998." Atlanta: American Political Science Association.

SAP AG. 2004. *Interview with Neil Beagrie, British Library.* SAP INFO Online 2004, [Accessed May 19 2005]. Available from http://www.sapinfo.net/index.php4?ACTION=noframe&url=http://www.sapinfo.net/public/en/index.php4/article/Article-3089140c577c931a92/en/articleStatisti.

Schatzki, Theodore R. 2001. "Introduction: Practice Theory." In *The Practice Turn in Contemporary Theory,* edited by T. R. Schatzki, K. Knorr Cetina and E. von Savigny. Routledge: New York.

Schatzki, Theodore R., Karin Knorr Cetina, and Eike von Savigny, eds. 2001. *The Practice Turn in Contemporary Theory*. New York: Routledge.

Schier, Steven E. 2000. *By Invitation Only: The Rise of Exclusive Politics in the United States*. Pittsburgh: University of Pittsburgh Press.

Schneider, Steven M. 2004. "Final Project Report: Library of Congress Election 2002 Web Archive project." Utica, NY: WebArchivist.org, [Accessed October 20 2005]. Available from http://www.webarchivist.org/Election-2002-Web-Archive-Final-Report.pdf.

Schneider, Steven M., and Kirsten A. Foot, eds. 2000. *Annenberg 2000 Election Web Archive*. Philadelphia: Annenberg School of Communication, University of Pennsylvania.

———, eds. 2003. *Election 2002 Web Archive*. Washington. D.C.: Library of Congress. [Accessed October 21 2005]. Available from http://www.loc.gov/minerva/collect/elec2002/.

Schneider, Steven M., Kirsten A. Foot, Michele Kimpton, and Gina Jones. 2003. "Building Thematic Web Collections: Challenges and Experiences from the September 11 Web Archive and the Election 2002 Web Archive." Paper read at European Conference on Digital Libraries Workshop on Web Archives, at Trondheim, Norway. [Accessed September 20 2005]. Available from http://bibnum.bnf.fr/ecdl/2003/proceedings.php?f=schneider.

Schramm, Wilbur. 1954. "How Communication Works." In *The Process and Effects of Communication*, edited by W. Schramm. Urbana: University of Illinois Press.

Seely Brown, John, and Paul Duguid. 2000. *The Social Life of Information*. Cambridge, MA: Harvard Business School Press.

Seiger, Jonah D. 2003. *Privacy, Security and Trust on the Political Web*. Institute for Politics, Democracy and the Internet, March, [Accessed June 28 2005]. Available from http://www.ipdi.org/UploadedFiles/privacy_security_and_trust_survey_final.pdf.

Selnow, Gary W. 1998. *Electronic Whistle-Stops: The Impact of the Internet on American Politics*. Westport, CT: Praeger.

Shannon, Claude E., and Warren Weaver. 1949. *The Mathematical Theory of Communication*. Urbana: University of Illinois Press.

Shannon, Victoria. 1994. "Despite Access Barriers, Internet is Worth Exploring." *Washington Post*, September 26, F19.

Siegl, Erica, and Kirsten A. Foot. 2004. "Expression in the Post-September 11th Web Sphere." *Electronic Journal of Communication* 14 (1–2). [Accessed August 20 2005]. Available from http://www.cios.org/www/ejc/v141toc.htm.

Simon, Adam F. 2002. *The Winning Message: Candidate Behavior, Campaign Discourse, and Democracy*. New York, NY: Cambridge University Press.

Spagat, Elliot. 2004. *Former Dean Campaign Manager Counsels Against E-mail Address Release*. SFGate.com, February 9, [Accessed October 2 2005]. Available from http://www.sfgate.com/cgi-bin/article.cgi?f=/news/archive/2004/02/09/financial0023EST0009.DTL.

Star, Susan Leigh. 1988. "The Structure of Ill-structured Solutions: Heterogeneous Problem-solving, Boundary Objects and Distributed Artificial Intelligence." In *Distributed Artificial Intelligence*, edited by M. N. Huhns and L. Gasser. Menlo Park: Morgan Kauffmann.

Starr, Paul. 2004. *The Creation of the Media: Political Origins of Modern Communications*. New York: Basic Books.

Stokes, Donald E. 1963. "Spatial Models of Party Competition." *American Political Science Review* 57:368–377.

Stromer-Galley, Jennifer. 2000. *Candidate Websites Foster Debate, Not Negative Campaigning*. NetElection.org, February 24, [Accessed June 20 2005]. Available from http://web.archive.org/web/20001120063345/http://netelection.org/commentary/2000009.php3.

———. 2000. "On-line Interaction and Why Candidates Avoid It." *Journal of Communication* 50 (4):111–132.

Stromer-Galley, Jennifer, and Kirsten A. Foot. 2002. "Citizen Perceptions of Online Interactivity and Implications for Political Campaign Communication." *Journal of Computer-Mediated Communication* 8 (1). Available from http://jcmc.indiana.edu/vol8/issue1/stromerandfoot.html.

Taylor, James R., and Elizabeth van Every. 2000. *The Emergent Organization: Communication as Its Site and Surface*. Mahwah, New Jersey: Lawrence Erlbaum Associates.

Tedesco, John C., Jerry L. Miller, and Julia A. Spiker. 1998. "Presidential Campaigning on the Information Superhighway: An Exploration of Content and Form." In *The Electronic Election: Perspectives on the 1996 Campaign Communication*, edited by L. L. Kaid and D. Bystrom. Mahwah, NJ: Lawrence Erlbaum Associates.

Trippi, Joe. 2004. *The Revolution Will Not Be Televised: Democracy, the Internet, and the Overthrow of Everything*. New York: Harper Collins.

Wellman, Barry, and Caroline Haythornthwaite, eds. 2002. *The Internet in Everyday Life*. Oxford: Blackwell.

West, Darrell M. 2001. *The Rise and Fall of the Media Establishment*. Boston: Bedford/St. Martin's.

Westlye, Mark C. 1991. *Senate Elections and Campaign Intensity*. Baltimore: Johns Hopkins University Press.

Whyte, William Foote. 1943. *Street Corner Society: The Social Structure of an Italian Slum*. Chicago, IL: The University of Chicago Press.

Wiese, Danielle R., and Bruce E. Gronbeck. 2005. "Campaign 2004 Development in Cyber-Politics." In *The 2004 Presidential Campaign: A Communication Perspective*, edited by R. E. Denton. Lanham, MD: Rowman & Littlefield.

Wikipedia. 2005. *Meetup*, May 11 2005, [Accessed June 28 2005]. Available from http://www.absoluteastronomy.com/encyclopedia/M/Me/Meetup.htm.

Williams, Andrew Paul, and Kaye D. Trammell. 2005. "Candidate Campaign E-mail Messages in the Presidential Election 2004." *American Behavioral Scientist* 49 (4):560–574.

Williams, Andrew Paul, Kaye D. Trammell, Monica Postelnicu, Kristen D. Landreville, and Justin D. Martin. 2005. "Blogging and Hyperlinking: Use of the Web to Enhance Viability during the 2004 U.S. Campaign." *Journalism Studies* 6 (2):177–186.

Williams, Christine B. 2004. *Bentley Study Analyzes E-campaign for 2004 Presidential Elections and Clark Meetups*. Bentley College, January 12, [Accessed June 28 2005]. Available from http://www.bentley.edu/news-events/pr_view.cfm?id=1316.

Williams, Robin, and David Edge. 1996. "The Social Shaping of Technology." *Research Policy* 25 (6):865–899.

Xenos, Michael, and Kirsten A. Foot. 2005. "Politics as Usual, or Politics Unusual: Position-taking and Dialogue on Campaign Web Sites in the 2002 U.S. Elections." *Journal of Communication* 55 (1):165–189.

Yates, Joann. 1989. *Control through Communication: The Rise of System in American Management*. Baltimore: Johns Hopkins University Press.

Zaller, John. Forthcoming. *A Theory of Media Politics*. Chicago: University of Chicago Press.

Index

This index includes the names of candidates and other site producers whose sites are cited in endnotes. The page on which the endnote reference appears is provided in the corresponding index entry.